What do you get
when you cross
a Dandelion
with a Rose?

What do you get when you cross a Dandelion with a Rose?

The True Story of a Psychoanalysis

VAMIK D. VOLKAN, M.D.

Jason Aronson, Inc.
New York and London

Library of Congress Cataloging in Publication Data

Volkan, Vamık.
    What do you get when you cross a dandelion
with a rose?

    1. Psychoanalysis—Cases, clinical reports,
statistics. 2. Physicians—Psychology. I. Title.
RC509.8.V64 1983   616.89'17'0926   83-6332
ISBN 0-87668-638-2

Contents

The Third Year

The Fourth Year

Preface

This book is the true story of a psychoanalysis, written by one physician about another, his patient. The analytic process, which took four years, was like a pot of water placed on the fire. At first it only simmered. Later it began to show a few bubbles that burst when they came to the surface. Then it rose to a full, furious boil, in which the heat of the transference neurosis brought about turbulent motion. All of this ultimately subsided into a still pot of water.

Those aspiring to excellence in the healing professions traditionally undergo apprenticeship: the young surgeon works for some time at the side of the master surgeon to observe how the latter performs, reacts to crisis, and arrives at decisions. But the nature of psychoanalytic treatment and its requisite privacy, which encloses analyst and analysand, make it impossible for the young analyst actually to observe the master analyst. This book is an attempt to show the reader the analytic process unfolding. It begins with my first meeting with the patient to the final day of our highly intimate journey, when we shook hands and separated. We subsequently met in preparation for the publication of this book. The emotional interaction, both verbal and nonverbal, between analysand and analyst shows clearly. The meaning of dreams adds to the "therapeutic story," which is not a logical but a psychological disclosure.

After I wrote this manuscript, I gave it to the analysand for his review and permission for its publication. Not only did the analysand grant this permission, but he wrote a long letter about his own understanding of what had taken place during his treatment. This letter, the best lay person's description of analysis that I have seen, appears in the last chapter of this book.

The title of the book derives from the analysis. The analysand's mother, who had been adopted as a child, had conveyed to her son the fantasy that her natural father had been a nobleman. But the analysand sometimes feared that his mother had come from humble stock and possibly from gypsy parents, since she was swarthy. Accordingly, he was sensitized to the differences between those things, people, and aspects of himself that he categorized as "roses," that is, as valuable and pleasing, and those he saw as worthless, common "dandelions." During his analysis, he learned to "cross" dandelions with roses and provided a hard-won and surprising answer to the question: "What do you get when you cross a dandelion with a rose?"

This book, I hope, answers many questions: how the analyst systematically formulates meanings from the patient's communications; how the interpretation of dreams fits into the *total* "therapeutic story"; how the analyst handles dreams of his own in which the patient appears; how the analyst responds to issues that are apparently extraneous to the analytic work; and how the analyst handles an accidental meeting with his patient at a social gathering.

For the professional therapist, this book provides a highly detailed model of how one psychoanalyst works. It is likely to provide a point of departure for the discussion of many technical and theoretical issues, but it also allows for the comparison of different therapeutic styles and different technical frames of reference.

For the young therapist, this book can be a guide for studying an entire therapeutic picture, from outset to termination. It is not limited to vignettes concerned with the unfolding of one or more psychological constellations.

For the lay reader curious about Freud's "impossible profession" or about what psychoanalysis might be like, this book may be useful. It uses little psychoanalytic jargon and reads like a fictional account of a journey into the depths of one man's mind.

Psychoanalysis proper and psychoanalytically oriented psychotherapy have come under close public scrutiny during the past several decades. Insurance carriers and other third-party payers in a poor economy have raised questions about value. A public confused about the proliferation of "new" therapeutic approaches claiming to alleviate emotional discomfort and to convey psychological benefit has raised other questions. This book explains in detail the hitherto mysterious analytic process.

The Black Panther

The psychoanalytic process involved two men, the analyst and his analysand, who met four times a week for about four years, with only occasional, unavoidable interruptions. When together, the two were bound by the time-tested rules and techniques of Freudian analysis: the analyst did not address his analysand by his first name, for example, although the psychological journey they took together was long and most intimate.

I report the story here as I learned it—as new information came to my attention in piecemeal fashion, as we became aware of the meaning of previously unconscious material, and as we reconstructed the nature of the analysand's inner world, his conflicts, and their resolution. The panther dream would prove central to the analysis.

The sleeping child could see his own small body stretched out in his bed, and he saw the luminous fog that covered the snowy ground outside his window. He knew that something was drawing near through the moonlight, something with footsteps too light to hear until they began scuffing along the snowy crust. He fancied himself joyously sledding down hills of ice cream, and he saw himself disappear in blue smoke.

But the panther came closer, until he could see her black fur shine in the moonlight. He felt cold. The snow had turned to ice, and he trembled with fear, tossing like a kite in a cold wind and tugging at the slender thread that moored it to the earth.

Suddenly the panther leapt onto a branch of the leafless tree just outside the child's window. She spread her legs and rubbed against the sturdy tree trunk until she seemed to merge with it. Her silhouette suggested two people in close embrace. The child could see the panther's eyelids flutter in the moonlight, and he felt their alluring, seductive power. He could not get enough of looking at the animal in her tree; his heart pounded with an excitement he could not understand. He looked until he thought he would go blind.

Then the tree shook violently, and the panther dropped onto the snow. He heard her padding footsteps, and she suddenly appeared before him in his room, her mouth open wide. It was a strange mouth that opened vertically; it was moist and pink, with thick lips that opened and shut slowly. The child caught a glimpse of sharp teeth. Certain that he would be snatched up and consumed, he felt terror. He lay paralyzed on his bed, only his eyes following the movements of the panther's eyes and mouth.

Suddenly the animal's fur became noticeably denser and silkier. As it concealed the threatening mouth, the child's fear left him, and he felt hypnotized by her glowing, seductive eyes. She moved so close to him that he caught her scent, that of a soft, clean blanket that he would have liked to pull over his body. As he became aware of her warmth, he wanted to unite with her; he was no longer afraid of being consumed. But terror swept over him once again when she opened her mouth and exposed her strong, sharp teeth. He screamed.

The child was in his father's arms, which seemed as strong as the branches of the naked tree in his dream. His father reassured him: "Hush! Hush! You've just had another bad dream!" The boy opened his eyes and clutched his father, drawing security and strength from the embrace. Then he saw his mother and drew her toward him with one arm. As her hair fell across his face, he breathed in its familiar, reassuring scent and felt even more secure. After his father had gently put him back to bed, his mother sat on the bed and stroked his back until her husband called to her. By then, the child was drifting off into a world of bright bubbles and quiet sleep, though not before he glimpsed through half-open eyes the black panther slipping out of his room. By morning he had no memory of the dream. The dream recurred, but in the absence of a conscious memory, he did not question its meaning. Nonetheless, the fearsome black panther and the ambiguous power of her glittering eyes made an impression on the child's developing character.

It was years before he lay on a psychoanalyst's couch and became accustomed to speaking of his dreams. When he first attempted to report a dream from the night before a session, he could report *no content,* only a feeling of terror. After four years as his psychoanalyst, I sought to reestablish the content of this empty dream. I had concluded that it was about a black panther and that it had been a repetition of a dream (or dreams) he had had as a child. His psychoanalysis had begun unearthing his childhood memories, but this particular dream remained too terrifying to be remembered. I had to piece together the panther dream from the multitude of circumstances and perceptions of childhood experiences that evolved from his analysis. (If the particulars of the panther dream represent the assumptions of the analyst, so be it. In no other aspect of the analysis did I embellish actual transactions or disclosures.)

There are usually three phases in the therapeutic process of psychoanalysis: an opening phase, a middle phase, and a termination phase. The first starts with the initial contact between analyst and analysand, during which the latter's problems and aims are evaluated, the basic rule of analysis explained: that the analysand is encouraged to let his (or her) mind wander and to report anything coming into it without deference to social conventions. During the opening phase, the basis for an alliance between the two persons is laid, an alliance seeing into the analysand's mind as he undergoes a therapeutic and transient regression and expresses forbidden desires and forgotten memories in current ideas, feelings, or bodily sensations. The first phase occupies the time required to establish a more or less enduring "transference neurosis." This involves the analysand's making his analyst a kind of "reincarnation" of people who had been important to him in his childhood. The transference neurosis also brings about a transfer onto the analyst of childhood feelings, reactions, and wishes—as well as the defenses against such wishes.

The middle is the longest phase in an analysis; it involves keeping the transference neurosis "hot," as it were, in order to work on its various manifestations over and over. A transference neurosis brings the past into the present with extraordinary vividness, and the analysand begins to see the validity of his analyst's interpretation of his unconscious processes. The analyst offers interpretations systematically and usually begins with an interpretation of the analysand's reluctance to face the nature of his conflicts before the analyst identifies the issues they involve. The analysand typically talks in his sessions about external events, memories, fantasies, and the like but emotional interaction with the analyst is the central concern. External events serve as a backdrop for the unfolding of the analysand's internal story and thus reflect the psychoanalytic process. Dreams provide highly important communications when their deeper meanings are explored through the analysand's associations to their surface (manifest) content.

The analyst does not have an opportunity to explore with his patient the deeper meanings of all the dreams reported. Sometimes the analysand reports a dream too close to the end of a session, and sometimes the unfolding of other important psychological constellations take precedence. Nonetheless, dream interpretation remains a chief therapeutic tool for unlocking that Pandora's box, the mind. The therapeutic story can advance when dream communication is linked to other material offered simultaneously by the analysand.

As the analysand's childhood experiences, whether recalled accurately or partly or altogether dependent on fantasy, repeat themselves in the interaction between analysand and analyst, the latter slowly becomes "a new person" who, as time goes on, is less and less confused in the analysand's mind with figures from his childhood. Thus the analysand experiences something new within the analytic process and assimilates selected aspects and functions of the analyst, thereby enriching his own mental world.

Liberation from old emotional ties and responses is perceived as "losses," and such losses bring to the psychoanalytic process one experience of mourning after another. It is not until the third phase, however, after a termination date has been set, that mourning is the focal issue. During this phase, the analysand recapitulates the transference neurosis and experiences the resolution of his conflicts. Resolution of the oedipal conflict is the crowning point in this process, this conflict involving the child's early striving for sexual union with the parent of the opposite sex and the fear of being punished for entertaining such a goal. Only through mourning can the analysand successfully separate from his analyst and prepare to consider a new beginning.

Any analysis includes the analyst's response to his analysand's expectations and presents the possibility that the analyst will transfer his own childhood desires, along with the defenses he used against them, onto his analysand. To minimize this possibility, analysts include personal analysis as part of their training and monitor their own emotional reactions to their analysands insofar as they are consciously perceived.

It is much harder to write about this side of the psychoanalytic dyad than to relate the analysand's conflicts, their reactivation, and the way in which they were interpreted; nonetheless I have tried here to say something about my reactions to my analysand, and I include later the one dream I had about my analysand. Needless to say, I refrained from burdening him with my reactions during the treatment, although I did use derivatives of my responses when appropriate.

Writing about the psychoanalytic process necessarily emphasizes the analyst's intellectual understanding of his patient, but it somewhat misrepresents what actually takes place during an analysis. The analyst regresses, as in a creative endeavor, to be receptive to his analysand's subtle communications, and his emotions and empathy for the patient become a necessary tool to confirm his perceptions. This process takes place automatically often without the analyst's awareness, and therefore is difficult, if not impossible, to chronicle here.

It is to the analysand's ultimate advantage that his analyst refrain from taking any active role in his life and from directing his daily activities while the analysis is going on.

As a treatment, psychoanalysis certainly offers neither salvation from all misery nor the transformation of an analysand into a "superbeing" immune to the pain of the human condition. It is well to consider analysis a process that better equips the analysand to deal with his inner and outer world, that better prepares him to respond to the major and minor cruelties of life, and that prepares him to compete openly, without guilt, instead of dissembling. Psychoanalytic theory expands as we learn more and more about the mental functions and their development early in life. In treatment, we aim not only to resolve systematically the neurotic or other compromise formations concerning childhood desires and the defenses against them, but also to strengthen the foundation of the analysand's identity. Thus we study how an analysand developed his concept of himself and others and how primitive representations of the self and others may hinder his efforts to relate fully to himself and other people.

Introducing Dr. Chris Albert

I will call my analysand "Chris Albert." He embarked on his psychological journey with me reluctantly. When I first saw him, in the autumn some years ago, he was 35, or about ten years my junior. He was rather tall, with curly, dark red hair and a thick mustache that brought to mind old pictures of British military men in India. His face was Goyaesque and unsmiling when he first walked into my office.

Chris Albert was a physician who worked at another medical center in the city. I had never met him before he came to my office and knew nothing about him. He had been married for eight years and had a six-year-old daughter named Pamela. A few months before his first visit, his wife Mamie, had announced that she was leaving him "to find herself." She said that she felt that her marriage was inhibiting her development as a person. When she moved into the apartment of a woman friend, she left Pamela with her husband. He was entirely unprepared for any of these developments.

Not understanding Mamie's remarks about "needing to find herself," he tried to get her to return to him, even drawing up long lists of his virtues and shortcomings as a husband. (His idea of "a good deed" was to take out the trash regularly, and his notion of a bad one was to come home late from work at night.) He asked Mamie to go over these lists to prove that the good outweighed the bad, but she refused to return. He found himself bewildered and depressed, unable to concentrate on his work.

At the suggestion of a colleague, he consulted a psychiatrist, who told him during their first hour that he believed Mamie was having an affair and that he would do well to divorce and forget her. This recommendation horrified him. He felt uneasy without knowing why but came to the conclusion that his dissatisfaction arose from the psychiatrist's having offered a solution "without scientific evidence." He did not return to this psychiatrist, but when my name was given to him he made an appointment for consultation. The professional person who had given him my name at a social gathering did not know me but had told him that I was considered a reputable analyst and that I am Turkish by birth. When he came for consultation, he pretended not to notice my accent.

My office was then located on the second floor of a unit of the university hospital in Charlottesville, Virginia. It was modest, with one window always curtained since a painter, brush in hand, had one day delightedly leaned forward on his ladder to get a better view of a female analysand on the couch. The room was lighted only by a floor lamp; it was unpleasant to have the ceiling light shine down on my patients as though they were being forced to face an inquisitor. I rather fancied in any case that the dim light gave a womb-like feeling to my small office and that this helped my patients to regress, to go back to earlier phases of their lives, as people must do in analytic work. There was just room enough for my desk, a bookshelf, and a chair in addition to the chair I occupied behind the couch during sessions. The box of tissues within easy reach of the couch was the only other therapeutic instrument I needed.

My office door opened onto a hallway lined with the offices of other psychiatrists and our secretaries. There was no waiting room, and my patients quickly learned that if they came on time they would find my office door open in anticipation of their arrival. I did not have my secretary deal with my analysands and took pains to have no intermediary between myself and my analysands. The hallway was often busy and sometimes noisy, but I tested and found that my patients could not be heard in the hall. I reassured each patient *once,* very clearly, if he or she began to worry about being overheard.

Dr. Albert's mother had been adopted at the age of 3 months by a physician whose family enjoyed good standing in the small town in Southern Maryland where her son had been born and where she still lived. Although her adoptive father had died many years before she had a son, she idealized his memory and named her child after him. Dr.

Albert was aware that his mother had favored him over his siblings, a sister eight years his senior and a brother four years younger than he, and that she sought to keep alive through him the "glory" of his grandfather. He was the only one of her children urged to go on for advanced education. At the time of our first interview, his mother was still smothering him with attention. When she visited him, she brought extravagant amounts of food, made him extra meals, and virtually forced him to eat. He reported that by age 14, he had become obese and remained so until he went away to college, where he managed to slim down and developed what he called "an allergic reaction" to his mother. On the way home to see her he would feel the onset of symptoms such as sinusitis and dermatitis, symptoms that disappeared when he left home. Until four or five years before our first meeting, these symptoms had been an inevitable accompaniment of trips home.

His father, who died when Dr. Albert was 26, after suffering great pain from lung cancer, was perceived by his wife as an ineffectual man who could not hold a job and who drifted from one project to another. Once he had embarked on a get-rich-quick scheme involving a small machine to laminate valuable documents in plastic; once he managed a modest motel. Dr. Albert said that although he had accepted his mother's view of her husband's character and abilities, he now understood that it was at the insistence of his mother that his father had ventured no farther than the little town in which her adoptive father had been so admired and that this had severely limited his chances for employment.

His mixed comments about his mother, who had encouraged him to obtain a good education but also continued to mother him, enabled Dr. Albert to speak with the same ambivalence about his wife, until he caught himself and insisted on his idealized love for her. I felt he wanted me to witness his worth as a husband and the many incidents that proved it, but I offered only a few words of encouragement for him to continue with his story. His recital of good deeds led me to observe how often he had acted like his wife's slave. He said that she had come from a broken family and was beautiful, slender, intelligent, and creative. But I noticed that his image of her was unconsciously contaminated by his own mother's perception of his father: in the same disparaging way as his mother had spoken of her husband, he would describe Mamie's inability to complete any project she undertook. He described how Mamie had planned to be a real estate agent, then an artist, and how he had always supported her plans despite her drifting about. He seemed almost to have a mission to make her happy. I sensed that certain elements of both of his parents were being projected onto her, and that he was trying not only to please them by pleasing the mental representations of them he saw in Mamie, but also to repair them. He seemed masochistic in this endeavor, but it would have been belittling and tactless of me to have communicated such observations to him at that time.

As he talked to me, it became evident that he was agitated and had low self-esteem, but in an interesting way his agitation would disappear whenever he spoke of such grandiose and only partly concealed wishes as one day winning the Nobel Prize. The possession of what psychiatrists call "obsessive character traits" was suggested by his manner of deliberate, cautious speech and extremely logical thinking; by his lists balanced by other lists; by his ambivalence about important people in his life; by his unsmiling face; and by his neatness. His desire to accomplish remarkable things in the world—and his belief that he could do so—pointed both to strong narcissistic tendencies to glorify himself and to defenses that would support his basic character in dealing with stress. His wife's defection had affected daily life; it had lowered his self-esteem and depressed him; but at the same time, it had promoted his escape to grandiose wishes and beliefs.

I surmised that his mother might have pushed him to be "perfect" in an effort to compensate her for the injury of knowing that she was an adopted child. Thus later in life he undertook, both consciously and unconsciously, a mission of "saving" women. This mission alternated with feelings of hostility toward women. Women were like the panther I imagined he had dreamed of as a child: he was afraid of them but searched constantly for their love. He seemed willing to submit masochistically to them, as though hypnotized by the need to "buy" their love.

During our first interview, Dr. Albert sat before me in a chair, showing no alteration of expression as he talked. He described being ill, as a three-or four-year-old, when his mother had been pregnant with his brother. He recalled having "choking spells" that he now realized had come from holding his breath. Thus it was clear that as a child he had displayed retentive symptoms that affected his relationship with important people in his life. I surmised that just as he had tried to hold his breath, so had he attempted to hold back his feelings for other people. Since symptoms that involve holding back are considered obsessional, I concluded that his childhood obsessional neurosis and his adult obsessional characterological structure were related. I also felt that his obsessional character traits involved aspects of his identification with the mother of his childhood, who, according to his description, clearly had such traits herself. She was greatly preoccupied with cleanliness, although an untidy housekeeper, and her marked horror of touching excrement and her interest in the bathroom appeared in his stories of his home life. For example, when her son got his M.D. diploma, his mother gave him the diploma that had belonged to her adoptive father and had the two hung side by side in the bathroom.

Since Dr. Albert seldom mentioned his father, I thought it possible that the physician he had never seen—his adoptive grandfather—might be serving as a displaced oedipal father. Recalling the two diplomas side by side, I speculated that he felt that, as his mother's special male relative, he was obliged to compete with her other male favorite, his grandfather, for her affections. As Dr. Albert, his grandfather's namesake, said "He [the grandfather] was always number one in my mother's life! She pushed and pushed me to excel, but I knew I could never be more than second best!"

I surmised that the unresolved oedipal issues appearing symbolically in his references to the mother-child-grandfather triangle returned him to an exaggerated use of mental mechanisms from an earlier, anal level. (Psychoanalysis sees the so-called "psychosexual" development of the individual as involving a series of stages—oral, anal, phallic, and oedipal—that are relatively fixed in time. The child who, having entered the oedipal stage, is unsuccessful in resolving the issues pertaining to it, may revert partly to a previous level in order to escape oedipal conflicts and thus exhibit a clinical picture indicative of the presence of psychological representations of the preoccupations of that level.) In the case of Dr. Albert, this regression along with the events of his life—the birth of his brother and the impact of his mother's characteristics—when he was at the anal level (age 1½ to 3½) accounted for his obsessional personality structure. His ill-concealed longing for the Nobel Prize and his desire to be number one in the eyes of the world (and his mother) reflected his still fervent search for oedipal triumph. He was a good medical researcher and therefore had sublimated his desires to a considerable extent; through sublimation, energy required for his search for oedipal triumph had been redirected into advancing his professional goals.

I wondered during our interview about the "psychological mindedness" of Dr. Albert. It was important to assess this, since the more psychologically minded and curious about the workings of his mind a person is, the more suitable a candidate for psychoanalytic treatment he is. Although he was voluble and expressed a great deal verbally during the hour, I felt as though Dr. Albert were communicating with me from behind a wall of glass. He showed no warmth; he used many cliches. Although he was consulting me because of a recent depression, his personality was heavily armored. Patching up or painting over that armor, I thought, would not bring relief. He needed to replace his armor with something lighter and more flexible. Psychoanalysis was no doubt the treatment of choice, yet I felt misgivings about the success of psychoanalysis in his case. I suspect that I was mirroring some of his own ambivalence, but my misgivings also arose from his great difficulty in gaining access to his emotions and from his history of psychosomatic illness (obesity, sinusitis, dermatitis, and asthma during puberty). I wondered whether the regression inevitable in analysis might evoke similar symptoms.

He offered nothing in the consultation that would account for his wife's defection. Although he had spoken of it as his reason for consulting me, he went on quickly to discuss his life in general and did not return to the matter of his wife's departure. I told him that his relationship with her seemed to have been contaminated with conflictual elements from the relationship he had had with his parents as a child; that his difficulties with her—above and beyond her own motives, about which I could know nothing—might be influenced by some long-standing difficulty he had in relating to women. I recalled some of the terms he had used in describing his relationship with his mother and told him that further exploration would be necessary for any understanding of the meaning of the events that had so distressed him. I shared my belief that his characterological problems would not be much alleviated by short-term therapy and that psychoanalysis was the treatment of choice. I also told him that within two months I would have the time to work with him in a psychoanalytic setting.

He thanked me dryly but insisted that all he needed was short-term crisis intervention. I explained that I was not a specialist in crisis intervention and added that, even were the crisis to be resolved, he could still examine its elements. It seemed to me, I explained, that they had been a part of him for a long time. He listened politely and then asked if I could recommend someone who would give him crisis intervention or family therapy. I gave the name of a psychiatrist interested in crisis intervention who might take him as a patient or direct him to someone else who would be suitable. Thus I was surprised when he called a month later and announced that he was ready to begin analysis, but made an appointment for him.

When he came, in mid-February, I learned that his depressive symptoms continued, that he had been in extreme psychic pain, and that, after considering the possibilities, he had decided that I was the only one who had listened seriously to him and had explained that his domestic problem was part of a chronic phenomenon, the understanding of which would require serious and lengthy work. Thus I seemed to him the only "scientific" prospect, although he still had doubts about psychoanalytic treatment. During this session, he asked repeatedly if I had no shortcut to offer or if it were not possible for me to hypnotize him, find his problem, and solve it. I repeated my belief that psychoanalysis was the treatment of choice for him, and he agreed to try it. We discussed financial terms and planned to meet four times a week. I explained that he was to lie on the couch and to report freely to me whatever came into his mind and any bodily sensations and feelings he might experience. He tried lying on the couch on the following day, and we began together the journey about which we both felt some reluctance.

The First Year

A World Full of Dandelions
and Roses

Mid-February to Mid-March

An analyst starting the psychoanalysis of a new patient feels an odd excitement. If a male analyst were sufficiently candid to admit being jealous of women, he might describe his feelings as coming very close to those of a woman who has just been told that she is pregnant and faces a nine-month commitment to another life. An analysis commits both parties to long, intimate work together, culminating in the rebirth of the analysand and his separation/individuation from the dyad.

The analytic setting is artificial, designed to be therapeutic. The opening and closing of each session are carefully scheduled; the analyst seldom changes the appearance of his office, in which people meet and "talk," although not in the usual social exchange. I know of no other situation, real or artificial, in which one party is expected to open his heart while the other sits behind him, speaking only when he considers comment useful for both, although some might see in this situation shades of the confessional.

Dr. Albert began with a session on the couch on February 17. The day was cloudy, and my dark office was darker than usual, even depressing. I sat silently behind him as he began to speak in a monotone about his wife's departure.

"Why am I not rewarded?" he asked. "I have a good position, and I have been a good husband." The rest of his utterance was composed of such platitudes as "Love is giving and sharing," or "Love is a sacred word," or "Advancement for the sake of achievement is not fulfilling."

I learned that he had dated little until his first year in medical school and that then he had had a love affair that seemed to have foundered on his inability to say "I love you." Then he had met Mamie, just as she was ending an affair with another man. He explained that he had married her *"because I admired her father."* Although I thought this a peculiar statement, I did not interrupt his recital of the details of his marriage to Mamie.

Beginning with his second hour on the couch, he alternated between complaining about his wife's leaving him and telling me his history. He seemed to have wanted to be "a good child" and to have performed according to what he thought his mother expected of him. He explained that he was telling his early memories because in medical school he had read that that is what one does in psychoanalysis. His early memories came out in sterile fashion, without emotion. He spoke of his mother's excessive attachment to him, itself based on her own starving for love, as would become clear to me later. Aware of her special concern for him, he felt it to be so excessive that he had come to distrust all women lest they smother him.

Too great an interest on my part in his formulation of his relationship with women would encourage further intellectualization (a term for highly logical reasoning erected as a defense against confronting unconscious conflicts). Intellectualization was a manifestation of his character organization. However, because it was necessary at first to let him know that I followed closely all he said, I made noncommittal sounds of encouragement, or said, "Go on." I asked few questions and then only those calculated to encourage his story without probing: "Have you finished your sentence? your story? your description?"

During the first weeks of Dr. Albert's analysis, I learned that his mother was a small woman, too small, he thought, to have punished him physically when he was a child. He nonetheless held her accountable for the almost daily, ritualized whippings his father had given him after demanding that he bend over. His obesity began in the sixth grade and remained a problem throughout high school. He had trained himself to conceal emotion by practicing a noncommital expression before a mirror. I suspected that in due course I would hear particulars of a deeply traumatized childhood. I had already noticed how successful he was at hiding his emotions, in accordance with his belief in being in command of one's feelings. When he disclosed childhood experiences that might have been expected to evoke emotion, he adroitly turned to an emotionless recital of his difficulties with his wife. This relationship began to seem more and more but the tip of the iceberg. But because our goal was to grasp the total situation, I did not interfere with his limited description right then.

Dr. Albert compulsively had been checking a calendar his wife had left behind and some short stories she had written, in search of clues to her departure. The circling of certain dates on the calendar suggested to him a code: for example, a note that said "H. I." suggested "Holiday Inn," and the letters "W. L." became Wood Lane. Gradually he admitted that he thought his wife had been having an affair with a married friend, and that the circling of certain dates and references to what seemed to be place names referred to assignations. Although he entertained the possibility that Mamie had been unfaithful, he sought evidence to prove him wrong. Although he thought that he had competition for Mamie's affections, he decided that he was the only man in her life. The oedipal sound to this triangle did not escape my attention, and I considered again that any active investigation of it would induce more intellectualization. My patient needed to understand the real-world reason for his wife's departure.

In the meantime, he was seeing Mamie almost daily, either at her new home or inviting her for coffee or tea in his. Their meetings reflected denial and other neurotic interaction: they behaved as though nothing were happening to them, as if to cover over their emotions and conflicts.

Throughout the first month of his analysis, Dr. Albert acted as though his purpose in coming to me were to report on either his current, daily life or events of his childhood. I was to learn much later that in childhood he had ritualistically reviewed each day's activities with his mother after school. As he reported events to me, I had the feeling that, as far as he was concerned, he was alone in the office, even though occasionally he abruptly would ask me a question like, "Are you a basketball fan?" In hindsight, I later realized that during the opening phase of his analysis, Dr. Albert related to me as he defensively and ritualistically related to his mother, in order to conceal his emotionally conflicted feelings toward her, and that his questions about my interest in sports had to be an attempt to relate to me as to his father. I replied at the time to such questions with, "Let's be curious about it," and instead of dwelling on getting an answer, he would resume his routine of reporting.

Hostile fantasies about his wife surfaced as March began. Although he still spoke of her without any display of emotion, I noticed that any report of a hostile daydream in which he might, for example, shoot his wife or her presumed lover, was followed by grandiose fantasies, in some of which he saw himself as a virtual superman. Sometimes he fantasied winning the Nobel Prize, sometimes finding a cure for cancer (and I remembered that his father had died from cancer). In other fantasies, Dr. Albert had the love and admiration of practically all the women in the world. When asked his associations to the latter fantasy, his tentative efforts produced the family legend that his adoptive grandfather had been a ladies' man and had pursued every woman in town. He could associate no further at this point in his analysis.

A few days after reporting his fantasy of finding a cancer cure, Dr. Albert referred again to this disease: a year before she left him, his wife had had a hysterectomy when her Pap smear had showed cancer cells. His mother had commiserated, saying, "Now, my son, you can never have a son of your own!" He had felt accused of failing to provide a son to carry on his adoptive grandfather's glory. I suspected that he also heard his mother admonishing him, "Divorce this woman who cannot give you a son. Find another woman, and perpetuate my father's image."

At the time of her hysterectomy, Mamie allegedly had been greatly upset. She would later attribute the loss of her love for Dr. Albert to his failure to support her in this ordeal. Here was the first clear explanation of her departure that I had heard. But Dr. Albert then remarked that he did not think the hysterectomy had been so stressful for his wife, because after she spoke of having lost her love for him, he consulted a diary she had kept at the time of her operation and found an entry saying, "The hysterectomy may have some effect. But no major problem!" Nevertheless, he stopped his narrative abruptly, as if waiting for my agreement or disagreement. I said nothing, but I observed the first reappearance of the agitation he had exhibited in our initial consultation. He quickly recovered, however, and reported that the song line "Life is a cabaret" had just popped into his mind, as if activated by a button, and that it had lifted him out of his agitated, depressive state.

The next day, Dr. Albert said that his mother had had two spontaneous abortions before he was born and that she had almost lost him, too. I then suggested to him that his mother's difficulty in childbearing may have contributed to her seeing him as "special." He then reported what he said was the most vivid memory of his childhood, that of a *black panther* coming to his hometown in southern Maryland when he was 3 or 4 years old. Although he never saw it, he had heard that it climbed into a tree in the yard. This memory, which he said was like a dream, was associated with fear.

Traumatic events that occur before a child is 5 are customarily repressed, in a process called "infantile amnesia." What are known as "screen memories" symbolically reflect a condensation of forgotten and important memories from this time of life. Screen memories may be altogether false or a mixture of the false and true. I considered the tale of the black panther a screen memory and was interested in how Dr. Albert had told the story just as a session was ending. He may have used an unconsciously defensive maneuver against probing into this memory and generating anxiety.

A few days later, on March 7, he reported a dream for the first time. But it had no content. He simply described it as a strange sensation that terrified and awakened him. "There was terror in the room," he said. This brought to mind the possibility that the dream with no content might have some connection with his screen memory, but he could offer no associations.

During the next hour, Dr. Albert reported a dream *with* content. In the dream, he was performing research previously performed by a Dr. Boyd, a "super researcher." Then the scene changed, and he found a silk-screened elephant, which he hung on the wall. When he was encouraged to associate, Dr. Albert said that Dr. Boyd had successfully remarried after a divorce. In reality, Dr. Albert had some years earlier purchased a silk-screened elephant at an art gallery and had given it to his wife. She had hung it in their living room and then had given it to her father. The empty hook had remained on the living room wall for years.

The dream had a number of oedipal elements: a woman had given his elephant (which was probably a phallic symbol) to another man—a father—and this had left the patient's "hook" dysfunctional. I did not mention my formulation at this point in Dr. Albert's analysis. I was also impressed by aspects of this dream that pertained to resistance. Although Dr. Albert had voluntarily undertaken psychoanalysis with me, he was unconsciously resisting the dredging up of repressed material into consciousness. In this phase of his analysis, I had to pay attention to his resistance and to bring it to his attention. Once resistance toward the disclosure of certain material is worked through, it can be brought up or reexperienced in the patient's relationship with his analyst.

The dream with content had followed a dream so terrifying that Dr. Albert literally could not see it. The dream with content allowed him to tell me that Dr. Boyd had gone through a divorce and successfully remarried without psychoanalysis. Moreover, the elephant, by reappearing on the wall in this dream, indicated that his "hook" was no longer empty. After reporting his dream, he said he wished that he might have a successful "one-day" analysis. Guided by the manifest content of the dream, I told him that his dream might indicate his wishes to succeed without analysis and to play down his emotional problems. I also told him that reporting material from his unconscious had terrified him in the earlier dream. He agreed.

In mid-March, I heard his analogy of "the dandelion and the rose" for the first time. It was offered in connection with the refusal of one of his friends to marry a girl because she lacked social prestige. He spoke of prestige as making one a "rose" and the lack of it as consigning one to being a "dandelion." He implied that no intermediates existed between these two absolutes. I suggested that we examine this analogy, and he responded by telling about his mother's adoption. Her *black* hair and *dark* skin justified, he felt, her fantasy that she was the daughter of a Spanish nobleman whose travels had brought him to southern Maryland, her birthplace. Dr. Albert believed that his mother could establish the identity of her real parents, and he believed that if he checked certain records in the state capital, he could identify them. Neither he nor his mother ever had tried to do so, however, preferring the fantasy of a noble connection that made her a "rose."Mother and son shared the wish that she be a "rose," and that he be one also, by extension. All characteristics that might have identified him as a "dandelion" were either hidden or projected onto others. Thus his mother often had told him that he was superior to this or that person. Just as he had practiced before a mirror repressing any display of emotion, he worked consciously—and successfully—to lose his southern accent, which he equated with being "a dandelion." I began to think that his "mission" of saving women had to do with repairing his unfavorable image of his mother as a "dandelion" because she was adopted.

Childhood's Deaths and Mutilations

Mid-March to April 25

On March 15, Dr. Albert suddenly went beyond making guarded remarks about me and began to call me "the Duchess of Windsor." Here was the first open manifestation of his "transference." (This term refers to the analysand's unconsciously "transferring" to his analyst patterns of feelings, attitudes, and expectations originally associated with important figures in his early life. Transference is a kind of repetition of these, although the analysand is not consciously aware of replaying aspects of his early life. Such transference involves a therapeutic story as the analysis becomes highly charged, and then we speak of "transference neurosis.") He found me inaccessible, as inaccessible as the Duchess of Windsor. I saw in his explanation the first unguarded, direct reference to the mother transference. Except when he fantasied his mother as having royal Spanish blood, he perceived her consciously as a kind of gypsy who had penetrated a well-known, wealthy family just as Wallace Simpson had penetrated England's royal house, becoming the Duchess of Windsor. I suggested that we examine his use of this name and pointed out that the Duchess was sufficiently powerful to have made a king surrender his throne for her. He cried at once, "Yes! An incredible sacrifice. I once thought of giving up medicine and devoting my life to making Mamie happy!"

Once he understood that he was displacing onto me some perception from the past, he behaved, at least for a while, like a child who had found a new toy. He then went on to call me a priest. Before meeting his wife, he (a Baptist) had dated a Cuban girl who had sent him to a priest about the possibility of his joining the Catholic Church for her sake. In his interview with the priest, whom he thought of as "ominous," he had been unable to reveal the particulars of his life and feelings. I thought that the "ominous" priest might embody some of his childhood perceptions of his father and his mother, and I felt that he perceived me as dangerous to him, but I did not say so, for too much explanation of transference can interfere with the development of the transference neurosis and its systematic interpretation and resolution.

Although Dr. Albert was making me ever more powerful and ominous, he was at the same time trying to reduce me to nothing. "I don't think of you," he said. "You are . . . you are . . . a *black void.*" Now he had referred to the color black with the panther, his mother's hair, and with me. When I asked what "black void" brought to mind, he declined, with his usual caution, to make any association.

The rather open manifestation of transference was enough to give him his first somatic reaction, a repetition of his childhood means of absorbing anxiety. On the following day, he was sneezing when he came to my office. Acknowledging that he had "a cold," he declared at the start of the session, "I am not ready to die!" When I suggested that we probe the meaning of that remark, he said that his life was "full of death." Listening to him, I felt that death symbolized psychological danger for him and that he felt a need to be ever on guard against it.

He reported that when he had been in the fourth or fifth grade, a tough and foul-mouthed classmate named Jack had died of a cerebral hemorrhage. I thought to myself that he had communicated that punishment comes to foul-mouthed and aggressive boys. He listed all the people he had known who were now dead: a girl he had dated a few times in college, his father and other relatives, and his patients "by the hundreds." Since his medical specialty brought many dying people to his attention, this remark was understandable. He said that he had always been fascinated by death and connected it with "black magic."

Then Dr. Albert turned to hardships and misadventures that he had experienced. He spoke of having been a sickly child who rotated the thermometer in his mouth in order to elevate the reading and get to stay at home from school with his mother. At age 14, he had "accidentally" amputated a toe with a lawnmower. I wondered whether my patient had not unconsciously punished himself by losing his toe, whether he might have been symbolically playing out a form of self-castration. We know that the male child expects punishment in the form of castration by the father, whom he sees as his rival for his mother. Just before describing the loss of his toe, Dr. Albert had reported maneuvering to stay at home with his mother. He had wanted to keep his toe as a grisly trophy, and did keep it in a jar for a while, but a minister had finally buried it. Thinking him unready for the castration symbolism condensed in this incident, I said only, "You feel that part of you is dead and buried."

Dr. Albert had been unable to walk after he lost his toe, and required months of training to walk normally again. With gentle probing, I learned that the accident came after he had been chosen to officiate at a school ceremony and that he had had to officiate on crutches. I made the formulation that he saw success as attainable only if it were accompanied by self-mutilation. (The excessively obsessional person thinks like a bookkeeper, demanding that everything balance, and Dr. Albert had taken pains to balance the misery of his amputation by noting that his insurance for it had paid him enough to buy his first car. A car for a toe—another example of "success" gained as a result of self-mutilation!)

He continued talking about death and mutilation, speaking of the death of pets and recalling another "accident" that had taken place when he was 4, in which he had stuck a knife in his eye while trying *to cut a branch from a tree.* I noted that this event coincided with the birth of his younger brother. The injured eye had bled profusely, and his mother had rushed him to a doctor in alarm. Although it turned out that only the eyelid was damaged, he felt sure that his mother had expected him to be *blinded* by this accident.

Then Dr. Albert produced the story of Danny, a strange boy a few years his senior, who liked guns and fast cars and whom he had befriended in high school. I recalled that as a teenager, he had lost his toe, become obese, had no dates, and regarded life with extreme caution. Surely he had believed that if he were aggressive, foul-mouthed, or jealous of a new baby brother, or even if he succeeded in officiating at a school ceremony, some danger would come to him! Danny was clearly everything he was not: rebellious and liberated from parental domination in an exaggerated way. He represented aspects of Chris Albert's own aggressive drives, and through his friend's guns and fast cars, young Chris could have vicarious pleasure and safely discharge his own aggression. I thought that he had tried to identify with Danny to save himself from both realistic and fantasied parental domination. Chris detested the girl Danny soon married. She had once almost run him down with her car, and he perceived her not only as a woman who interfered with his attempt to identify with Danny, but also as a person dangerous in her own right.

Danny bet Chris that he himself would die within ten years, and told him that if he survived he would owe Chris ten dollars. If he did die within ten years, Chris was to take ten red roses to his funeral. Danny did die, riding a motorcycle his wife had encouraged him to buy; the accident was apparently his own fault. As Chris took the roses to Danny's funeral, he was devastated and was convinced that Danny's wife had killed her husband by abetting his self-destructive tendencies. Chris resented her for ruining his chance to learn "how to be a man" from Danny.

All these memories of death and mutilation were offered in the same hour, and by the end of the session I sensed an eerie feeling in the air. My analysand seemed anxious, and as the hour ended and he got ready to leave my office, he said, "I do hope you didn't catch my cold. . . ." I finished the sentence for him: "and die!"

By the next day, Dr. Albert's anxiety had given way to grandiose fantasies of omnipotence, another way he habitually dealt with anxiety. He began the hour by reporting that he was "one hundred percent okay now." He had fantasied the previous night that an ex-patient of his, who was socially prominent, had left him millions. The devastation he had felt over Danny's death and over my death from his cold was transferred into jubilation over being so rich that he need not worry about anything. He fantasied using his newly found millions to gamble in Las Vegas and multiply his fortune! His fantasy included going to New York, where he and Mamie had lived when he was a young doctor and where he recalled buying Mamie *black* pearls and a dress to make her happy. His generosity would include his brother, too; he fantasied helping him with his restaurant. His fantasy made him a "good boy," so there was no reason for him to be anxious. When I interpreted the function of this fantasy, he listened without comment.

When he began his next session, Dr. Albert was able to talk more openly than before about his "mission" of repairing Mamie and making her "a queen" (recall the Duchess of Windsor). Spontaneously but without much feeling, he connected this behavior with his status as a special person, chosen by his mother to bring her glory. This open appreciation of his psychic processes was accompanied by a sudden preoccupation with draperies, the lack of which in his living room, he said, made him feel naked when he was in the room. He spent a week talking about draperies before finally buying some. At this point, I suggested that my "looking into" him in the analysis might be making him uncomfortable. This constituted an interpretation of the draperies as his resistance to analysis. I commented that we would work together in looking at issues that he might perceive as uncomfortable, that there was no hurry about this, and that our working together might make the examination of hitherto unknown issues easier for him.

He reported a dream at the start of the next session: "I had holes in my underwear and wanted to buy the best to replace it. Then I was buying Hanes underwear. I wore them; they were sparkling clean!" His associations involved a babysitter's checking the genitalia of a friend's daughter by removing her underwear. The thought came to me that if I looked through the undraped window, or through the holes of his underwear, I might see something in his genital area that would make him uncomfortable. Choosing not to dwell on any discomfort he might have about sexual matters—or, possibly, anal soil—I spoke of his resistance to the psychoanalytic process in the case of the draperies and pointed to his insistence on buying the best underwear to protect himself (by a grandiose defense). The "sparkling clean" aspect of his new undergarments might reflect a perceived absence of any need for psychoanalysis to wash his dirty linen.

I could see that he was responding favorably to my handling of this dream material, because he activated the image of a good father and recalled how, as a child, he had received help from his father when he had nightmares. Since his father had often awakened and comforted him, I thought, in piecing together his dream of the black panther, that it had been his father who comforted him on that occasion.

Dr. Albert's warmth toward the good father/analyst was accompanied by anger toward the mother, and he said, "I saw my father only through her eyes for a long time!" After saying this, he was spontaneously able to give more associations to the dream and recalled having peeked at the genitalia of a young girl cousin when he was about 10. He had been so curious, but "there was nothing there!" I then suggested that he might be anxious about my finding something missing if I looked into him. The anxiety my tentative suggestion caused him was neutralized that night when he dreamt of his adoptive grandfather's pistol—a phallic symbol—which was now his.

At about this time, toward the end of April, his mother came from southern Maryland to visit him, and I thought this event stimulated him to talk of his interest in German literature, notably a detailed story, connected with oedipal issues and the primal scene (a child's real or fantasied witnessing of his parents engaged in intercourse). His story was of a rather retarded 16-year-old boy, in love with a headmaster's wife. The boy saw her making love with her husband and concluded that they were fighting, and so he burned their house and killed them both in the fire. This theme reappeared in further fantasies about Mamie and her supposed lover, both of whom Dr. Albert killed.

Although he was no longer fat, because he had been fat as a child he imagined himself as too heavy whenever his aggression became so strong that it required neutralizing. Associations to this reaction indicated that this was his way of feminizing himself, of ridding himself of the derivatives of his aggressive drive. When oedipal competition was displaced onto the image of the grandfather, his real father image could be invested with warm feelings. One day he wept—for the first time in his analysis—over his father's death. He became for me a suffering human being, one whom I could feel close to. Dr. Albert noted that his mother had always called her idealized adoptive father "Daddy Doc," and he had felt betrayed by her when he found that Daddy Doc in fact had been an alcoholic philanderer who had succumbed to tuberculosis. My analysand felt that he had been deprived of the opportunity truly to know his own father by his mother's substitution of falsified images of Daddy Doc.

The day after he had wept, he began a habit of removing the box of tissues from the head of the couch to its far end before lying down. I observed to him how he kept balancing one session or event with another, balancing an occasion for expressiveness with something to conceal his expressiveness.

It was at this time that he made passing reference to a childhood trauma he had not previously reported. He reported that when he was very small, he had been diagnosed as having thymus trouble, for which the prevailing treatment was radiation therapy. His fragmentary re-collections of this period in his life implied that his mother had been very anxious about the radiation therapy, that she had insisted he wear a straw hat when he went out to prevent radiation from the sun from adding to what he was receiving in treatment. Thus he wore a constant reminder of his mother's anxiety and of her perception of the world around him as dangerous. I made the formulation (to myself, the memory having been expressed unemotionally) that dread of daily danger had exacerbated both his anxiety over separating from the mental image of his mother/protector as he became an individual on his own, and his castration anxiety over losing his manliness (penis) as punishment for competing with the father or grandfather for his mother.

Reaction to Separation: the Bedbugs

April 25 to the Beginning of August

The first separation of my analysand and me came in May, about two-and-a-half months into his analysis. A professional meeting required my absence for a week. When, toward the end of April, I spoke of the coming separation without giving a reason for it, Dr. Albert began toying with the idea of having his first date with a woman since he had separated from his wife the previous fall. I wondered to myself if this were a response to our separation.

Since he and Mamie had separated, they had occasionally made love during her visits to him. In her absence, he masturbated. He recalled that when he was a young man his mother had warned him, "If you make a girl pregnant, you may have to marry her. Be careful!" It occurred to him that his mother might have made his father marry her because she was pregnant with his sister, and this suddenly seemed to him a true insight. He concluded that his mother had indeed been pregnant at the time of her marriage.

On April 26, he dated a woman, and as they made love he thought, "Volkan, I did it! Screw you!" Although I could hear overtones of his rebellion against an overly cautious mother and some identification with an aggressive father in response to our coming separation, I was puzzled about his need to date a woman at this time. Was she a substitute and available mother figure during my absence? (The importance of his having union with a woman at a time of separation [death] from the father/analys would become clear much later, when I learned the circumstances of his father's death.)

As the time for my departure grew near, he was able to verbalize with some anxiety his death wish for me, indicating at the same time that he dreaded that the wish might come true. "See, Volkan, your plane will crash!" he said, after reporting his thought that I would fly somewhere for a vacation. Since I was in fact going to fly, an expressed wish that my plane would crash jolted me for a moment. Most separations from the analyst are very difficult for the analysand, and Dr. Albert was certainly not the first of my patients to wish me dead. He was not emotional about his wish, and I have been subject to more venomous attacks. Experience has taught me not to be flattered by such perverse indications of my importance to a patient; I know that I assume, in their therapeutic regression, the role of persons in their childhood who had been important, even indispensable. I was, however, amused to observe in myself a fleeting emotional response to Dr. Albert's "attack" on me. I was not, after all, some machine sitting behind him, but a human being. I did not burden him with my response to his wish for my death. I saw another expression of his anger toward the "rejecting" analyst in his constant reference to me as "Volkan," choosing to disregard my professional identity.

That evening he felt compelled to buy new Hanes underwear. I thought of him as fearing my retaliation and needing to protect his penis in a way that recalled his preoccupation with the draperies in his living room and his dream about new underclothing. I did *not* interpret this to him at this level, although I did tell him that in view of his dream about the underwear and his preoccupation with draperies, it seemed that he felt obliged to cover himself, to conceal any anxiety or anger he might feel over my departure. I thought that separation anxiety was closer to the surface than castration anxiety during this phase of his analysis and that he could bear my remarks about his panic over the separation as contrasted with his relative intolerance to any discussion of castration anxiety. Because of the stories Dr. Albert told about illness during his childhood, I thought that he clung even in adult life to the notion that he would be unable to survive without his mother's protection, however much he felt smothered by her. He was repeating this idea in reference to the two of us due to his therapeutic regression and my impending physical separation from him.

He said to me, "Fuck you, Volkan! You are constantly on my mind. I can't even have a haircut because of you!" He went on, "Why, *why* do I have to think of you?" He explained that he had forgotten to get a haircut because his mind has been so crammed with fantasies about me. I surmised that not getting a haircut was his defense against his fear of my retaliation for his anger toward me and against my castrating him. By displacement, his forgetting to have his haircut protected him from having any part of his body cut!

He was omnipotent in his fantasies, exhibiting typical narcissistic defenses. He felt able to control anything, particularly the aggression abroad in the world. Knowing of my Turkish origin, and having read of Turkish–Greek conflicts, he fantasied making peace between the two hostile countries. The aggression of his Turkish analyst was thus under control. Once again he was defending himself from my possible retaliation. But he could not fully control his sadism toward the rejecting analyst. He thought of me as the target of his dartboard at home whenever he hurled darts at it. Impulsively he bought a pair of boots, and the tune to, "These boots were made for walking all over you" came to his mind. He plugged in my name as well as that of Mamie's supposed lover.

I noticed on my return that the skin of his hands and arms was covered with red spots. I recalled at once the skin allergies he had reported suffering when he had come too close to—or sometimes, gone too far from—his mother. Now he was separating and reuniting with me. Instead of saying this to him, I waited for him to tell his own story. During my absence, he had taken a trip and had had intercourse with a woman he met. Once more he thought of me during intercourse and afterwards, saying to himself, "See, Volkan! It was enjoyable. No big deal!" This thought had alternated with his mother's warning, and he felt anxiety lest the woman become pregnant. Out of bravado, he had taken no precautions against pregnancy, and he understood that she had taken none. The next day his skin broke out; he explained this rash to himself by thinking that their bed had had lice or fleas. When the rash failed to clear, he consulted a physician. The two physicians decided that bedbugs were responsible. I did not challenge this but remarked that he had once spoken of having a rash whenever he was reunited with his mother. I let him make whatever associations to this he could.

That night (May 10), he dreamt of a room deodorant. He associated this with his mother's having recently brought him a deodorant-germicide for his bathroom. He laughed nervously when he realized that this deodorant might kill bedbugs. That morning he had suspected that there were bedbugs in his trousers and had hesitated before putting them on. I told him I had no way of knowing whether there had been real bedbugs in the bed where he had slept with this woman, but I wondered if he could help me understand "psychological bedbugs," that is, whatever had gotten under his skin in relation to our separation. Because bugs often symbolize children, I suggested that he might have been disturbed when his mother left him to deliver a new child and that he might have wanted his younger sibling to be exterminated. This was probably a premature interpretation; he did not respond to it, but he was ready to give his own association. He spoke of his mother's admonition that he always wash his hands after using the bathroom and acknowledged that after having had intercourse, he had thought of getting up and washing himself but had refrained from doing so. Dr. Albert was condensing anal and phallic "dirt."

There followed more bathroom memories. He had been constipated as a child and had been made to sit on his potty until he defecated. Reality underlay his retentive childhood symptoms at the anal level and his holding his breath. He also remarked that on the couch, he became "verbally constipated" and that "psychoanalysis is like learning to paint," substituting paint for feces. Our separation had led him to use an anal mechanism—psychological retentiveness. Because he had failed to wash the "phallic dirt," his rash, whether due to real or imaginary bedbugs, was perceived by him as punishment. Once all this was discussed, his rash disappeared within the week.

He was now able, with my help, to observe how he had been using omnipotent narcissistic defenses against his anxiety. During the next month and a half, in the absence of any noteworthy occurrence, he and I learned how such narcissistic defenses had once brought him close to a break with reality. At the age of 13, he had believed that he could influence others by prayer and that he had a mission to make others happy. I surmised that by "others" he really meant his mother. I also gathered that the mission was basically in the service of covering up his rage against her.

In one session, he fantasied taking a trip with me suggested by a movie he had seen, which he identified as *Barry Lyndon*. I told him that Barry Lyndon was like the Duchess of Windsor, a gambler who married wealth. I told him that on "our trip together"—our analytic work—I had come to understand that his mother had idealized her adoptive father and that after his death she had gambled that her son, my analysand, would grow up to fill the void left by his death. My analysand raised his voice and said, "Yes! My mother put her stakes on me in order to have high self-esteem herself. That pisses me off, because she also tells me I'm second best!" He meant that he could never fulfill her expectations and surpass his adoptive grandfather. Dr. Albert again used the dandelion-rose analogy. On one level, he apparently had thought of himself as a dandelion. His mother had spent hours teaching him table manners and trying to make him into a rose. Her attention had been centered on him, and look where it had gotten him!: to an analyst's couch, while his sister was happily married and his happy brother "fucked the world."

In mid-June, Dr. Albert and his wife signed the papers for legal separation. At about this time, the local newspaper ran an article on a dangerous laboratory animal that had bitten someone. Although this event had not taken place in his laboratory, he fantasied killing rabbits and cats there. Cats, he said, reminded him of the black panther of his childhood. On the following day, he "accidentally" killed a cat.

At the end of June, Dr. Albert and his father-in-law, with whom he had made it a point to stay friendly, went off for a week-long fishing trip. I had told him that I would take my vacation in August and that it would be useful for us both if he could postpone his fishing trip to a time when I would be away. He seemed to want to argue about which was more important, his need for a good vacation at that time or his sessions with me. I simply said that I did not consider anything more important than his analysis at this phase of his life and refrained from any argument. During the hour just before he left, he complained that his contact lenses hurt him. He sat up, removed them, and lay back on the couch. Just before he left at the end of the hour, he put the lenses back in. I said nothing, and although I did not know it at the time, this action marked the start of a behavior pattern that would express important aspects of his transference neurosis during the second year of his analysis.

During his vacation, when his mother had cared for his daughter, the two men had disparaged Mamie and women in general. I felt that Dr. Albert saw his father-in-law as a father representation. I recalled how he had said during his consultation hour that he had married Mamie because he liked her father. Now, after being legally separated from her, and after symbolically killing her (mother-woman-panther), he could reach for closeness with a father figure. "Dead" women could not interfere with the relationship developing between a son and his father. Nonetheless, the other side of his ambivalence about his father and his father-in-law persisted, and he displaced his own father's propensity for

get-rich-quick schemes onto Mamie's father, with whom he entered
into a pact involving the promotion of certain plants to cure warts. (At
this point I was unaware that the father-in-law was a very rich man.)
Later, his father-in-law sent him a sample of the plants in question, and
although he had great ideas of testing them in a laboratory and even
going to the patent office in Washington with a remedy, the scheme
slowly faded away.

Dr. Albert began telling me about a young woman, Sabrina, who had
been a patient of his for some minor difficulty. She was separated from
her husband, also a physician. Dr. Albert began to date her in midsum-
mer, in what was again an association with a separation between us in
August; my vacation was approaching. He became deeply involved in
his "Dr. Albert mission," as he put it, a mission to repair Sabrina. He
tried to improve her accent, her teeth, and the way she kissed. I felt that
his concern over her accent might have something to do with me and my
accent. His interest in her mouth and teeth was in the service of
"taming" the cat's (black panther's) possible aggression. By now, I was
sure that the black panther represented the mother, and, by extension,
all women with whom he was intimate. At the same time as Sabrina was
dating Dr. Albert, she was also dating a psychiatrist, and this gave Dr.
Albert's relationship to her an oedipal tinge. But the main issue at hand
was our impending separation and his finding a new "object" to relate to
as a substitute for me.

I took my vacation in August after he had reported "frozen images"
of things from his daily activities. I interpreted to him that he was trying
to "freeze" our interaction until the separation was over.

The Renovation of a Sun Porch

August to December

When we met for our first meeting after my holiday, Dr. Albert made no direct reference to our three-week separation. Instead, he began the session by reporting a dream in which his reaction to the separation was concealed. In the dream he had seen a number of knobs in the open drawer of a wooden desk and also many knobs in a cart someone was pushing. A black man began picking up these knobs and crushing them in his hands, which were prodigiously powerful.

In association to this dream, Dr. Albert spoke of an activity in which he had engaged while on a vacation he took during my absence. While he and his daughter were staying with his mother in her home, he had thought of "tearing down and rebuilding" the old empty house in which Daddy Doc had lived and had immediately begun the project, doing the physical work himself.

Because of his tuberculosis, Daddy Doc's last years in the house had been passed in a wheelchair on the sun porch Dr. Albert was now busy tearing down. Dr. Albert associated the cart in his dream with Daddy Doc's wheelchair, and the old desk with a desk on the porch that he had wrecked in the general demolition he carried out so zealously and spoke of so obsessively. The black man in the dream—especially the black hand that crushed the knobs—reminded him of a black murderer in a James Bond movie he had seen (Live and Let Die), who had killed with a karate chop a bystander at a faked funeral procession, putting the body in the empty coffin to be carried away.

With my help, my patient came to understand that he himself might be the black killer. Black was a color he associated with his mother; although he had fantasied that her dark complexion came from noble Spanish blood, he had also perceived her as aggressively bad. He was engaged in tearing down family myths and destroying powerful images from his childhood that had continued to influence his personality and behavior (in psychoanalysis we call such images "introjects"). They appeared as knobs in his dream—like nipples and testicles. Thus, during my absence, my patient had become the killer in his effort to resolve his conflicts *without* my help. I interpreted the "do-it-yourself" aspect of his attempt as an omnipotent measure to defend against the separation.

On the following day, Dr. Albert was overcome by fear that I might retaliate for the aggression expressed in his dream. During this session, his hand and arm "went to sleep," and he talked about his longstanding fear of going blind. I recalled that at the age of 4 he had stuck a knife in his eye after being separated from his mother, who had just had a new baby. He seemed anxious as he lay on the couch and told me that he carried a Medicalert token saying that he wore contact lenses. I did not communicate that he might be afraid of my blinding him. In consideration of his history of self-punishment, I wondered if he were repeating the story of Oedipus, who had blinded himself after learning the identity of Jocasta. Since I wanted his psychoanalytic course to evolve spontaneously, I refrained from giving him explanations. Two days later he reported having failed to remove his lenses before going to sleep and dreaming of "a white hand." I interpreted his defensive change of color from black (aggressive) to white (tamed).

He was now able, with my help, to appreciate that any "muscle-flexing" on his part would be followed either by fantasies of being so omnipotent as to be safe or by self-mutilating behavior that hurt him too badly to invite retaliation. He then reported another dream in which he had *felt* as though he put his hand on something hot, although the dream had no further content. He associated this with punishment he had often suffered at his father's hand.

In mid-September, Sabrina, with whom Dr. Albert had had a few sexual encounters, moved in with her other lover, the local psychiatrist. On the couch, my analysand declared, "Psychiatry is fucking me!" The imposition of my image onto that of the other psychiatrist became that of the punishing father and reactivated Dr. Albert's oedipal fears. He felt diminished by the psychiatrist, and as he described this triangle the following day he felt sick, and regressed in what I understood as a bid for the kind of attention from me a child would get from its mother.

Everything I knew of him pointed to a real fear of the punishing oedipal father, with whom he was unable to compete. He felt a need either to bypass his father by claiming at least transient omnipotence or to submit to him. He could, however, regressively retreat from the oedipal situation toward a relationship with a woman of his pre-oedipal period (or her representative). This option was also unsatisfactory, because his strong dependence on such a woman made him fear being smothered and losing his individuality. Dr. Albert had very little psychological room in which to maneuver in respect to his personal relationships.

His regression to the arms of a caretaking mother/analyst seemed to soothe his anxiety for a while, but the "mother" soon became dangerously powerful, a castrater. After playing *hand*ball one day toward the end of September, he had a dream about a woman with red hair. When associating to the red hair, he began singing a verse from *Porgy and Bess:*

> A redheaded woman
> Can make a choo-choo jump the track;
> A redheaded woman
> Can make it jump back.

When he recalled that Porgy was a bilateral amputee (symbolically castrated), he began suddenly to complain that his hips hurt. He thought that he must have hurt himself playing handball. I made the interpretation that the redheaded woman might represent his powerful mother; his mother's favorite colors were red and black. That night he dreamed of another woman, one combing her hair. He recalled how depressed his mother had been after her husband's death and how he had made her go to a beauty salon. The day residue of this dream—that part of it derived from something that had occurred in the real world on the previous day and that was unconsciously connected with his infantile sexual and aggressive drives—reflected his having made love to a woman he had just met. While making love to her, he had thought of her hair as being like his mother's. He reported that she had made "crazy gyrations" during intercourse. They had disturbed him, and he had "burned" his hand (the one he used for masturbation) by friction against the bedclothes. I summarized for him this association with hands that had appeared since the August vacation, suggesting that his anxiety arose from facing another man—the other psychiatrist and, perhaps, me also—in clean competition and his coming face to face, while backing away from the confrontation, with women who themselves became powerful and dangerous, able to hurt him (his penis) with "crazy gyrations."

On the following day, he declared that women were without sexuality. He had received a request for a reprint of one of his articles from a woman physician, and in referring to this he commented, "It's hard to imagine a woman in *hard-core* medicine." I suggested that he needed to deny the sexuality of women because of the threat it posed.

In mid-October, he recalled having as a boy compared the size of his penis with that of other boys. He then made disparaging remarks about me, declaring that psychoanalysts, like chiropractors, were not real physicians. He was symbolically reenacting the comparison of penis size. When he gave me his check, I noticed that although he had carefully added "M.D." to his name, he had not added it to mine. I brought this to his attention without telling him that he was disparaging the size of my penis, declaring himself the real doctor and casting doubt on the professional standing not only of myself, but also perhaps of Daddy Doc.

His fear of retaliation was evidenced by Dr. Albert's taking up weight lifting at about this time. He alternated grandiose gestures with self-castrating remarks or behavior, but I refrained from interfering with his struggle, which was becoming heated. He spent fifty minutes of his session one day talking about an article he had read on the hermaphroditic nature of women; then he voiced objections to the many articles on sexuality that appeared in scientific journals.

That night he made love to Mamie, with bravado. Then he had feverishly lifted weights although he had felt some concern about the possibility of a heart attack from such exertion. He let me know that he was not yet ready to die and spoke of a psychological symptom not previously reported, his fear of climbing a ladder. I thought that this fear might have something to do with protecting himself from the oedipal father's retaliation for his climbing above him via (sexual) success. I did not share this formulation with him, preferring to have him relive the course of his original childhood struggle; I still believed that too much interpretation at this point in his analysis would lead him to defensive intellectualization.

He prepared to return to Daddy Doc's house for a weekend of strenuous physical work, which clearly, in my view, had psychological aspects and indicated resistance to revelations about his childhood perceptions. The work he proposed would inevitably involve climbing a ladder, since it had to be done on the roof, and at the end of the session he lingered at the door, saying, "I hope I don't fall off the ladder!" I made no comment.

He returned on Monday without having fallen. He then spontaneously recalled my interpretation of the black hand crushing the knobs in his dream; he implied that, after all, the work at Daddy Doc's house might indeed have something to do with his resistance to the analytic process. I made sounds of agreement. During the weekend at home, his mother had kissed him again and again, priding herself on the renovation he had accomplished as though she herself had brought it about. Dr. Albert reported that her claiming credit made him angry.

He still lay on the couch so stiffly that if he had not reported feeling states, I might easily have thought him incapable of feeling. He claimed that his psychoanalysis was beginning to help him observe his mother; he now realized how she longed for him to be unmarried so she could have him as a replacement for her dead husband. At about the beginning of November, he told me that as an intern in a New York City hospital, he had been told of his father's approaching death and had gone home with Mamie to be at his bedside. While there, he had had sexual intercourse with her in a room under the dying man's; he believed that their daughter had been conceived then. I connected this with his having intercourse when faced with separation from me later, although the full meaning of the episode at the time of his father's dying was not yet fully evident then. The death and his own birthday remained somehow connected in Dr. Albert's mind, since the death occurred less than an hour before the son's birthday. Telling me this, he cried openly at the thought that his mother's exaggerated, smothering love for him had kept him from knowing his father well. "Why," he complained, "do I remember so little about him?"

Considerable blocking of his thinking was evident in subsequent sessions, in which he was often silent. He reported that his divorce would become final in December and that he counted the days. He became increasingly concerned about his little daughter, Pamela, who was in his custody but went to her mother's occasionally for overnight visits. Hitherto he had spoken of Pamela without any reference to her feelings. Reading my notes on Dr. Albert's psychoanalytic process years later, I came to the conclusion that at the time I subtly encouraged his concern for his daughter, I unconsciously identified her with the daughter of my first marriage who was separated from me at an early age. Although I believe I was able, by and large, to maintain a psychoanalytic position with Dr. Albert, it seems likely that events in my own personal life kept me from being altogether neutral about Pamela, who seemed to be having difficulties with her parents' separation. Dr. Albert took her to see a child psychiatrist.

He himself was undergoing considerable anxiety about separation and death, provoked by the impending finalization of his divorce. He once had maintained that he could dismiss from his mind anyone who died, but he now realized how deeply both his father's death and Danny's had affected him. Although there seemed no possibility that Mamie would return to him, he continued to feel that he had done something to estrange her; guilt over psychologically "killing" her persisted. These feelings led him to disclose that his brother had been accidentally responsible for someone's death while with the army in Belgium. Although the brother had been acquitted of responsibility, Dr. Albert feared that aggression could kill. He decided that his mother enjoyed violence. Her telephone conversations, he recalled, often included accounts of violent injury such as the loss of an arm accidentally caught in machinery.

The representation Dr. Albert had of Mamie was certainly contaminated by the mental images of both his parents, but I thought that he perceived his mother as plotting against his wife because she was unable to bear a son. The divorce threatened the extreme danger of removing all obstruction to psychological reunion between mother and son, a reunion, I thought, he both desired and dreaded.

The Case of the Missing Fish

December to Mid-February

The finalization of the divorce in the first week of December failed to completely separate Dr. Albert and Mamie, who continued to see one another. He was sometimes angry with her, sometimes submissive to her wishes. When she gave him for Christmas a sweater she had charged to his account, he dreamed of returning it to a clothing store that was transformed, as he dreamed, into a general store in which an old man sat behind a desk. He told the old man that Mamie was no longer entitled to use his charge account. He could recall from his childhood just such a general store, one that was also a post office, and he remembered having been shown a drawing there that began with the shape of a heart, to which the "artist" had added two legs and a tail, declaring that the result was a picture of "a jackass going south," as when he himself had left Maryland for a college in the Deep South. What on the surface had seemed an affectionate gift (represented by the heart), had made the recipient a jackass since it had been paid for with his money. He cried out the word "Jackass!" as though addressing himself. He declared, however, that he still loved Mamie and felt their separation had not really taken place, just as he felt that neither Danny nor his father had really died.

When he said, "Cicero said that you cannot do without women, but you cannot do with them," I thought that although he was giving a fair stapement of his dilemma, his reference to Cicero was a reversion to clichés to conceal his emotions. What he sought in his dream, I thought, was the self-assertion to go to the store and take back his "mail" (maleness). He actualized this dream later by canceling the charge accounts he had shared with Mamie, but on the couch that day he was overcome by self-pity and anger, saying that he was like the dog on a railroad track who lost its head while it was trying to see the train that had run over its tail.

I felt that he was now developing an "observing ego"—the capacity to assess and understand his own behavior and feelings. He summarized his situation by saying that he repeatedly got himself emasculated by women "in order not to lose their love." Yet it was because of a woman, his mother, that he had been unable to get close to his father, whom she had represented to him as both weak and dangerous. He had come to believe that his father had spanked him regularly at her insistence. Thus the father/aggressor really had been a tool of the mother/aggressor.

I felt that this session had been a good one, because of his ability to summarize what he was learning in his analytic experience. As he spoke, I made approving sounds and felt empathy for him in his distress, which he attributed largely to the hazards a man faced in dealing with dangerous women. He was in search of a "good" father to help him out of this quagmire, one who would act as an ally against his mother.

At the approach of Christmas, the first since the start of our analytic work, he ordered boxes of special candies to give to some friends. He announced one day that the boxes had arrived, that he had set aside one for me, and that he would bring it to the last session before we separated for the Christmas holidays. He went on to describe the color and taste of these candies in the belief that I would love them. I felt as though he were inducing in me an appetite for such wonderful goodies and wondered if he were turning me into the hungry infant as he became the overfeeding mother. Perhaps, in view of our impending separation, the hungry infant needed to be fed! I also had a nagging feeling that he wanted something from me in return. "It might be useful if we try to verbalize the thoughts connected with your desire to give me a box of candy," I said. But my effort to bring his gift-giving into analysis angered him.

"It has no psychological meaning," he said. "I just want to give you a box of candy. By implying that I have some unspoken motivation in doing this you spoil everything. Okay, I won't bring you the candy, but it's your loss." Remaining negativistic, he resisted my attempt to have him associate about his wish to give me the candy.

On the following day, he reminded me that his father had died a few days before Christmas, on a date when we would not meet because of my holiday schedule. I sensed that he was angry that we would be separated—that the father would die, without receiving his son's gift of love, the candy, with its potential psychological meanings. He was too angry to work with me on these hunches, however, and he still felt negative toward me when we resumed work in the new year. Yet during our first hour in the new year, he reported having enjoyed his New Year's Day celebrations and seemed surprised that he could have had such a good time in the midst of emotional turmoil. He was dating several women and had attended a party, but he was very cautious about developing any feelings of closeness that might lead to commitment. I thought that any commitment to a woman would lead him to see her as a smothering, dangerous mother.

As Dr. Albert lay on the couch, a picture that had always hung on the wall nearby came to his attention, and he decided that the man in it resembled Mao Tse-tung, the dead Chinese leader whose widow was then in danger of being ousted from the Chinese government. Behind these remarks I could hear his desire to "tame" the widow, his mother. In early January, our sessions were given over to his accounts of the different women he was meeting and dating. I felt that he saw them as interchangeable and lacking in individual identity. Without any sense of direction, he would review their names and ask himself why each attracted him. He reported having lectured each one about her aimlessness, thereby establishing himself as a "woman salvager." He repaired them to reflect well on his grandiose self and at the same time made them suitably good mothers in case he needed their attention. I thought that he was also telling me that although I had not accepted his candy, he could find others willing to accept his gifts!

On January 11, he dreamed about a woman with dark hair and alabaster skin. The word alabaster, he took pains to tell me, came from *á la baste;* that is, *á la bastard.* His mother and his sister might be bastards, but being a bastard's son was unacceptable to him. I observed to him that whereas he idealized all women at first and tried to rescue them, whenever he was frustrated he quickly discarded them. His reply was, "Big cycle, huh!"

On the following day, Dr. Albert reported dreaming of being stopped by a policeman while he was driving his car. The day residue in this dream came from his having received, on the previous day, a government inquiry into some aspect of his laboratory work. He said that he must "stop talking about pussies" and get down to the business of his analysis. When I asked him to elaborate, he said that he had felt reprimanded by my observation of his "big cycle." He had pondered my interpretation of his work on Daddy Doc's house and had realized that he was trying to resolve his conflict about women by his "big cycle" and his activities. He had perceived my remark as an order to stop resisting and get down to the work of his analysis. I was the policeman who policed his analytic work and as such made him fear the dangerous, castrating, and "bad" oedipal father. This fear was condensed with a fear of the dangerously smothering mother.

Dr. Albert suddenly began to speak of his aquarium, in which an algae eater had disappeared. He wondered aloud if the frog had eaten it. He seemed apprehensive and recalled that when he had looked at the aquarium the day before, "Nothing seemed to be violent there, but . . . but. . . ." (I had to urge him to complete the sentence.) "But mutilation and killing occurred!" When I asked him to let his mind wander about the disappearance of the algae eater, he reported feeling that when different kinds of fish were confined together, their natural animosity must lead to violence. I suggested that it might have been his thought of violence in that tank that had led him to dream of a policeman. He then reported that when one guppy in the tank had seemed aggressive, he had "executed" it.

His account of executing the aggressive fish brought him memories of having been an aggressive child until the age of 12, when something he could not recall had changed him. At 14, he had cut off his toe. With some embarrassment, he then disclosed that he had begun to masturbate when he was in the fourth or fifth grade. Feeling guilt, he recalled with even greater embarrassment having, at the age of 4 or 5, sucked the penis of a small friend, who then had returned the favor. I suggested that event might be another version of the frog eating the fish, but he screamed, "That has nothing to do with the fish! Nothing! Nothing!" After calming down, he spoke of the black panther and his belief that it would eat people. He then recalled having heard as a child about a fanatical minister who had amputated his penis and eaten it. I told him, "The case of the missing fish may be connected with the case of the missing penis. Let's be more curious about this."

By the next day he was able to tell me that concern about a missing penis might have something to do with a date that a friend was arranging for him with a *psychoanalyst* in a nearby city. Giving me her name, he asked anxiously if I knew her. I did, but instead of replying, I encouraged his fantasies about her. I felt that he was unconsciously contemplating a sexual encounter between us, the female psychoanalyst being symbolically my extension. In such an encounter, he would anticipate that his father/analyst would castrate him, but that the mother/analyst might eat his penis. Although at this point no clear reconstruction of the meaning of the black panther was available, I thought of sharing with him later, when appropriate, the possibility that the panther reflected his perception of a devouring vagina, one with sharp teeth.

Dr. Albert thought of the psychoanalyst, who in reality was slim, as a physically large woman with whom he would have intercourse. The prospect made him anxious, and on the couch he shook visibly. I told him to put his bodily reaction into words, whereupon he reported having had the notion that her vagina might be like a bear trap that would amputate his penis. On the following day, en route to my office, his car stalled in heavy snow, so our session was only ten minutes long. Although he was unaware of any conscious design in stalling his car, I suspected that he had been anxious about facing me, associating me (the castrater) with the panther or the frog. In any case, this session was effectively "castrated"!

His date with the psychoanalyst never materialized, but he took another woman to a professional meeting and missed two sessions with me. While away, he dreamed of lying in a drunken sleep when someone entered his house to kill him. He was unable to defend himself and awakened with anxiety. On the first night of February, he drove one of his girlfriends to her home late at night. She lived in the country, and he thought of me on the drive back to town, worrying lest I lived near her and might have seen him with his date. He had smoked marijuana with her, and even after his return home I remained in his mind as a "frozen picture of a judge wearing a judicial robe." Throughout a restless night he had moments of wakefulness in which he would see me again as a judge.

Dr. Albert had been in analysis with me for about a year, and I had learned a great deal about him. Although many of his childhood memories were reflected in transference, I knew that he had not yet developed a full transference neurosis. Although he continued to be overcautious, to speak monotonously, and to lie motionless on the couch, he had begun to experience and to show emotion, and I awaited the "heating up" of transference manifestations and his perception of our relationship as the core of his analysis. I knew that when this took place, I would be able to understand his childhood mind not only through his memories, some of which had previously been repressed, but through the interaction between the two of us. Only through such interaction and the eventual resolution of its conflictual aspects would his analysis be accomplished. I was excited that his "real" analysis was about to begin.

The persistence of my image in his mind against his will made him anxious, so I told him (using suggestion to promote the developing transference neurosis), "If I tell you that the core of the analysis is the analysand's thoughts and feelings about his analyst, would that be helpful to you?" He replied that he had already gathered that "the interaction between us" was highly important, but he was afraid that if he talked more about me I would think of him as homosexual, whereas he had only once in his lifetime, in college, kissed a gay man. "But that was all!"

Soon he reported a dream of parking his sports car, which reflected his macho image, in a parking lot at the local shopping center to attend a meeting of the military reserve. After the meeting, he could not find his car. A police station appeared in the parking lot, and policemen watching him seek his car concluded that he was somehow responsible for its disappearance. At the start of the dream, he wore men's clothing, but after the loss of his car, he was wearing a woman's pink robe. He then became aware of a tumor on his neck or shoulder; it felt like a breast when he touched it.

He was visibly shaken by this dream and began to talk about recollections of wearing his mother's shoes as a child (I thought he was referring to his conflictual identification with his mother and wondered if he had been wearing them when he stabbed at a tree and hurt his eye.) "Why do I remember this whenever I want to remember something from my childhood?" he asked. He thought that the tree he stabbed was the one *into which the black panther had climbed.* He remembered having objected to having a pet dog or cat altered. "It wasn't fair to snatch their nuts off. I have a type of empathy for them" he explained. He made no further direct associations to the dream about the parking lot, but he did remember that on the day before he dreamed about wearing a woman's pink robe, he had bought a pink robe for his daughter. This fact suggested that in his dream he was partly identifying with her.

That night, as Dr. Albert told me the next day, he had gone bowling and had bowled poorly. It had occurred to him that his performance had been poor for "psychological reasons." When he had got home, he had had a drink and gone to bed. When he had awakened, he had found himself in *the bed of his daughter,* who was spending the night with friends, and his hand touched her pet cat (pussy or panther). He knew he had not switched beds out of his drunkenness; he had simply played "musical beds" without conscious awareness, as in sleepwalking. (In technical terms, his experience could be called a "dissociative reaction," since he was not consciously aware of having switched beds.) Although his daughter had been away and her bed therefore empty, he was greatly embarrassed and able to report the episode, in trembling voice, only after considerable hesitation. I suggested that he let his mind wander over the meaning of this incident.

He recalled that on the day before the bed incident he had gone to pick up his daughter from her psychiatrist's office and had seen her talking to him in the waiting room. Their chat had seemed affectionate, and he had felt jealous. Desirous of his daughter's affection, he suddenly saw a triangle in which he was at a disadvantage. "Even baboons need affection," he grumbled. I understood that one reason for his wearing a pink robe in the dream and for sleeping in his daughter's bed was to gratify his desire to get affection through identification with her.

He talked about his mother's showering him with affection when he was very small. How nice her hair had smelled! "Maybe some time in the past I couldn't tell if I were a boy or girl," he said. I thought he referred to a wish for merging with his mother in order to possess her totally, and I suggested this to him. He then said he was having a very strange sensation on the couch, a sensation of floating so marked that he actually clung to the edges of the couch to steady himself. "If I let myself go I'll float!" (Unafraid, he was expressing an experience I had had myself in therapeutic regression during psychoanalysis. I recognized his pleasure in floating.) I told him that he was perhaps expressing a desire to be lifted up in my arms and to receive my affection. He smiled.

That afternoon, as he cleaned out his refrigerator, he suddenly thought to himself, "I can't let another woman look at my refrigerator!" When he realized that he had been referring to himself as a woman, he felt very upset. On the couch next day, he shouted at me, "I don't want psychoanalysis! Why should I learn more about myself? The last thing I want to find out is that I am a homosexual or that I want to be a woman!" I said nothing by way of response, and he quickly calmed down and let his mind wander.

Dr. Albert recalled having seen his daughter dressing a few days earlier, and he was reminded of once as a child having seen his mother's genitalia. "She exposed her cunt, totally without concern!" he said with some excitement. He then reproached himself aloud, "You are not interested in seeing her tits and pussy!" He said that he had entertained the notion of having been a husband surrogate to his mother and shouted at me, "I know that. I told you that!" He suggested that he was also a surrogate for Daddy Doc, whom his mother admired so much. "It would shock my mother to know that I am not perfect," he mused.

After a silence, he unrepressed the memory of what had taken place before he "accidentally" amputated his toe. Some older boys had held him tightly to force him to "do a blow job" on another boy who had taken out his flaccid penis. He had resisted, but his captor had touched his forehead or cheek with his penis during the struggle, and he recalled, with appropriate feelings, the anger and humiliation he had felt, saying that the place that had been touched might be a mark of feminization. I told him that the place had been displaced to his shoulder (the site of the tumor or breast of his dream), where it indicated a psychological burden: confusion of sexual identity and fear of homosexual tendencies.

The first year of Dr. Albert's analysis ended in mid-February.

The Second Year

Even Baboons Pick Lice from Each Other

Mid-February to April

Dr. Albert made no reference to the beginning of his second year of analysis; I said nothing either. I did tell him that it would be necessary to cancel three sessions during the month since I would be away during the third week. Just as he had done earlier in the face of an impending separation between us, he found a woman with whom to have intercourse. He learned that just a week earlier she had had a tubal ligation. When he spoke of her to me, he dwelled on the notion that she was "castrated"; he found this shocking. The session was full of silences, broken only by his narcissistic defenses, exemplified by his regarding himself as superior to this person or that.

His need for intercourse with his wife when his father lay dying and the present repetition of this pattern was intriguing. I sensed that it had several determinants. On the surface level, it seemed that when he faced the death of someone, it reminded him of a dreaded separation and made him anxious. Making love to a woman reassured him that he could still be "united" with another, and relieved his separation anxiety. He had impregnated his wife to balance a death with a birth. I also caught implications of oedipal conflicts and hoped-for solutions. Although his behavior could be seen as providing Dr. Albert with an oedipal triumph as he conquered a woman and killed the oedipal father, his behavior also seemed to involve an effort to keep the father alive.

Although castration anxiety is a major source of conflict in the course of a child's development, it also contributes to the resolution of the

Oedipus complex. Unable to conquer the father, the child joins him! A healthy resolution of the Oedipus complex accomplishes healthy identification with selected aspects of the father. Dr. Albert had not fully resolved his Oedipus complex because of early disturbances in his relationship with his mother. When he faced his father's impending death, he had tried, in a sense unconsciously, to provoke his father to come after him, feeling that the enactment of a triangular situation would keep him alive. Thus his hope of resolving his Oedipus complex persisted.

Two days before our brief separation, Dr. Albert reported that on the day before he had put his hand into a sack of cat food and had been suddenly terrified lest the sack contain mice or spiders. This incident released memories of a childhood fear that some creature would bite his penis. After telling me this, he said he wanted to take a "catnap" on the couch. I suggested that he might be angry at me, regarding my planned departure as rejection, and that the cat represented the aggressor, a creature who might retaliate by biting him. I suggested further that by wanting a "catnap" he was identifying himself with the aggressor (his analyst) and thus protecting himself from danger.

During the last session before I left, Dr. Albert lost the boundaries of his body and felt that he merged with my couch (in a representation of his attempt to become an extension of me). He also felt that the couch was a pool in which he was floating. One of the types of regression occurring in analysis involves the return to an early traumatic experience and an attempt to master it. The analyst can help resolve the conflicts involved in such an experience as they are reflected in the transference neurosis. Another kind of regression is in the service of an attempted return to an earlier state of real or fantasied gratification, in a retreat from conflicts of a higher level. My analysand, in the second type of regression, was experiencing a merging with me in order to avoid conflict with the anxiety and other feelings evoked by our impending separation. He gave further evidence of avoidance of anxiety when he reported a fantasy that had just occurred to him in which Groucho Marx, smoking a cigar, held in a pink blanket an infant with a moustache. I, who often smoked cigars, was Groucho, and he was the baby. I sensed that his cartoon fantasy devalued his need of me. I became a ridiculous caricature.

After my return, Dr. Albert reported having had laryngitis during my absence and commented that it was a good thing I had been away, since he would not have been able to talk to me in any case! Soon, and seeming more relaxed, he spoke of how strange our last session had seemed to him, evoking sensations in him like smoking marijuana or dreaming. He felt high recalling being held in the arms of Groucho Marx or floating in a pool of water. I interpreted his regressive way of avoiding unpleasantness, but he insisted that this defensive regression had not enabled him to handle his aggressive impulses toward me altogether. During my absence, he had accomplished one of his "self-castrating" acts in order to escape the retaliation he expected from me: he had had his hair cut very short. As he spoke his neck, he said, felt naked, cold, and exposed to me. I might chop off his head! This made him anxious, and toward the end of the session he again retreated to the pool. As though in a trance, he reported feeling weightless. He fell silent for a while and then confided that he had felt the sensation of being rocked.

On March 3, he reported having dreamed of cards like tarot cards, with words written on them. He then talked about his supernatural beliefs, and it seemed to me that he was revisiting that period of life when the small child's mind is omnipotent and "oceanic" and the child can relate to others through merging. In regression, he was able to recall clearly his old belief system, which had endowed him with magical powers and encouraged him to believe in reincarnation. He had thought himself in command of "electromagnetic energy" or "thought waves." In fact, in his daily life he still entertained vestiges of such a belief when he gazed steadily at a bowling opponent in the belief that he could thereby damage his performance. As a child riding in a bus, he had stared at the necks of those sitting in front of him, certain that this would make them turn their heads in response. Until he began analysis, he had had many daydreams of owning an impenetrable spaceship in which he moved about the globe, forcing everyone to surrender arms and give up waging war and destruction. I perceived that his use of narcissistic, omnipotent fantasies was in the service of denying the aggression in the world—including his own—while, at the same time, protecting him in an enclosure.

The words on the tarot cards in Dr. Albert's dream were *feeling, masking,* and *warmth.* He explained that he had been masking his warm feelings. He said that he had experienced a "different kind of loneliness" in our last separation and that he had begun feeling warmth toward me. On the previous day, the cigar scent that lingers in my office (although I refrain from smoking while seeing patients), had filled him with feelings of affection that he had masked until now. He said he wanted to feel warmth toward me "in order, later on, to have affection toward women." He had, in fact, begun to feel close to his daughter Pamela. Although he had formerly thought of me as "it" or "psychoanalysis," he now perceived me as a person. He still feared having sexual feelings for me, however, and one day while urinating he had wondered how I would look in the same act. He spoke of how feeling warmth toward me would enable him to take a woman to bed and feel warmth toward her. When recently he had felt some warmth toward two women he had just met, he had checked himself. Yet he declared, "Even baboons pick lice from each other. I need affection!"

He wanted affectionate relatedness to me as long as I was perceived as a woman, but any involvement with me "as a man" would threaten homosexual surrender. He had had a strong attachment to his mother up to and including his oedipal phase. He had not resolved his oedipal conflicts by healthy identification with his father; instead, he had partially identified with his mother. This in turn made him fear homosexuality; it would lower his self-esteem to know that he might submit to his father as his mother had done, but on the other hand, he unconsciously wanted such submission in order to avoid dangerous rivalry with his father and to escape the castration he feared at his hands. This unconscious wish became evident in a dream in which he saw one of his older superiors in the hospital, a Dr. Sanders, make love to Mamie in his office. Dr. Sanders practiced the same specialty as Dr. Albert did. Once, in reality, Dr. Albert had knocked on Dr. Sanders's office door and, thinking that he had given due notice, had entered, only to find the doctor fondling a female laboratory technician.

I told him that his dream about Dr. Sanders concealed his fear of homosexual surrender by his offer of his own woman to the older man. Interpretation changed his usual posture on the couch; now he opened his legs, as though conveying a desire to receive me. I said nothing about this and awaited the unfolding of the analytic process. He talked about how hard it had been for him to have an affectionate relationship with his father and noted that although he felt no interest in touching or embracing me, he did feel affection for me. With considerable embarrassment, he confessed that he had recently masturbated while daydreaming about homosexuality. His masturbating hand felt cold as he spoke of this.

Around this time, Dr. Albert suddenly realized in conversation with a friend who spoke of me that I am Turkish. The person who originally suggested that he come to me had made this clear, but my foreign accent until then apparently had not excited his interest in my origins, although during the previous summer he had briefly and with an omnipotent manner spoken of finding a solution to the Turkish-Greek conflicts. Now he began to talk about surrendering to that "terrible Turk," his analyst. He had never known a Turk well, in spite of having perhaps run into one or two while in college, and like most Americans, was quick to activate the sterotypical view of such a foreigner as being ominous, dangerous, and powerful. As a way of dealing with his fear of submitting to me and to deny any such possibility, he became hyperactive heterosexually. Mamie had left town to start a new life, and he felt free. I sensed that "pussy collecting," the going from one girl to another, bolstered his self-esteem and protected him from the painful acknowledgment that he was working through a homosexual position. Besides defending against homosexual surrender to the oedipal father, he seemed to be demonstrating rebelliousness against the controlling mother. From being a virile man he would quickly change into a child in a dangerous and submissive posture. He kept telling me that I was "so damned nebulous" and that after more than a year I should be more active and give him "direction," and he tried to arouse me to take action against him in order to obtain "direction." He demanded to know what "the rules and regulations" of analysis might be, and when I did not reply, he remained silent for as long as 30 or 40 minutes, his legs apart in a passive and seductive way. In one session, he had an image of himself as a white laboratory mouse. He felt then that if he moved he would be shocked, so he lay immobilized on the couch. The second half of this session compensated for this; he screamed that he was, after all, perfectly all right, that it was others who were "all fucked up," and he wanted to know "what in hell he was doing on my couch."

As we approached the end of March, Dr. Albert continued in his sessions to be abruptly aggressive toward me, especially in his tone of voice. He felt anxiety over my retaliatory aggression against him. Then he would become anxiously submissive and experience homosexual panic. This behavior continued in a cycle of alternating moods. One way to interrupt this cycle was for him to regress further, but although regression had pleasant aspects, it was not without danger.

Dr. Albert felt rage against the psychiatrist who was now living with Sabrina; he was my displaced representation. While driving his car, he had thought of running down some pedestrians, and the notion had evoked guilt and panic. When he reported this on the couch, he felt that if he moved his dangerousness would be unleashed. He expected me to reprimand him and then reported having a strange sensation, which I asked him to describe. Dr. Albert said that he thought of me sitting behind him, growing bigger and bigger all the time (and thus ever more dangerous to him). Soon my face was enlarged in his imagination, becoming a flat plain with a ditch in the middle. He shrank and put his face under the flat plain, which he watched with fascination.

Since I felt that the flat plain with a ditch in the middle represented an early perception of his mother's breasts, I explained how his anger in a triangular situation, his competition with me, and his fear of my retaliation made him regress all the way to being a nursling. His alternation between facing the oedipal father (my growing bigger and bigger) and trying to find a pre-oedipal mother (my having breasts) continued. He saw me as representing both of these figures in the developing transference neurosis, in spite of the fact that he could hear my interpretations and observe with me the experience he was having. At times, his experience of reactivated childhood events and appropriate accompanying feelings overrode his ability to observe what was taking place. Although I did not interfere at such times, I offered clarification for him. He became unable to reach a climax in a sexual encounter, and his relationship with his mother brought anxieties about a vagina with teeth *(vagina dentata)*. The couch was affecting his personal life.

At times, the analytic process is a very trying business. The analysand's ability to continue in his ways of dealing with the world may deteriorate as he gets ready to cope in new ways. This deterioration is accompanied by anxiety, and were it not for the therapeutic alliance, the analysand might decide to discontinue therapy. Dr. Albert had seen a painting illustrating *vagina dentata* and cried out, "Why would anyone paint such an incredible thing?" His mind seemed full of stories of monsters, and it frightened him to lie on the couch because it was there that he allowed these frightening thoughts to come to him.

When he had news that he had been promoted at work, he called his mother, only to find that the parent who had so pushed him to excel was excited very little by the good news. Dr. Albert felt that she was unable to understand the meaning of his promotion, that her encouragement of him had little to do with the real world and much to do with using him psychologically as an extension of the idealized Daddy Doc, to patch up her own deficient (adopted) self.

I kept hearing that he was searching for a good father who could pull him away from the frightening images of his childhood. This was no easy job; he would be willing to take "directions" from me, but he had to pay a price for this by submitting to me. I explained this to him, and for a while he seemed relaxed, producing memories of the good father. It was then that I learned that his "weak" father had had a strong side, being an excellent athlete who had been a basketball star in high school and had played with good teams. For the first time, I understood why at the start of his analysis he had asked me if I liked basketball; he was looking for a good father, one good enough to help him, to analyze him. The image of the good father seemed to split off from the image of the frightening one. I sensed that he was not yet able to put the two images together into a realistic view of his father (or of me).

Musical Beds and Stories about Bears

Early April through May 16

Early in April, Dr. Albert reported feeling like "a blood pressure apparatus wrapper with prickly ends that wouldn't stick together." He felt "cut loose" and sensed something opening up. He could not describe what was occurring in his analysis except that his ability to feel fear and sadness gave him a sense of security. While in bed the night before our meeting on April 3, he fantasied that a bear attacked his daughter Pamela. He was bitten when he came to her rescue, and lost an arm. A woman who lived next door came to help him, and he suddenly realized that he loved this neighbor.

On the previous day, Mamie had been in town for a brief visit, and the couple had had intercourse, after which he had felt remote from her, liberated—"cut loose"—but saddened. On the night of the fantasy about the bear, he had had a sense of the intertwining of Mamie's image with those of his mother and his daughter. Pamela was having trouble with schoolwork, and it bothered him when she brought her difficulties to him. He had been horrified to think, while looking at her, "If I kill her, she will not be in trouble at school." He explained that *he* was the bear attacking Pamela in his fantasy. He was trying to save her by trying to kill his angry self.

I asked Dr. Albert to speculate about the loss of his arm in the fantasy. His reply was that he paid a heavy penalty for his anger and understood that he must be mutilated in order to be worthy of a woman's love. "I am a slave to my peter!" he cried. He observed that he had to be in a position of castration if he were to use his penis, and shared with me his perception that his lovemaking was usually an act of aggression. He felt a conflict between being aggressive toward a woman and being her savior. "I have both attitudes," he said.

During his childhood, his mother sat by his bedside and told stories as he went to sleep. The stories were often about a family of bears: the papa bear, the mama bear, and the baby bear. These stories were connected with eating and tidying up. He spoke again about the sweet smell of his mother's hair, but these recollections made him uneasy. It would take more time for him to be "cut loose" and uncover fully his memories about his mother's visits to his bedroom and his unconscious "interpretations" of the bear stories.

He began the next session by reporting that he had just seen his name listed on his hospital's roster with the wrong middle initial. He was surprised to realize that it was his father's initial, and for a moment he thought that I was playing a trick on him. He felt merged with his father briefly and thought of his father also as having been a physician. I asked him to speculate about this. It seemed that he wanted to identify with a strong father and so in his fancy made his father a doctor who could hold his own with his wife. This wishful fantasy was selfish inasmuch as the strong father met Dr. Albert's need to break away from his mother. He gave details of his mother's disorderliness and, for example, told how his father had had to put the house to rights after his daughter's wedding. These memories degraded not only his mother but Daddy Doc also, as he went into particulars about how often he had been drunk and philandered.

At the next session, instead of simply closing the door and taking his place on the couch, Dr. Albert closed the door and picked up the telephone on my desk to reach a nursing station in his hospital to give instructions about one of his patients. I suggested after he stretched out on the couch that he speculate about why he had done this. He had little explanation to offer except that his patient was in critical condition and that it had not occurred to him to ask permission to use my phone.

He reported a dream in the following session, saying, "I was a very young-looking doctor listening to a woman's chest with a stethoscope." The night before having this dream, he had thought that he was coming down with a cold and blamed me for a psychosomatic reaction to what was going on in his analysis. The next morning he recalled that as a small boy of about 1 or 2, he had been taken to an allergist for shots. The allergist had let him use his stethoscope and pretend to be a doctor. Although his mother had prodded him to become an extension of Daddy Doc, he had never as a child been allowed to play with Daddy Doc's stethoscope, which was locked away. His mother had been afraid that some tuberculosis germs might remain on it and harm him.

It was now possible to make psychological sense out of his dream in connection with recent events. He had "played doctor" in my office, identifying with the aggressor (the physician who had given him shots or the analyst whom he wanted to be his strong father). Discussion of this led him to speak of his reluctant acceptance of helplessness and weakness as a small child and how this feeling had persisted into his adult life. As a child, he said, he might have attempted to deny his helplessness: "I felt like my dog, Max. Max never looked like a puppy; he always looked grown up. But now I know he must have been a puppy once, even if he looked like a grown dog." His identification with Max brought to his mind how, as a small child, he had once defecated on the floor and a dog had tried to eat his feces. He had been fascinated, but his mother was greatly upset when she entered the room and saw what was going on. I suggested that we see what associations might come from this memory, and he thought of having used my phone; I had not seemed pleased with his doing this, and thus I was like his mother in not accepting his "shit." I think there was some truth in his perception, because his using the phone had taken me by surprise and had disturbed the analytic routine. Although I had said nothing about it until he was on the couch, he may have picked up my momentary disturbance. He then remarked that he often felt "like farting" while on the couch. A ceiling ventilator above the couch blew in air intermittently and somewhat noisily, and he had always fantasied that the ventilator was my anus and that if he passed gas while on the couch, "I would fart a bigger fart" at him.

Our sessions were now full of what is technically called "anal material," with much discussion of cleaning up "messes." I was aware that this material had begun to surface after his fantasy about the bear and his recollection of aspects of the bear stories his mother had told him at his bedside. I wondered if the introduction of anal material was defensive; from a developmental point of view, a child's anal phase corresponds to the time between 1½ and 3½ years, when he is learning to control his muscles, the anal sphincter among them, and to separate himself psychologically from his mother. In adult life, continuation of any extensive use of the psychological mechanisms involved in that period makes an individual obsessional, as I had initially felt Dr. Albert to be. The period between 1½ and 3½, with its characteristic psychological devices to deal with the inner and outer world, comes between early childhood and the more sophisticated psychic mechanism of the oedipal period. Clinical experience shows that an individual can be badly mired in anal issues whenever the original anal period was sufficiently traumatic to keep the child from rising to a higher level of functioning. Often the anal level and its accompanying psychic defensive-adaptive mechanisms become, in a sense, a reservoir of conflicts between the higher oedipal level and the lower, early ones. In other words, the child having difficulty in facing oedipal issues returns to the anal level he has already mastered; or the child with very early trauma will reach up to the anal level to escape the effects of a very early pathological mother–child relationship.

I wondered now if Dr. Albert were both "reaching down" and "reaching up" with his obvious anal preoccupation; but I also knew that he had been traumatized at the anal level, chiefly by the birth of his brother. Thus, initially, I did not try to find ways to interpret his preoccupation with anal material as a defensive maneuver against something, probably something hidden in his mother's bear stories, that was becoming highly charged. I wanted him to stay with the material so we could uncover actual memories and their reactivation in the transference. I thought that this course would add to our understanding; but I decided not to lose sight of what else might be involved in his "bear stories."

His anal preoccupation yielded a "fringe benefit." There seems to be considerable connection in the unconscious between feces and money, and Dr. Albert began to speak spontaneously of his financial situation, to review and revise it. He decided to buy a property that would give him a tax advantage.

Another benefit of dealing with the anal material was the opportunity to put together in a logical way aspects of Dr. Albert's personal history. During the anal period, the child begins to use logical thinking and to organize issues. Dr. Albert now embarked on a presentation, almost as if it had been packaged, of his family story. This presentation helped me greatly later in his analysis as I tried to formulate different symptoms, character traits, and inhibitions. The following account was given spontaneously in a series of sessions; I synthesize it here.

Daddy Doc had been a landowner when he and his wife had adopted Dr. Albert's mother. His wife was known as "Brownie" (a nickname that

I felt Dr. Albert associated with feces). Besides Dr. Albert's mother, the couple also adopted an illegitimate daughter of Daddy Doc's whom Brownie disliked. This daughter still lived at a distance from the family home. Brownie was no fonder of Dr. Albert's mother. Daddy Doc died long before Dr. Albert's birth, but Brownie, who remarried, lived to be 81, and he remembered her as an important figure of his childhood.

Dr. Albert's father had been the son of his father's second marriage, one of seven children, all of whom except himself ultimately became successful. By the time he was an adult, the family had lost its fortune, and Dr. Albert had come to believe that his father's youth and athletic prowess had seduced his mother and that her pregnancy with Dr. Albert's sister had forced their marriage. Meanwhile, Daddy Doc's family also lost their wealth, but Brownie retained a considerable fortune.

After his marriage, Dr. Albert's father had struggled to make ends meet, and his financial situation was at low ebb when Dr. Albert's brother was born. Dr. Albert recalled having gone into the fields with others in the family to gather *dandelion* leaves to eat out of necessity. Brownie was not interested in helping the family of her adopted daughter, although she continued living in the big house—the one that Dr. Albert was so preoccupied with "tearing down" and "renovating." Apparently a very narcissistic woman, Brownie favored young Chris Albert above all others in the family. He had mixed feelings about her. He thus perceived himself as not only the favorite of his mother, who was at the time a "dandelion," but also the favorite of Brownie, who clearly declared herself a "rose."

No misfortune could make Dr. Albert's mother stop idealizing Daddy Doc, however. His image always smelled like a rose. The family was made up of dandelions and roses, and Dr. Albert, thinking about his rich grandmother and the necessity of eating dandelion leaves, was confused on the couch and confessed to embarrassment over the pretentious facade maintained by some of his family.

Brownie died when Dr. Albert was 30. She left over $150,000 to his mother as well as property, including the house with the sun porch. Since this represented a considerable fortune in a small town of that period, Brownie's posthumous aid was substantial. Dr. Albert's mother managed her finances poorly, however, and in time the fortune dwindled away.

It was after his review of his childhood and his perception of having divided the people in his family into dandelions and roses that Dr. Albert became involved in putting together his two "sides." In his daily life, he presented himself omnipotently as a rose above all others, but he had come to see that this was defensive retention of a self-concept and that his dandelion self had persisted in the shadows. For example, he had young "redneck" friends, with whom he bowled regularly, and he regarded bowling as something only dandelions would do. His bowling companions included no professional people, and his weekly, ritualistic bowling engagement activated his dandelion self and kept him in contact with it. Moreover, his review of his background emphasized open reunion with his poor, dandelion aspect to the extent that he began dating a "redneck" girl. This connection did not last long, and when it was over he showed some humor in declaring, "She was not a dandelion; she was very little more than hominy grits!"

Just before the middle of May, I left for a week to attend the American Psychoanalytic Association meeting, as I had done the year before. I did not hear upon my return, as I had done then, of his dealing with the separation by finding a woman for a sexual encounter; I felt that the meaning of that behavior had been interpreted to him with some success. I was to learn later, however, that during my absence he had been with a woman who reminded him of his mother on a *conscious* level.

During the first session after my return, he complained of a stomach ache and salivated excessively, as he said he had been doing each night during my absence. He had had this symptom before, he explained, although not for a year and a half. He associated his stomach ache with fear, and the salivation with hunger, spontaneously suggesting that his new symptoms were associated with our separation. He seemed able to tolerate his own observation of his regression to helplessness. For example, he had a visual image of a bowl of spaghetti and was able to speak of his wish that I would feed him.

In the next session, Dr. Albert kept vacillating between acceptance of his helpless state and a desire to enjoy himself "as a normal person." He could show more empathy for his daughter and was responding to her needs. He vacillated between a desire to be fed by a good mother/ analyst and visits with his oedipal father (during his sessions), who was under the sway of a bad mother. The images of the bad mother made it hard to trust her (to be fed by her). He recalled how his mother had held him on her lap almost every week while his father had cut the child's hair. He could still visualize his dark, heavy locks falling on a towel, and he remembered how he had lived in fear that his father would cut off his ears. I interpreted to him that his hunger for his mother was complicated by his perception of her cooperating with his father to mutilate him. Fear of mutilation at the hands of his father compelled him to cling to his mother, but since she was implicated in his mutilation, the only way he could remain with her was to mutilate himself in a controlled, and hence less dangerous, way. It was fear of his mother that made him deny childhood helplessness. I congratulated him on becoming able to tolerate this helplessness and to experience how it had been for him to be a child in his own particular environment. Listening, he added another understanding to complete the picture, telling me that his mother's description of his father as weak also made him cling to her. "I stayed in a woman's world. Men were impotent, except Daddy Doc, who was a superman and unreachable."

When he visited his mother in mid-May Dr. Albert noticed that her basement was full of useless things that she had eagerly collected, and he felt like one of them. When he left, he was unable to kiss his mother on the mouth to say goodbye, although previously they had always parted with such a kiss. He said that he had had the feeling this time that if he kissed her in the usual way, she would grasp him and kiss him as though in an act of love. He had developed a revulsion for something that would be "too lingering, too thirsty, too hungry, and too desperate."

This feeling brought up many memories of his mother's kissing him on the lips when he was a small child. Dr. Albert understood that his following this custom with his daughter had its origin in his own childhood, and he acknowledged with embarrassment that he sometimes sensed Pamela's desire to hang on his lips. I told him that I heard him sensing how an aspect of a mother–son relationship had been transferred to the father–daughter relationship. I think my empathy helped him, and he reported more childhood memories, returning to the previously interrupted "bear stories."

When he was a child, said Dr. Albert, his mother seldom slept the night out in one bed. Although she went to bed with her husband, during the night she would slip into other beds in the house, usually empty ones. The meaning of Dr. Albert's awakening in his daughter's empty bed began to emerge. With that act—as I could soon tell him—he was recalling his mother's playing "musical beds" at night and his special way of perceiving and symbolizing this behavior. Young Chris had been very much interested in his mother's nightly moves. He remembered the sweet smell of her hair from those occasions when she came to his bed.

After saying this, he suddenly stopped and told me that he thought he had a cold since his nose was stopping up. I told him that this sensation meant that he could not smell, and that if he could not smell his mother's hair, he might not remember the feelings or thoughts associated with that fragrance. Although he responded to this with a nervous laugh, he continued talking.

It was, Dr. Albert said, when he was in the fifth or sixth grade that his mother went to his bed for the last time, told him a bear story, and gave him a "bear hug." She then lay beside him. Having heard something about "fucking," he asked her about this and about "how babies are born." He went on to ask if sexual intercourse was fun. Although he thought now that his question might have embarrassed her, she acknowledged that she enjoyed it. She never came to his bed again.

Dr. Albert then spoke in some detail about the bear stories and how the bears were always being lost in caves and rivers. I told him that the caves and rivers might represent the vagina, and that his mother had in fact been giving him a symbolic description of sexual intercourse, which had stimulated his question. Upset by this interpretation, he cried out, "All Freudian theory is bullshit!" But I considered my interpretation well timed and felt that his anger was displaced from his mother onto me. Because I said nothing, he became calm enough to talk further about the "musical beds." He recalled that his mother had carried her own pillow from bed to bed and that he had developed a "sleep disturbance" because of the need to stay alert for the sound of *his mother's footsteps*. He said that his "sleep disturbance" had continued until he was 10 or 12, when he had been taken to a doctor who gave him pills for it. I felt that young Chris had for years both hoped and feared that his mother would return to his bed.

On May 16, the following day, Dr. Albert was noticeably cautious. From the couch, he said that I felt "foreign" and that he had an odd feeling of being remote from me, as though he were not really in my office. I said that in view of the memories he had shared on the previous day, he might be trying to see if he could separate himself from the mother/analyst and remain independent of such undue stimulation as his mother's nightly activities had originally provided. This approach, with its positive view of his capacity, broke the ice, and he disclosed childhood memories, upon which he fixed an observant eye. His desire and dread of being with his mother led him to a discussion of a possible meaning of his having become obese in late childhood and to connect this obesity with the issues we had been speaking of. I suggested that although he wanted to be free of his mother, he had retained her as fat tissue, a defense against separation. He looked very solemn and, weeping silently, he asked at the end of the session, "Was the breakdown of my marriage my fault because of my faulty relationship with my mother?" I thought it well to acknowledge that that had been part of the reason, but since I wanted to relieve his guilt over being "at fault" in the termination of his marriage, I said that there might be other reasons, including Mamie's own contribution to its dissolution. "It takes two to tango," I reminded him.

A Visitation of
Incestuous Wishes

May 17 to the Beginning of June

During the latter half of May, Dr. Albert regressed even further, remembering painful childhood wishes, some direct derivatives of which had persisted into adult life. The only way he could admit them to his conscious awareness was to separate them from their affective correlates. The childhood memories that came pouring out in May were incestuous. It was evident that the diversion of his mother's attention to a new baby, when Chris was 4, had heightened his desire for her. He could remember neither his mother's pregnancy nor his brother's birth, but the feelings he had had about them were transferred to a pregnancy his mother underwent thirteen years later, when he was 17. This pregnancy was "accidental" and ended in a stillbirth. Dr. Albert remembered well how jealous of the unborn baby he had been and how embarrassed by his mother's swelling body. He could not recall how he had felt when what had apparently been a normal pregnancy resulted in a stillbirth.

At the time of his brother's birth, he had been further disturbed by his family's move to a new house, larger than the one they had been living in. In view of the many details about this house that Dr. Albert offered, I felt that his sibling rivalry was condensed in it and that his intense awareness of all its particulars represented a need to observe and control the newborn brother. The baby had activated his desire to have his mother for himself, and in his oedipal period this desire had become highly sexualized. The new house had three bedrooms, one occupied by his parents, another by the boys, and the third by Chris's sister, who was his senior by eight years. When the sister grew up and left for college, the mother began more and more often to sleep in her daughter's room.

Toward the end of May, Dr. Albert clumsily burned himself while preparing coffee at home, and "accidentally" cut his finger. It seemed to me that he was punishing himself for the incestuous wishes of his childhood, an open recital of which took place in his next session. As a child he had masturbated while having fantasies about his mother and sister. It interested me that he spoke of these fantasies in a monotonous voice without much emotion. He had succeeded in isolating his emotions while on the couch, but I could sense that he had had, when younger, a struggle between his desires and his conscience (superego). He had been preoccupied with religion then and oppressed by the fear that the church forbids the kind of fantasies he was having.

With some embarrassment, he acknowledged having had like fantasies until two or three years before beginning his analysis. I made sounds encouraging him to continue. He was ready to talk, albeit without accompanying feelings. He disclosed that he would think of women and, becoming sexually excited, would masturbate. He could not ejaculate, however, unless his thought involved those "forbidden" people, his mother and sister. His mother continued to appear in his fantasies as she had looked when he was a child. What follows is a typical masturbation fantasy from before analysis; his growing trust in me allowed him to recall it now on the couch.

In one fantasy he would be sexually rejected by Mamie, as in reality had often been the case. Then he would take a vacation with her, going to his home town, where he saw his mother. He would manage to separate himself there from Mamie and go to a room he had built himself while a teenager. There his mother would come to him and tell him she would do anything he asked. He would tell her that he missed sex, that Mamie was not a good woman, whereupon his mother would offer herself to him, and at this point he would ejaculate.

The mother of his early and late childhood was most seductive, he recalled, always wearing red. He recalled her wearing a tight night-gown, and in his fantasy she wore nothing underneath it. As a young child, and later, in adult life, he would have conversations with her in his mind as she moved from room to room and wound up at his bedside. He fantasied discussing the evil of relatives (sisters, brothers, children, and parents) becoming sex partners. Then their views would be reversed, and they would agree that there was no harm in this. When he was grown and had learned about hysterectomies, he fantasied his mother telling him that they could have sex together with no fear of pregnancy. I recalled that Mamie had undergone a hysterectomy before any serious problems arose in her marriage to Dr. Albert, and I wondered whether after her hysterectomy, Mamie might not have been invested by Dr. Albert with his incestuous mother image.

In his fantasies Dr. Albert would sometimes rape his mother, who, in other fantasies, simply offered herself to him. As a teenager, he had used such fantasies to stimulate himself and had masturbated into his socks and underwear. He now thought that his mother might have known about these activities, although she never spoke of them. He fantasied sending his father away, and the fantasies became easier to activate after his father's death. In telling of this, Dr. Albert referred to a recent event so I would know how these childhood fantasies were appearing in the transference; he had masturbated early in May during my absence. Two weeks earlier, he had met a social worker named Jane at a party and had felt a strong physical attraction. (Separated from her husband at the time, she would play an important role in Dr. Albert's life.) But instead of trying to date Jane, he invited a female medical student to his house, where he had sex with her. Thus, after all, there was a "union with a woman" at the time of his separation from me, although he had not spoken of it on my return. He was consciously aware that the medical student represented his mother; she not only resembled his mother when young but had the same pleasant smell. He had had an oedipal triumph when his father/analyst was away!

Dr. Albert reported having an odd sensation as he told me about his fantasies. When I asked him to tell me what it was, he replied that he felt as though his lovemaking with the student had not occurred just a few weeks earlier, but many years in the past. I told him that his peculiar sensation was due to his connecting a recent event with the childhood desires that he was reporting and that I represented the father he wanted to be absent. He was wrapped for some little time in his confusion of the medical student with his young mother; he needed to use logical thinking to separate the two. He spoke, for example, of how his mother had been much taller than he when he was a child, but that he was now taller than the mother/student.

His understanding that he was repeating in transference his desire for his mother and his fear of a father who should be sent away led to further regression and more unrepressed memories. He now recalled *childhood nightmares* that had terrified him, and strange feelings he had when he

awakened from them. He felt confused. Was he making up stories about
the nightmares? Did he really remember them? Although he was
overtaken by an initial confusion, his logic prevailed. He definitely
recalled waking up in tears and seeing everything as dark and
frightening. It was his father who came to his bed when he was
frightened and who picked him up and carried him in his arms, singing to
him. The two were very close in those moments. I observed how the
good father's image had been separated from that of the father who
frightened him in his fantasies or who in reality had whipped him. Dr.
Albert suddenly realized the nature of his nightmares; they concerned an
animal that would bite him. I was sure that the animal was the black
panther, which was included in his screen memory. I made the
formulation that the black panther stood for the aggressively sexual
mother or her black vagina, but I did not share this with my analysand,
who at that point could only remember the image of a dog baring his
teeth and trying to bite him.

I greatly appreciated his maintaining an observing ego in spite of the
degree of his regression. This was exemplified when he expressed
surprise over being able to recall such images and memories after thirty
years. But he still complained that feelings that should be connected
with such terrifying images were absent. He also felt surprised that he
did not suffer intense embarrassment after telling me about the masturbation fantasies about his mother. I told him that the conscious recollection of incestuous thoughts served as a screen for perceptions that
frightened him, such as being eaten by his mother. He was still without
any expression of feeling but said his eyes were watering.

When he went bowling that night, he began to fear an attack of
angina. Spontaneously, using his observing ego and the analyzing ego
that had shown how he was identifying with my analyzing functions, he
began to wonder if he might be experiencing guilty feelings about his
sexual fantasies. Although he felt nothing, perhaps he was punishing
himself by thoughts about threats to his body or his life. He began his
next session with me by confiding his insight about his thoughts at the
bowling alley. I suggested that through this device of self-punishment he
was protecting himself from feelings he regarded as painful. He spoke of
the severity of his conscience. When he spoke of wanting to renounce
God, as he sometimes did, I understood what a heavy burden to him his
strict conscience was.

The notion of loosening up his conscience was too much for him,
however, and within a few days he dated a "religious" girl (an external

superego), but the date was not a success, and he never saw her again. He then transferred his irritation to me, saying angrily in reaction to his psychiatric knowledge, "I knew my psychoanalysis would come down to the Oedipus complex." When he accused me of giving him no direction, I was silent. He complained that the fantasies he had recently reported had never come to mind at the beginning of our work together but that now they overwhelmed him.

Dr. Albert opened the May 26 session by telling how he had gone bicycle riding with his daughter. They had gone downhill, and he reported having said, "If we go down, eventually we go up." I considered this a reference to his recent regression and his hope of getting out of it. He went on to say that when he and his daughter had begun an uphill journey, a passing car had frightened her. There was danger in progress, too! His daughter's fear reminded him of the many phobias his mother had. She had been frightened by cows once and rescued by her husband. In recalling his mother's fears, he wondered if his identification with her accounted for some of his behavior. For example, he had been in the habit of hiding his money in his shoes when traveling, to which he associated his mother's fear of being robbed. I suspected that this fear of hers might have had something to do with her having been adopted and having had something (parents) taken away from her, and I suggested this to Dr. Albert. He seemed ready now to discard some of the unprofitable behavior patterns that had originated with his mother.

As the hour went on, Dr. Albert alternated the examination of his childhood fear, pertaining to identification with his mother, with contemplation of his psychosexual curiosity. He recalled noticing spots on his parents' bedsheets and thinking they were traces of their intercourse. As he spoke, his voice lowered and his speech dragged. Once again he was regressing. He recalled the death of his dog and how he and his father had carried the dog together. Although I did not pursue any symbolic meaning in the dog's death, I was greatly struck by his feeling state, one in which he had a memory of extreme closeness with his father. He began to weep, and I found myself telling him, "You missed your dad! You are crying for him!" He gave a heavy sigh and said, "Yes!" He whispered that his mother had kept him so close that he could not get near his father. Here the session ended.

We were separated over the weekend, during which Dr. Albert and Pamela went to visit his mother. There he dreamed of sexually penetrating his daughter, and when he awakened, he remembered my telling him that the mother-son relationship could be transferred to the father-daughter relationship. In a sense, he could now summarize his childhood wishes in the dream. Since it had not awakened him, I assumed that he was, to some extent, now able to tolerate his childhood incestuous wishes.

Playing Footsie
with a Rose Person

Early June through August 1

There were interruptions in Dr. Albert's second summer of analysis. I planned a two-and-a-half week vacation in early August, as I had done the previous year. His schedule did not fit mine. In early June, he was to give a scientific paper in a distant city, and on the way home he would spend a few days with his ex-father-in-law, who would be caring for Pamela while he attended the meeting. These plans would require his absence during the first two weeks of June. My notes indicate that I expressed no objection to the consequent interruption of his analysis, although I recall having made some remark about the resistance to analysis that seemed one aspect of his absence. I made no effort to examine this systematically with him. Certainly, he had a good reason to be away; his professional advancement was involved.

An analyst does not live in a vacuum, and I was facing a change myself at that time, having been assigned new responsibility at the university's medical center. I was to move to a new office in August to become the medical director of a satellite hospital about five miles from the one in which I had been seeing Dr. Albert. I had accepted my new post reluctantly and with some ambivalence, but it seemed the best choice open to me in view of the internal politics of the medical center. I realized that I was grieving over the loss of my old position in spite of a kind of promotion involved in the new one, and I was preoccupied with the coming change. I told Dr. Albert about the proposed move to another office, but I did not share my feelings with him; they may nonetheless have accounted for the fact that I did not undertake any systematic investigation of the resistance aspect of my analysand's departure in June. To some extent, events in my life at the time reduced my ability to maintain a truly analytic position, and in retrospect I think that my failure to communicate my preoccupation to him had much to do with my own denial of some feelings I had about the change taking place in my life. Technically, it might have been better to have acknowledged my preoccupation very briefly, had I been alert enough to sense that he was aware of it, although I certainly would have been wrong to burden him with the details or to insist that I was still capable of giving him my full attention, although this was largely true.

Just before his departure at the beginning of June, Dr. Albert opened a session with a dream about a big, powerful train that was taking him and Pamela on a journey. He felt anxiety in the dream and also in reporting it. He began his associations by stating that the dream might be concerned with the trip he was about to take in real life with Pamela. On the night of the dream, he had had a date with Jane, the social worker. In view of his anxiety, I suggested that he let his mind wander and try to put his feelings into words. He recalled a horror movie he had seen three years previously concerning a murderer stalking his victims on a train, his eyes turning red when he killed. Although the film was not an old one, he felt it resembled one from "the old days," and I could see that his feeling state about the train had some connection with "the old days"—his childhood.

This association brought memories of riding in a train as a child with Brownie and feeling that the train was a black and powerful thing. The Cuban girl he had dated before meeting Mamie had taken a train whenever she visited him. He recalled now having a "train phobia," being fearful of getting near the tracks lest someone push him into the path of the train. Before he had his dream, he had had a feeling that I would kill him by pushing him in front of a train if he got too near to Jane, whom he had begun to like very much. I reminded him of his dream about the redheaded woman and his song from *Porgy and Bess,* suggesting that he perceived his mother as powerful enough to move a train on or off its tracks, and that he was afraid of both his mother and father. Laughing nervously, Dr. Albert associated the train with a powerful penis, recalling another film he had seen, one about the Orient Express. Since the Orient Express was associated with Turkey, and I am Turkish, this represented my penis. My penis, or the powerful mother who could manipulate it, spelled danger. He continued his free associations by recalling the picture of a nude man, penis exposed, he had seen in a magazine. That man was a peacock, a showoff, someone seeking attention, and on his way to my office he had seen a policeman he thought was a peacock, too. Peacock also means "pea cock," or a little cock, he said. This association indicated ambivalence toward me: was I powerful, or was I tiny? Dr. Albert was defending himself from my powerful penis by turning a peacock into a "pea cock."

At the meeting, he would see a certain physician he considered "cocky," a "little Napoleon," with whom he had *trained* in his specialty years earlier. "I want to punch holes in his balloon. I want to punch holes in his cock," he said. Dr. Albert went on to say that the man's penis was bent, and when I asked how he knew this, he replied that he had observed it when they lived in the same fraternity house. At this point he began to count other men he had heard about who had bent penises, such as a certain famous baseball player. He fantasied that a penis became bent from "jerking off all the time." Then he calmed down and confided that his own was "curved slightly." As a child he had regarded his father's penis as "a big mystique," and he thought of it as large. Sadly, he recalled how his father at the time of death had had a Foley catheter in his penis and how "his penis was small."

I thought that in view of the impending separation between us, he was comparing our penises, fearing or degrading mine and protecting his by associating it with that of the baseball superstar and minimizing the guilt and punishment involved in masturbating by indicating that his penis curved "only slightly." I can see in retrospect that it was hard for me to know whether he sensed my grief over changing my professional post and was struggling because of it. He had wanted me to be strong, but my preoccupation made me seem weak to him. I was letting him leave his analysis without a struggle. We parted until late June.

He began his first hour after returning by telling me that the paper he had presented had been well received and that he had done well socially. He observed that the physician friend he had thought of as a rival had his own "hangups" and that in comparison with him, he felt good about himself. "I am pleased that I am me," he confided. He had had a good visit with his ex-father-in-law, and when his mother had phoned on his return, he was surprised to find himself having a most comfortable conversation with her.

I listened without interrupting. What I was hearing was a tale of a flight into health, as if everything were satisfactory and he had no further need of me. In looking back, I think it possible that he was "saving me" by "being well" (if he had indeed sensed my preoccupation with the coming change in my professional situation and the feelings, not all pleasant, pertaining to it). When his recital of "fun and success" was over, he reported a dream about which he retained only a vague recollection. He was sure only that the color yellow appeared in it and that it had something to do with a farm cultivator. Announcing that "cult" meant a group of people, Dr. Albert spoke of having seen "a group of hippies" camping near the home of his ex-father-in-law. They had reminded him of Charles Manson. When I asked who Charles Manson might be, he replied that *he* might be Charles Manson since he felt aggression toward his ex-father-in-law even though he felt a need to be close to an older man. But his ex-father-in-law might be Charles Manson, for Dr. Albert sensed a certain danger about him. "I respect him for what he does for himself," he said, referring to the older man's financial success. "But he is like a Nazi—really able to kill people. He is a fanatic. He derides women and hates them." He then recalled an incident in which his ex-father-in-law had been rather cruel to Pamela in a verbal exchange. He sensed that he himself was rather like Mamie's father, also angry at women. Now the color yellow in his dream reminded him of a field full of daisies and dandelions. As a child he had picked these flowers and had noticed their scent clinging to his fingers and wondered why people did not like these wild flowers. The answer now seemed to him to be "because dandelions take over the whole yard."

"Just like your mother," I said. "If you don't watch out, she invades you." He replied sharply, "I don't want to be threatened by her any more!" Toward the end of the session, he disclosed that a physician named Sharon, the wife of a physician friend of his, had been among those attending the meeting from which he had just returned. He confided that after dancing with her one night, he had "fucked a friend." "It was different," he went on. "No dependency, no obligation!" I speculated as to whether this "friend" might have been the woman he sought at the time of separation from his father/analyst.

He had a bandage on one of his fingers at the session on the following day, June 30, but I said nothing about it. Lying on the couch, he spoke of having noticed the scent of cigars as he approached my office. I had indeed been smoking there before his arrival. He had many "death wishes" for me. Since I smoked, I would die of cancer, like his father. When he spoke of the "great expectations" he had of psychoanalysis and of how he sensed that they were soon to be fulfilled, I commented, "If I die now your great expectations would never be realized. When your father died, you were left with some unfinished business with him." He was silent for a while and then reported an odd image: a snail that left a trail behind it as it moved. He associated this trail with semen and told me that after having sexual intercourse with his "friend," he had put a finger in her vagina and then smelled it. This was the finger he had accidentally cut and bandaged. I realized that he had repeated the pattern of self-castration. The color yellow in his dream referred to his being a coward, that is, "yellow." I was the dandelion, the invading mother or the Nazi father, and with his cultivator he could be rid of all these. This was his dream wish, but since the dream also implied a condensation of his "yellow" castrated image, he would take the matter of castration into his own hands, control it, and avoid being castrated by the hands of the father/analyst, which were being manipulated by the powerful mother.

That night Dr. Albert had a horrifying dream, which he reported to me at the next session, on July 3, after giving me a check. In the dream he parked his old car, which in reality he had turned in for a new one, on a snow-covered street in his Maryland home town. An officer with a mustache like mine put four parking tickets on the windshield. Dr. Albert had seen the officer approach and escaped from the car in a panic, running toward the house in which he had lived as a child. Then the snow melted away, and he felt himself seized and choked by the officer. He was overcome by terror, but some passerby, who might have been a superior staff member from his hospital, pulled him from behind and out of this terrifying situation. Then Dr. Albert saw himself transferring the parking tickets to his new car. His associations to the nightmare made a great deal of sense. He had had sexual intercourse with his married "friend" four times. "Oh, I parked my car in Sharon's garage four times!" he explained. The frequency of intercourse with her paralleled the frequency of his weekly sessions with me.

His guilt over sexual desire for a married woman (the mother of his childhood) and his desire to be punished were being transferred to a new situation, just as he transferred the parking tickets to his new car. I was the punishing policeman/father/analyst. It seemed that another woman besides Sharon made overtures to him. The wife of another colleague came to his house in the middle of the night to seek advice from Dr. Albert about handling her frustration with her husband. When he told me of this, he referred to his mother's coming to his bedroom when he was a child. "Women come to see me in the middle of the night!" he said and went on to say that besides consoling the second woman he had kissed her, "a tall woman who had cigarette smoke on her breath." In kissing a woman who smoked, he was kissing one contaminated with the mother/analyst, since we both smoked.

Dr. Albert considered the snow in the dream a symbolic "snow job" or cover-up. He had always covered up the meaning of his psychological struggles but could no longer do so. His frozen repression was thawing. I was pleased with his powers of observation in all this. The hospital superior standing behind him in the dream was his analyst in the guise of a savior. Although in the dream his superior had rescued him, Dr. Albert had transferred "punishing" tickets to his new car, giving evidence that in spite of his heightened powers of observation, he needed to continue his self-castrating behavior as a defense.

During the first week of July, his therapeutic regression led him to reinvestigate the "reality of his childhood." He visited his mother and asked her help in confirming some of his childhood perceptions. Had the family really been poor and obliged to eat dandelion leaves? His mother said yes, that his father had been very proud and had concealed his family's plight from Brownie. Friends and neighbors had contributed food. During this time, his father "accidentally" had cut off the tip of a finger and had then been out of work for six to eight months. Here was another issue: indentification with a mutilated weak father, the amputation of whose finger Dr. Albert had recently copied. The family's suffering had ultimately been relieved when they went to Brownie for help. As he heard his mother talk, Dr. Albert sensed that there had been love between his parents, and I felt that he took comfort in this knowledge. I thought that if his parents loved one another, the mother would not respond to Chris's oedipal, incestuous strivings, and thus he would be protected from feeling guilty as well as from the fear of his father's retaliation.

By the end of the first week in July, he began to reenact his oedipal dilemma in an active, symbolic, and colorful way outside the analytic sessions. Although I sensed from the start what he was doing, I made no remark to interrupt the process; I wanted it to ripen enough to be brought into the transference neurosis, to become charged between us, and therefore ready for interpretation.

He befriended a young man, not a physician, who worked in his hospital and had helped him prepare a scientific paper. He invited this young man, whose name was Joe, along with his wife Caroline, to his house for drinks one night, and the three continued to drink, talk, and socialize after Pamela went to bed. As the hour grew late, Joe fell asleep on the couch. It seemed to me that this episode repeated the situation of his childhood, when his father slept and his mother went to her son's bed. Unconscious of this, Dr. Albert was aware of having a death wish for the sleeping Joe and sexual desire for Caroline. He reported this, explaining how ready Caroline had been to be seduced. While her husband slept, he kissed her and smelled her hair, but they stopped short of sexual intercourse, finally falling asleep—but not in one another's arms.

This was the beginning of a triangle nonetheless, and other real aspects of the situation made it a vehicle for the external reactivation of an intrapsychic process. It was significant that Caroline was a "rose," the idealized mother, since she was wellborn, charming, and unattainable. Although Dr. Albert valued his friendship with Joe, he could see that Caroline, that rose, was interested in himself. Since her quality "emanated from her," in his words, "she deserved better than Joe." Dr. Albert was referring to himself. The three met every night, and Joe continued to fall asleep while Dr. Albert and Caroline sat at a table holding hands and "playing footsie," rubbing their feet together under the table. In doing this, Dr. Albert was very careful not to use the foot missing a toe, "lest it keep her from getting turned on!" He was pleased to learn that Joe had a webbed toe; Joe's defect seemed to make him less of a rival.

Throughout July, he continued acting out his oedipal struggle in his relationship with Caroline and Joe. I was put in the position of a spectator and felt that our impending separation in August helped maintain his efforts to deal with the oedipal situation outside his analytic sessions. He was intimate with Caroline but not to the point of having intercourse with her; she continued to be the rose (ideal) mother at a time when he was frantically seducing other women and having sex with them. I observed that he had split his mother's image in two, one part being idealized and beyond physical sex; the other part physically sexual but not idealized.

Dr. Albert was beginning to work energetically on his "fat boy" image. "I am liberating my body," he declared after he had danced all night with Caroline at a party. Usually shy at social gatherings, on this occasion Dr. Albert had summoned up enough courage to chat on the stage with the lead singer. When he had played volleyball, he had taken off his shirt and displayed his naked torso. I felt that he was asking witnesses to judge whether he was a fat boy. He talked in his sessions of the "roll" around his waist, saying that it was like a "spare tire." I could hear in his associations the unspoken statement that it not only represented the remnants of his "fat boy" image, but also included an extra penis in case his real penis were lost to castration. I gave the interpretation that he was asking people to look at his "roll" so they would not look at the foot with the missing toe. It was at this time, when he was trying to liberate himself from his mother by getting rid of his fat tissue, that he reported another kind of liberation attempt; he had stopped taking allergy pills, which, without my knowledge, he had been taking until then.

Pamela left home for a few days, and one night Caroline slept in her bed, while Joe slept on a couch in the living room. During Pamela's absence, on a night when Joe and Caroline did not join him, Dr. Albert had another episode of dissociative reaction: playing "musical beds" once again, he found himself in his daughter's bed.

On July 24, after reading an article about a psychiatrist who had testified against his patient, he opened the session with the question, "Would you ever testify against me?" I learned more about his current involvements when I asked about his free associations to this question. It became apparent that he felt like a criminal because he not only wished that Joe would die, but wished the same for three other husbands whose wives he was trying to seduce. He kept repeating murderous thoughts about Joe throughout the rest of the month. On August 1, at our last session before I left for my vacation, he reported having stayed up with Caroline until six o'clock in the morning, while Joe slept. He reported feeling that during my absence something drastic would happen to Joe. I gave the interpretation that his involvement with Caroline had begun after his nightmare about getting parking tickets and being checked by my representation, the officer with a mustache, probably for having sexual desire for a married woman. Since then, he had prevented me from considering the triangle involving Joe, Caroline, and himself. I told him that I felt that he was repeating *in action* his relationship with his mother, who had played "musical beds" while her husband slept. I explained that he had been greatly stimulated as a child by his mother's nocturnal visits to his bed, and that, wanting to have her for himself, he had desired his father's death. Since I was going away, relinquishing my control for a while, he dreaded that his wishes might take the upper hand. He listened to me attentively.

The "Wine Water"

We met in my old office for our first post-vacation session on August 21. Dr. Albert was suffering from an "allergy" and had taken pills for it. He reported having sneezed and having had a runny nose for three days. He himself suggested that the allergy might be due to his visiting his mother, and he observed that he was returning to his analysis with mixed feelings about "it." Once again I had become "the analysis" and "it" in his mind.

During my absence, Dr. Albert had had a long talk with Caroline. This led to her declaration that she would not leave her husband for him, and he felt rejected and depressed. The night before my return he had dreamed of Sabrina, who had rejected him earlier for a psychiatrist. In the dream, a tall man with a mustache had come to his door to tell him that Sabrina had been married, wearing a T-shirt. In the dream Dr. Albert then took to his bed, and the tall man lay next to him. It felt strange to have a man in his bed. After reporting this dream, Dr. Albert made reference to Caroline's rejection, saying, "I don't have a pussy. I depend on women. If they like me I feel like a man, but if they reject me I can only go to bed with a man." He associated the man in the dream with me and with his father. In the dream, Sabrina's T-shirt made her like a young boy in his associations; she had small breasts, "just nipples."

After experiencing rejection by Caroline in reality, Dr. Albert had an accident with his new car that cost him about $200 in repairs. As he drove to the garage to have it worked on, he found himself thinking that he was paying penance for desiring another man's wife and said inwardly, "I am punishing myself." I said I had observed that he felt women could make or break him and that he behaved as though everyone depended on women. I noted that when he reached for friendship with a woman, he sexualized it, and this led to competition with other men and feelings of jealousy and fear of them. He perceived Caroline's rejection as a narcissistic blow. I pointed out that by making Sabrina a "boy" in his dream, he was identifying with her in going to bed with a man, the psychiatrist/psychoanalyst. I added that although the homosexual notion might be unacceptable to him, it was in the service of his effort to protect himself from his own jealous feelings about the psychiatrist (who represented me) and Joe, whom Caroline seemed to prefer over him; it also served to fend off their retaliation. As if this protection were not enough, he had damaged his car—as he had amputated his toe—in order to prevent being hurt at my hands.

Dr. Albert then told me about the "horrible paranoid nights" he had recently experienced, during which he was afraid of being attacked by someone like Charles Manson. At the next session, he said that the man in bed with him in his dream reminded him of Lazarus, the dead man Jesus restored to life. I wondered aloud if he might want to bring his father back to life because he felt guilt over the idea that he had killed him for a woman he wanted—his mother. This remark led him to considerable rumination about his feelings of guilt for never having been close to his father. I told him that his fantasies about his mother had kept him from such closeness. He agreed and lamented anew that he had always seen his father through the eyes of his mother and so had misjudged him. He kept seeking memories of his father as a strong man.

On August 25, we had our last session in the office we had been using for about a year and a half. Some of the furniture already had been moved out. Although he had been prepared for this, he began sneezing and wheezing when he saw the office half empty and suddenly asked, "Are you leaving your PDR [the reference book for physicians that lists all medications] in this office?" I felt that anxiety over the change of office had led him to feel anxious that I myself might change and might leave behind what could be regarded as a symbol of therapeutic conduct. When I asked him to associate to this question, he spoke of having had double pneumonia at the age of 4, and of being given honey and whiskey by his mother, while his father gave him shots.

My new office was in what had been a tuberculosis sanatorium. The 200 acres of wooded hills, in the center of which the hospital is located, make it seem at first glance a resort rather than a medical establishment. Some of the numerous satellite buildings, some of which had housed sanatorium employees, had been renovated, but there were few patients, and the interior of the main building in which my office was located, although substantially built and well maintained, had something of the aspect of a ghost town. I was the newly acquired facility's new head, the representative of the university; I was charged with taking part in the development of new programs, opening units for new types of patients, including psychiatric patients, and had thus become more an administrator than an academician. Coming as I do from a family proud of its contribution to education, I had to adjust to a new self-concept.

My new office had not only a balcony from which one could see the beautiful wooded hills, beyond which stood Thomas Jefferson's Monticello, but a solarium, which I filled with plants. Unlike my former office, this one was full of light, often of that special changing luminosity characteristic of Piedmont Virginia on a fine day. The couch Dr. Albert lay on there was the same color as the old one but considerably more luxurious; my chair also was nicer than my old one and had a matching ottoman. I appreciated these amenities as well as the new freedom from outside noise.

Dr. Albert did not on the surface appear particularly excited about our new location, but I observed, as I settled in my chair and listened to him, alert for hidden meaning, that my move to a new office five miles distant from the familiar one had induced in him a wanted, but also dreaded, move away from the mother that the old office represented to him. He behaved as though he were now going to be alone with the father and away from his mother. He wanted me to be a strong father who would help him to move further away from his mother, but the dangerous possibility that I was a bad father with homosexual designs on him outweighed his wish to be close to me. The only way he could be close to me was to use his customary maneuvers, feeling omnipotent or castrating himself.

On his way to my new office one September morning, Dr. Albert felt that his eyesight had miraculously been cured. This was his omnipotent defense. But once in my office, he repeated his self-castrating behavior. On only one previous occasion had he removed his contact lenses before me, but in my new office he now established a ritual that involved his taking his seat on the couch at the start of every session, removing his lenses (symbolically castrating himself), and putting them in a box before lying down. At the end of each hour, he reversed the ritual. When I showed mild curiosity about his behavior, he would not let himself give me a psychological answer, telling me instead that although his lenses had been comfortable enough during the drive to his appointment, they were not comfortable when he lay on the couch. This made little sense, but since he was unready to explore the psychological reasons for this behavior, I did not then try to clarify them.

With his lenses removed, Dr. Albert seemed more comfortable in being directly involved with me in a father transference. He asked me to hypnotize him, "to open his memory bank." I took this as an invitation to enter him. Since he was already damaged—his eyes having symbolically been plucked out—such an invitation felt to him less dangerous and more tolerable. He could now relate directly to my sexuality. He fantasied that my penis was S-shaped. His associations indicated that S stood for shit, and he recalled his dog "eating his shit." I told him that he wanted me to enter him or wanted to eat me, feeling that if I were inside him he could identify with me and be equally strong. He then associated to my given name, Vamık, as vomitus. I told him that he was not yet sure that if he took me in I would be good for him, and he wanted to keep the option of vomiting me out. In spite of his having plucked out his "eyes," the fear that I might still hurt him persisted. Another association to my supposedly S-shaped penis was the curved Turkish sword; he thought he had seen Turks fighting with such scimitars in a film. Turks stood for his Turkish analyst. He expected Turks to behead people.

Dr. Albert seemed to experience therapeutic regression now with every session and to be involved in a hot transference neurosis, but only after performing his eye ritual. The father transference also helped him recall many memories of his father's death and his impregnation of Mamie under the deathbed. He now associated this with his desire to demonstrate to his father before he died that he had his own woman and no longer wanted his father's. In one hour, he identified with the dying man and was so fatigued as he lay on the couch that he was unable to move. I interpreted to him that this identification was in the service of protecting himself from a dangerous father but that identifying with a dying or dead father might reflect a wish to kill him. After this discussion, Dr. Albert came out of his temporary and disruptive identification with his dying father.

During the first week of October, a visit from his mother brought an end to the hot father transference. When Dr. Albert lay on the couch on

October 9, I felt as though I were miles away from him. He was sneezing and opened the session by wondering if his allergy had something to do with his mother's visit. The visit constituted the day residue of a dream in which a bug with a mouth like a staple remover made cuts on his skin, from which blood flowed. Without my help, he played with the word "staple" and associated it with provisions of food, in other words, with the mother he depended on and who fed him, but who also cut and injured him. "The bug is my mother," he said.

Dr. Albert was ready to review spontaneously his mother's smothering, which had continued up to that time. I continued to feel distant from him, and I decided to share this feeling. His response was that while he complained about his mother, he feared that I might be jealous of him were I near, since he loved "to be his mother's number one baby." I was being kept at a distance as his sibling or father would be.

As he went over his feelings about his mother, he wondered why he could not even now integrate his opposing perceptions of her and half jokingly he asked me to give him a "pill for integration." His mother went home on October 11. Throughout her visit, he had had "allergic reactions" daily. On the day his mother left, he opened his session by saying, "I had to use five handkerchiefs last night." He attributed the severity of this, his worst allergy attack in years, to his decision to sit down for a talk with his mother and to try and learn more about what had actually happened in his childhood. What follows is a summary of these revelations.

When he was 1 year old, he was thought to have thymus trouble and was given radiation therapy. Pressure of the thymus on the trachea was supposed to have caused the choking spells he had at age 2 and 3. Dr. Albert told me that he had realized for some time that these choking spells had been caused by nothing but his holding his breath. His mother told him that he also used to retain his feces. When he was 2, the doctor advised that he be left on the potty until he defecated. When he was 3, he had pneumonia. He felt now that because of these physical problems his mother had given him excessive attention, and her absorption in him had been interrupted by the birth of his brother when he was 4. It was then that he stabbed his eye with a knife while trimming a tree and was taken to a hospital when it bled profusely. No permanent injury had resulted. Dr. Albert realized that I had heard all of this before, but he had been surprised by learning in conversation with his mother that some of his symptoms, like his obesity, his allergic reactions, and his need for glasses dated back to age 5 to 7 instead of from 12 to 14, as he had supposed.

After making this report, Dr. Albert seemed relaxed and said that the talk with his mother had helped him to feel comfortable. Although he still thought of me as a judge, I no longer seemed menacing to him. I was "a benign judge," helping him to put things together.

On the previous day he had played tennis with Joe and in the locker room had noticed that Joe had sound genitals. He was able to realize that he was jealous of them. Recalling that his father's had looked equally sound until his terminal illness, Dr. Albert told himself that Joe's genitals should not give him cause for jealousy. He recalled having made a slip of the tongue the previous night when he had called his mother "Honey." He remembered then how she sometimes made slips of the tongue in calling him by his father's name. He seemed excited over his new ability to make sense of all these observations without being afraid of them.

Toward the end of the session, he recalled a song in which a man telephones his old love to talk about old memories, which they describe as being like "diamonds and rust." Dr. Albert then recalled the loss of an old tree that had stood in front of his home and waxed nostalgic over the losses involved in "giving way to modernization." He said the memories of his childhood were like diamonds and rust and wondered aloud if there might be others that were "between diamonds and rust." As the hour concluded, I realized that whereas he had recently asked for a pill to help him to integrate his perceptions, he was now exploring on his own the possibility of filling the gap between diamonds and rust—or, to return to his usual terms, between roses and dandelions.

This attempt to integrate things was followed—and balanced—by anxiety on the next day, when he again asked that I hypnotize him. Until October 18, when he reported a significant dream and returned to his attempted integration, he frantically vacillated between father and mother transferences. On Friday, October 13, he began his session by speaking of the bad luck associated with Friday the thirteenth. Regressing to mumbling, he reported an image of a small mannequin that had been beheaded. His associations disclosed that a doctor had once told him about circumcising an infant and mistakenly cutting off the head of his penis. The baby's family took the matter to court and won a substantial judgment, but as an adult, the injured male had married and begotten children. There was hope for him, too! But he mumbled, "I don't want to die without knowing what is *in front of me!*" I suggested that in speaking of what was "in front of him," he might mean his penis. He then recalled having examined his mutilated toe, which symbolically represented the castrated state of his penis, with a mirror that morning, and finding it ugly.

On October 16, the following Monday, he saw me put a paper cover on the pillow on which he was about to rest his head. Ordinarily, I do this before a patient's arrival, but this time he found me doing it just as he walked into the office. This was enough to induce a mother transference and to recall to him how his mother had brought a variety of toilet tissues for him on a recent visit. The next day he began his session by saying how anxious I had made him recently. He spontaneously referred to his smothering-loving mother, to his fear of his father, and to how both appeared in the interaction between the two of us. He noted that although he had reported several instances of self-mutilation, he had forgotten to say that when he became officially engaged to Mamie, he had smashed a finger so badly that he almost lost it. But he was still unconsciously involved in a balancing act. For example, as soon as he reported his self-castrating behavior during his engagement, he told me proudly how lately he had been going barefoot and that the skin of his feet was becoming thick and impervious: hard to cut.

After being silent for a while, Dr. Albert reported a memory of his father's anger over a man's having parked his car in their yard. Recalling his dream about the parking tickets, I told him that he had thought his father would be angry at him for wanting to park with his mother. It had been only a wish, not an act, but he felt nonetheless that he had committed a crime. All this time he had been feeling guilty over a crime that he had not actually committed!

Then Dr. Albert asked if I knew why it was always his left side that he mutilated. I suggested that sometimes people consider the left side to be feminine. This brought to mind a memory of his sister's buying him a suit. In order to insure a good fit in the trousers, she had asked him which testicle was larger than the other. Now he was suddenly unable to recall the proper answer; he seemed anxious and reported confusion. I told him that he was seeing me as the Terrible Turk, and that if I did not know about his testicles, I would be less accurate when I plunged my sword at them. He began to laugh nervously. I continued talking and stated that while I was a Terrible Turk, he himself behaved like a Turkish wrestler who oils his body to foil his opponent. If he could trust me more, I might be able to help him further to put things together. It was because of this exchange, I think, that he brought a dream on the following day, October 18, which was indicative of another effort to put things in perspective.

Dr. Albert said that this dream was a "mixture of the old and the new." In it he found himself in Daddy Doc's house, where Brownie had lived. She appeared briefly in one of the rooms, alive. The dreamer then went on to see the kitchen, where there was a jug of ice water on the window sill. There were big, old-fashioned mugs of the kind that had been in the kitchen in the past, and he filled one repeatedly with water and drank. Finally, when he poured more he noticed that in the mug it was *brownish* and murky. Then his mother and his brother entered the kitchen. When his mother asked him how he liked what he was drinking, she told him that it was not water, but "wine water." Never having heard of such a thing, he asked what it was. His mother explained that it was something his brother had obtained from a nearby country club.

The day residue of this dream came from his having bowled the previous night with one of his "redneck" friends who tried to arrange a date for his sister with him. Dr. Albert had been curious about this woman; he thought she would be a dandelion, but he felt some anxiety, as though he needed to check his own background. He then envisioned my disembodied head which remained before him as though on a screen. A helpful, externalized, analytic "introject," it gave him confidence. In reality his mother had reached him by telephone when he returned home from bowling, and he felt that the dream that followed their conversation was in the service of looking at his background with my analytic guidance and integrating things.

Dr. Albert was interested in the meaning of wine water, and talked about how Jesus had turned water into wine. "Wine and water are like dandelions and roses," he said. The color of the wine in his dream reminded him of Catawba grape wine, which he and his friends had drunk when he graduated from college. At the time, he had considered the wine suitable, but after he tasted champagne he could clearly see that Catawba was to champagne what a dandelion was to a rose.

His mother had been in the habit of giving Brownie mugs and aprons at Christmas, and he remembered Brownie wearing layers of aprons topped by layers of sweaters. He recalled also that she had kept her special teaspoons packed away in tissue paper, and these recollections now led him to declare that she was not a rose after all. At best, she was a mixture of rose and dandelion; although she had come from a well-connected Maryland family, she was a miser.

Lost for a while in thought, Dr. Albert finally reported watching a gray fog. He claimed that he could see the top and bottom of the fog but discern nothing in it. He then said that his perceptions of his mother, Brownie, and even of people at work were like the middle of the gray fog. He could see their good and bad qualities, but he found it hard to believe that there was any gray between the two extremes of black and white. Logical thinking required him to know that most people function "in the middle." He was putting wine and water together but could not yet see what to expect of such a mixture, a mixture like the dandelions and roses in his own background.

The Taming of the Black Panther

October 19 to Mid-December

After his wine water dream of October 18, Dr. Albert seemed even more deeply plunged into a therapeutic regression, as if he were determined to get to the bottom of conflicts that had disturbed him for so long. Although he displayed courage in doing this, he could not help "having cold feet"—as he actually did on the couch. When, beginning on October 19, his allergy reached a peak and he was sneezing, wheezing, and having a runny nose, he asked me to take care of him. I indicated that I was standing by him but made no particular reference to his symptoms. At the end of the hour, he compared me with his mother, who had recently said to Pamela on a visit, in some excitement, "You have an allergy!" when she sneezed. Although he had been conspicuously sneezing in front of me, I had not remarked on it even once. He then said, "You know, I like your *not* paying attention to my symptoms!"

Dr. Albert's "allergic" symptoms continued, and toward the end of October he reported having had an attack of terror, about half an hour long, in the middle of the night. "I was afraid of something. I noticed every sound in the house. I was afraid of being killed." He had a feeling that as a small child he had suffered terror attacks. "The experience brings to mind my fear of the black panther," he explained. Regressing, he felt that he was in the bedroom of his childhood; this time the panther was *in* his room, "just sitting there." He looked as though he were in a trance as he went on, "But it wasn't menacing. I felt attracted to it." His voice dropped, and he began to recite a poem, "Panther, panther, with gleaming eyes!"

"Now I can see the eyes of the panther," he said. "They are *black*. It is a big cat. Yes, yes, it is a pussy!" He was overwhelmed with anxiety, but I did nothing except to utter reassuring sounds. After relaxing, he reported having seen his mother's black pubic hair when he was 5. "I was very much interested to see that she did not have a penis, but I wasn't surprised. Therefore I must have been exposed to a penisless person even earlier!"

Dr. Albert then reported that he had begun to examine the "pussies" of the women he bedded. He was fascinated but anxious at the sight of female genitalia, as though he were seeing them for the first time. He dreamed of a comb with missing teeth; this reminded him of *teeth in vaginas* that had alarmed him as the mouth of a panther would. He said, "You know, I feel guilty using all these women recently. They are sacrificial lambs. I use them in order to learn how to tame a panther!"

During the first week of November, Dr. Albert watched with fascination a television show about a hunter and a tiger (panther) and the struggle between them. As he sat in his room that night, he wanted to reexperience his terror attack, but all he could manage was anxiety lasting only a few minutes. It seemed as though he had mastered the terror, which had now become a toy he could play with to demonstrate his mastery. Nonetheless, I noted that this mastery was accompanied by something I would call a symptom; he was taking a drink or two almost every night before retiring. His references to Jane, the social worker, now came more often. It seemed to me that she was not to him just another "pussy" or sacrificial lamb. He was sufficiently involved with her to report feeling jealous when another man began paying her attention.

His voyages to his childhood, now accompanied by genuine felt emotion, continued. On November 12, Dr. Albert dreamed of being operated on; someone was cutting the tendons of his right ankle. He talked about the Achilles' heel and spoke of how Achilles' mother had dipped him in the river Styx to make him invulnerable but had missed wetting the heel she held him by. He talked once again about being subjected as a child to medication, radiation, and surgery. He had had his straw hat to protect him from the sun. How horrible it had been for him to live in a world of dangerous expectations! He knew that in his sessions with me, in his dreams, and even when awake at home, he was reliving the feel of his childhood.

Dr. Albert stopped suddenly, and I suggested that he continue when he was ready. He then said that a childhood memory had just come to him: he had been playing with some other children, who were happily jumping into a sand pit ten feet below. Although the thought of jumping terrified him, he was able to jump after all when it was his turn. I told him that he might be conveying to me his ability to regress even further to discover the things he had perceived as dangerous. Going into a deep regression, he began talking in so slurred a way that I could hardly understand him. He began to weep, but when he emerged from this experience I was delighted to see that his observing ego was functional. He told me that he was recalling the way chairs had squeaked when his mother walked from bed to bed in the middle of the night. He felt like a canvas sheet stretched between different hooks. He was afraid that he was about to be slashed, cut, and torn apart. "I had no teddy bear to soothe me," he said. "I had a little boy doll; I don't remember his name."

On the way to my office on the following day, Dr. Albert said that he had fantasied losing his contact lenses during his eye ritual, and my rising from my chair and joining him on hands and knees to look for them on the floor. In other words, he had fantasized that I would care for him like a mother. Then he spoke of having developed an itchy area on the skin of his penis. It might, he said, be a fungus infection. I understood that he wanted me to cure his blindness or the disease on his penis. When I told him this, he said that the reverse was also true, that he still could not trust me fully, and that whereas I might find his lenses for him, I might equally well smash them.

We then spoke in psychological terms of his ritual with his lenses. Dr. Albert once again reviewed, with feeling, the accident in which he had stabbed his eye, and his mother's anxiety. But this time he reported a new and significant memory: he had had a mole on his penis, and his mother took him to a surgeon, who removed it. This operation had taken place just before he reached puberty. "I have a scar one inch away from the root of my penis," he said.

After falling into silence, Dr. Albert reported fantasying a bird—an eagle or a hawk—with a red neck, flying up into the air. "I know this bird represents me," he said, "since while I had this image before me I felt air all around my body, as though I were flying." The bird had hair in place of feathers. "I know it was my penis, mutilated and red with blood." He wanted me to repair it. I told him that I heard his wish and knew that he wanted me to help him but was cautious about me and did not fully trust me. I told him that the bird with its "red neck" also represented his image as a dandelion. I could now offer the interpretation that his being a man—as opposed to his being a mutilated man (a woman)—was condensed in his self-perception of being a rose, as opposed to being a dandelion (redneck).

Dr. Albert told me then that he could now understand why he had had trouble dating as a young man in high school and college: he had been trying to hide his dandelion aspect. But on one date, he had felt compelled to make love to his partner twelve times in one night to show her what a rose he was! "I would go from one extreme to the other. I would like now to be able to function in the middle," he said.

In mid-November, Dr. Albert was able to experience the black panther terror on the couch, with me nearby. As soon as he lay on the couch, his speech became slurred, slow, and incoherent. I said nothing. He began rambling about Dante's hell. He saw visions of his body parts floating around and images of black holes. Then he described seeing his mother coming nearer and nearer; *she turned into a panther with teeth bared.* The teeth were larger and larger as she approached, and he felt anxious. I continued silent, knowing that he had already tolerated such an experience and that any unusual interest on my part about it might cause him to use the experience now as a regressive game. It could change function and become a regressive defense against other issues rather than a regressive experience in the service of mastering his fear. In the face of my silence, he emerged from the experience on his own and reported that while he was regressed and saw his mother as a black panther, he also kept an image of her as he had seen her recently, a tiny elderly woman who was not at all alarming. He wanted to meld the different images of his mother and noted that attempts to do so protected him from real panic. It was evident that he was performing his inner psychological work and that I was right in not becoming excited at his regressive experience.

On the previous night, Dr. Albert reported, he had sat in his dark bedroom and relived his childhood. He felt someone (his mother) sitting in a chair next to his bed, and he felt himself to be small, a child. On the following day, his mother in fact visited his home. During the time of all these regressive experiences, both on and off the couch, he had been undergoing successful change in his daily life. His conflicts were more and more brought into his analytic process; as his involvement in the transference neurosis increased, he was freeing himself from his neurosis in his daily living and learning to deal with the real world in a much improved way. His research gained recognition, and he was awarded a substantial grant. He no longer felt anxiety when talking to or negotiating with his superiors or when going before a group to express his views. But in his analytic sessions, he continued his eye ritual, and I noted the development of another symptom—weight gain, which was temporary. I recalled that he had become obese after the incident involving his eye in childhood.

Dr. Albert was becoming more and more involved with Jane, whom he now referred to as his "girlfriend." They had been sexual partners for some time, and he now planned to take her on a trip to a meeting at which he was to present a paper. He planned to take her to the restaurants for which the city in question was famous and generally to show her off. His mother's current visit had been planned for Pamela's care during his absence with Jane. This was the first indication that his mother and Jane had met. He suspected that his mother was jealous of his girlfriend.

In his desire to learn more about his childhood, Dr. Albert had asked his mother to bring his baby book with her. He learned little from it, but he discussed his childhood with his mother and discovered from her that her pregnancy with him had been hard and that doctors had recommended an abortion. When she spoke of having been determined to bring him to term, he thought that she spoke as though she had life-and-death control over him.

That night when he went to bed, he deliberately forced himself to imagine the panther. It gave him no anxiety or terror. That afternoon, after his session, he left town with Jane. On his return, he was hesitant to tell what had happened while he had been away. His caution was increased by his having seen, just before he went away, the announcement of my book on the psychological aspects of the turmoil between Turks and Greeks in my homeland, Cyprus. Although he said that he was pleased at my success, he seemed puzzled over other feelings he could not identify. Dr. Albert then reported a dream, in which he had been fishing in a creek and saw a large frog. When I asked for an association, the phrase "a big frog in a small pond" came to him. I suggested that his dream might have something to do with his learning by accident something about me; was I the big frog in a small pond? Perhaps he wanted to upgrade and downgrade me at the same time. The usual phrase is "a big fish in a small pond," and I was curious about the introduction of the frog image. Dr. Albert's association disclosed that as a small child he had gone hunting frogs at night with his father, who had taught him how to *blind* frogs by using a flashlight in order to catch them by hand. He said he had caught only big frogs and that he had decapitated (castrated) them. He seemed to want to mutilate me in his dream, but I thought that in that case, he would fear retaliation from the father/analyst. He missed his next two sessions, offering as an excuse some change in his hospital schedule that made coming to my office at the usual time impossible.

On his return, Dr. Albert reported a dissociative experience again. He had had a wonderful weekend with Jane while Pamela was visiting friends. When he went to bed after Jane's departure, he awakened in Pamela's bed. He seemed much confused, puzzled, and disturbed. It had not made him feel better when he awakened in his daughter's bed to recall his mother's "musical beds." He sensed a personality in himself that was beyond his control and felt that he should have punishment at my hands, that he should "bend over and be spanked."

I reminded him that before leaving for his meeting he had been recalling and experiencing, in the service of mastery, his childhood fears of his mother, especially his fear of her genitalia. His separation from me (and I noted his hesitation in speaking of what had passed between himself and Jane), his reading about me just before going away, and his notion of my being "a big frog" might have stopped his dealing with his mother and led to facing his father instead. I wondered aloud if a frog was like someone bent over to receive punishment. I suggested that coming face to face with the father might have something to do with the reason he went back to his daughter's bed, in an act that represented a symbolic return to the mother. He reported feeling desperate and helpless about what was taking place. Tears came to his eyes. He recalled his mother's being in the room and the pleasure it had given him until his father loudly summoned her to return to his room and drink beer with him.

Dr. Albert was frightened when he went to pick up Pamela on the following day at the home of one of her friends. He wondered what would happen if his nocturnal wandering continued, whether he might sexually molest or even kill his daughter. He gave up drinking in order to control his impulses, and I told him once again that the father–daughter relationship was being contaminated with the mother–son relationship of his childhood.

One night in his room, Dr. Albert prayed that the panther would actually materialize so that he could see it and be rid of his bothersome feelings. He was openly distressed in reporting this and said that he felt as though he were holding back something. "I can't hold it any more," he cried. I told him that I was in no hurry and asked if we were moving too fast for him. He indicated that he would rather undergo whatever was necessary. Tears filled his eyes, behind which was "monumental pressure"; in broken sentences he spoke of mothering, violence, sex, and destruction, weeping all the while.

At the next session in the first week of December, Dr. Albert said that he was well and comfortable, but his voice was very flat as he spoke. He had been with Jane on the previous night and had told her that he was reexperiencing childhood events on the couch and having a difficult time. I said, "Hm! Hm!" and repeated my observation of his playing yo-yo, facing danger from his mother and from his father, and of the small space he seemed to have in which to maneuver between the two. He then could tell about what had happened on his trip with Jane: one night she had performed fellatio on him, and he had ejaculated into her mouth. Only now did it become evident that his black panther fantasy continued while he was away from me. This was the first time in his life that he had allowed his penis to be taken in by a mouth with teeth (*vagina dentata*). Yet after the fellatio, his penis had been intact! He was fascinated with Jane and with her ability to enjoy him sexually in a new way. He also felt very different sexually. "In the fifteen years I have been having sex," he said, "I have had nothing like this!" He had begun to feel relaxed in sexual relations. When he abruptly stopped talking, I asked why this was so.

Dr. Albert said that in his relaxation after ejaculating he had recalled hearing about certain people in India who could relax their rectal muscles in a way that permitted them to take in water through the rectum. As the notion of taking something in through his rectum came to him, he seemed embarrassed and anxious. I had an image of him bending over like a frog, as when his father had spanked him. I thought he expected punishment from me in the form of anal penetration for having enjoyed Jane and for making his partner's mouth not dangerous, but I decided to make my interpretation in reference not to this expectation, but to his identification with the aggressor in his fantasy of anal incorporation. I felt that such interpretation at this time would enrich his development of new ways of dealing with the internal and external world. In other words, emphasis on the identification with me would grant "permission," as it were, to use my analytic functions as though they were his own.

I reminded him of his wish for various "pills" and "directions" from me, and he listened without anxiety, saying that at the start of his analysis he had thought of himself as perfect; later, he had expected to become perfect with the completion of his analysis. Now he wanted to take me in, but he did not think of me as perfect; so, after all, with the completion of his analysis he might not be perfect. A realistic assumption!

On the following day, December 8, he seemed again to be consolidating his recent experiences with me. He began the hour by coughing and sneezing, saying that he had a "frog" in his throat. I reminded him of his frog dream and of his thinking of me as a frog, and our talk about fellatio as well as about taking something in through other orifices. I suggested that we put into words what was *stuck* in his throat.

Clinical experience has shown that when we unconsciously make an effort to be like another person (to identify with him), this psychological process is usually accompanied by some cannibalistic reference, which may be direct, but is more often symbolic. It is as though we would eat the other in order to unite with him. Here I thought that what Dr. Albert was "eating" had stuck in his throat! He talked about his attempts to get to know and to identify with his father and how they had been thwarted by his mother. The psychological meaning of his habit of taking liquor before going to bed was discussed. I suggested that he was symbolically clinging to his mother by taking her in every night. He said that his "fat tissue" might also represent his retention of his mother. It was hard to give her up, he explained, since without her the sun would shine on his forehead and bring dangerous radiation: he would be unprotected from the external world. He noted that he now realized that when he had worked out his problem with his mother, it would be easier to face up to his father. Would his father be jealous of him because he was trying to be a rose while his father remained a dandelion? Was his father going to decapitate him?

This summation, which he made with little help from me, relaxed him, and he began to tell me that he was noticing more changes in himself. He could not yet put words to these changes, but he saw things now "somewhat differently" from the way they had appeared to him in the past. He spoke of having heretofore made decisions about very ill patients as though he were a computer but of how he now came to decisions of this kind in full realization of a patient's human feelings. "I feel much better inside, you know!" he said before falling silent. His next remark described his sensation of being in the water with his mother; this time he was actively swimming toward the shore and emerging into the *sunshine*. He no longer feared sunshine but enjoyed feeling warm and gratified.

Grieving over Losses

Mid-December through January 4

Members of the American Psychoanalytic Association meet annually in New York City for what is called the Fall Meeting, although the event takes place shortly before Christmas, when the weather is wintry and the Waldorf-Astoria, our meeting place, glitters with Christmas decorations. In order to attend the meeting that year, I had had to cancel a few of Dr. Albert's hours. I did not explain the cancellation to him. At his first session after my return, he came in, sat on the couch, removed his lenses, and put them in a new box before lying down. He mentioned that he had had the new box for some time but that this was the first time he had used it.

In the past, Dr. Albert seemed to respond to our separations without emotion, although there had been symbolic expression in the material he gave me. This time he was openly angry. I felt excitement over this more direct response. He was now able to express anger toward me over something I had done that displeased him. Loud and sarcastic, he said about my absence, "You have been *tooling* around while I had eventful days and needed your presence and advice." As I said nothing, he went on to describe his "eventful days."

Pamela, now 7, was being cared for by a woman who had another child in her care, a boy of the same age. The babysitter reported that she had found the two children on top of each other, kissing and giggling. The boy's mother told the babysitter that on the day before this episode occurred, she had been "in the sack with a boyfriend" and had been seen there by her son. The assumption was that the boy was trying to act out with Pamela what he had seen.

As I heard this, what came to my mind was that in the past when Dr. Albert and I were separated, he would be "in the sack" with a woman himself. I said nothing and awaited his reaction. He said that after hearing from the babysitter, he had made it a point to talk to people he knew who had daughters Pamela's age, asking how they perceived their daughters' sexuality and what they would do in his position. After such consultations—and I was aware of his sarcasm in demonstrating that when I was not at hand, he could find others to consult—he concluded that his daughter was discovering her sexuality and needed his help. He had given her books on subjects such as "where babies come from," and had also given her an illustrated lecture on male and female genitalia and on sexual intercourse. Once more I noted that he might be symbolically repeating in the father-daughter relationship the stimulation he had derived from his relationship with his mother. Although it was his mother who had been responsible for such lectures during his father's "absence," due to external events he had become the lecturer to Pamela.

I did not interrupt, and Dr. Albert went on to say that since his "lecture," Pamela had been drawing naked people, pointing to their penises, breasts, and so forth. He decided to go even further with her and "not hide my own sexuality from her." Accordingly, when Jane visited him and went to bed with him, he permitted Pamela to see them together in bed, although *not* while they were engaged in sexual intercourse. Pamela's response was, "I like Jane very much, but I like my own Mom much better!"

He asked me to "guide him so that Pamela will not have guilt about sexuality." I now realized that he might be using Pamela as a representative of himself as a child, as though she would cope on his behalf and externally resolve his own problems with sexuality. Since I refrained once more from commenting, he continued, saying that his mother might have a sixth sense because when he was in the midst of instructing Pamela, she had called to say that she was sending a book on sex to her granddaughter. I wondered to myself if, during his telephone conversation with her, he might not have been indirectly and symbolically trying to get her to do just that.

After a brief silence, Dr. Albert recalled that as a young child he had been very conscious of vaginas and of the penises of other little boys. He remembered bouncing on a bed with his younger brother while they checked each other's genitals. With sadness and anger in his voice, he declared that when he was growing up he associated sex with guilt and that this had harmed him because it had led to his being sexually inhibited as a teenager. "I was so frustrated because everybody was getting laid, and I wasn't. I used to think 'if I get laid once, it would be all right to *die* the next day!'"

Suddenly Dr. Albert yelled, "What should I do? What should I do? Should I tell the babysitter that the children should stop their sex games, which are just like picking one's nose in public?" I gave no direct answer but said that Pamela's sexuality seemed to stir up the mixed feelings he had had as a child about his own sexuality. I also suggested that he might be looking for someone to tell him what limits one should draw around excessive stimulation. I was not involving myself with his dilemma about his daughter directly but was dealing with his displacement and connecting his dilemma with the difficulties he was having himself.

He yelled again, "Give me advice about what to do with my daughter! Stop tooling around while I am having a heavy trip!" When he had calmed down, I commented on his repetition of the expression "tooling around" and asked what it brought to his mind. He said he might be referring to my penis as a tool. It occurred to him that "tooling around" had been a popular term when he was 8 and even when he was in high school. I suggested that he might be wanting to tell me something that had happened when he was 8.

Dr. Albert recalled having gone for Sunday drives with the rest of his family, but he shouted, "I don't ever remember my parents doing anything together!" "Except perhaps in bed," I amended. "Yes," he said. "Except in bed!" Then he added, "I don't know! I don't know!" When I asked what it was he did not know, he said that recently as he collected information about little girls' sexuality from friends, he also asked if these friends remembered "seeing their parents screwing in bed." None of them had. Sarcastically, he shouted, "They were moms and dads; they didn't fuck!"

On the previous night, Jane, lying beside him in bed, had started to giggle. When he had asked her why, she had said that she had been remembering a man she had known who could have an erection but could not ejaculate. The idea that she had been with another man, even with one who did not perform sexually as well as he did, suddenly gave him enormous pain. "I believe in monogamy," he yelled; then, as though lecturing to himself, he began a long recital about how he should accept anything regarding anybody's sexuality. I told him that he had thought of me as "tooling around" when I was away, and now I was hearing that

Pamela, Jane, and his parents were all "tooling around." "You are left with stimulation. You seem to have a conflict between wanting to respond to them—a course that might be dangerous or dirty in your mind—and denying their existence. Your dilemma is how to put a comfortable limit on such stimulation."

Dr. Albert then could tell me that when he heard the babysitter's account of the activity of Pamela and her playmate, his first impulse had been to shake his daughter and stop her from further games of this kind; instead, he had gone to the other extreme. He now recognized his anger at not having had appropriate guidance as a child about his own sexuality. "I no longer feel rage," he said. "Now I feel hurt!" He fell silent and then said that he had momentarily forgotten what we were talking about and had heard nothing I had said about his dilemma. "Please repeat what you said a while ago," he asked. Instead of repeating myself, I decided instead to deal with the reluctance that made him forget our exchange. Angry, he cried, "That pisses me off! I am so fucking dumb!" When he calmed down, I told him to recall that our session had started with his "taking his eyes off" to blind himself; now he was "taking his ears off" to make himself deaf. He was also "taking off" his "brain synthesizer" (his term) so that he need not consolidate what was happening. In effect, he was repeating his self-castration, trying not only to make himself an idiot, but to make me one, too. The reason was that his childhood sexual experience contained some still unspoken things that made him anxious.

"The whole thing still feels like a life-and-death struggle for me," he said, referring to sexual conflicts, which he accused me of failing to solve with one good interpretation and one piece of good advice about how to handle Pamela. I was instead just "dangling a candy cane before his eyes." I commented that he seemed to have mixed feelings about the candy cane, saying, "You see me as an old wise man and hope that if you take my candy cane, you will learn something from me. But at the same time you see it as valueless, perhaps dangerous. This is the way you blind yourself and turn yourself into a 'fucking dumb person'." As the hour ended, he sat up and put his lenses in. His custom when concluding a session had been to leave without comment, but now as he rose from the couch he murmured, "I hope you have nightmares tonight!"

During the sessions that followed, Dr. Albert continued reporting acts performed outside our sessions; I thought that they represented an effort to resolve aspects of his childhood sexuality. On the one hand, they reflected his attempts at mastering different impulses pertaining to his childhood wishes, but on the other, they reflected resistance to keeping these conflicts within the hours we had together. The week of Christmas was approaching, marking the anniversary of Pamela's conception. Life and death for him seemed linked to sexuality. Although Jane planned a visit home to Kentucky for Christmas, he succeeded in having her postpone it as long as she could, and they gave a party together to celebrate his birthday. When he made the punch he put something in it with an almost conscious desire to make Jane sick. She did become nauseated, and he agreed with me that he had "poisoned" her in revenge for her leaving him. Just before she left, he invited her to a dinner he was giving for his ex-father-in-law and second wife, who were in town. When it turned out that Mamie was in town also, he invited her and urged Jane to come anyway. He told me that he had realized that it would be awkward for the two women to come face to face over the dinner table, and took pains to tell me how polite, sociable, and considerate he had been, trying to please both women, and offering a meal he had cooked himself. I realize in retrospect that I was greatly struck by his sadism and responded to it rather than seeking to explore with him the meaning of his story. I told him of the Turkish sultan who gave a blue bead to each woman in his harem, assuring each that this was a gift he made only to his favorite. The sultan's strategy made for peace in the harem until one woman dropped her blue bead in the sight of the others, who saw the ruse. I told Dr. Albert that he had, in effect, given a blue bead each to Mamie and Jane because he feared women and their anger and that in spite of his superficial politeness to them, he wanted to poison them. His sadism was showing! Since we were to separate for the holidays, I ventured to suggest that some of his sadistic feeling toward me might be displaced onto the women in his life.

When Dr. Albert began behaving "like a nice boy," I realized that I had not only spoken too soon after his report of the dinner party, giving him no chance to think about it, but had spoken in a harsher than usual voice. I was perceived as a "superego" (conscience) to which, on the surface, he submitted. He was accepting punishment from the analyst/ external "superego" in order to feel good, and this was not a good analytic development. He asked if the Turks celebrate Christmas. I made no reply but asked about his fantasies. As the session ended, he turned to me, smiling, and wished me a happy Christmas. It was only after he left that I realized that he had treated me as he treated Mamie and Jane, being sweetly sociable and hiding his sadism beneath a smile.

We met for the next time on December 28. His ex-father-in-law, with his second wife, had been his house guests during the holidays, and Mamie, although staying elsewhere, had been a frequent visitor. He spoke of having kept the illusion of a good, united family. I told him his performance was a farce that hid angry feelings. He resisted this at first and became openly angry at me for my "attack" on his illusion, but the dam broke on the following day when he told me that in spite of all his efforts to be "a nice man," his rich ex-father-in-law had given him only a token gift for Christmas. The whole reunion had been strained, an illusion, and he had felt terribly "left out." He now saw Mamie in a new light, as a confused woman who could not take responsibility, a bad mother for Pamela, one who had left the marriage perhaps because of an inability to care for the little girl. Her visits to him were a way "to have her cake and eat it, too!" He was angry and sad and kept going over and over his investments in Mamie and their life together. I sensed that the family get together had been in the service of his testing the reality of a departed "togetherness" and that he was ready to separate himself more effectively than before from previous investments.

I saw Dr. Albert next on January 2, when he came with a fantasy of opening his first session in the new year by yelling and screaming at me. He said that he was ready to examine the meaning of this wish. He was now at home alone with Pamela, who reacted numbly to all that had taken place. I sensed that because of his own conflictual involvements, he was little help to her; in fact, he made only a passing remark to her reaction to the "Christmas visit." Jane had spent the New Year with him. When, after drinking, he had burst out crying, Jane had said, "You are crying over the end of your marriage. You are grieving about it now!" I thought Jane perceptive, and he apparently agreed, saying of her, "She is a combination of a rose and a dandelion. I don't even notice her accent any more." (Her local accent had previously bothered him. It should be remembered I have an accent.) "This scares me," he went on. "She is different, and I would hate myself if I were to use her, too, as a sacrificial lamb on my way to recovery." He added that it was perfectly true that he had never before grieved for Mamie's loss openly and directly.

In the course of his grieving, he realized that he disliked the house he lived in, which he had once shared with Mamie. It was in a neighborhood he considered poorly reflective of his professional standing. "But I feel stuck there," he noted. He had been too angry to grieve about Mamie earlier. Since he had had unfinished business with her and could not surrender her, he could not grieve over her. Moreover, he did not know how to grieve properly. In a sense, he could not grieve over letting his mother go, but was psychologically stuck with her; he was unable to grieve over his toe, with its psychological significance. Once he had cried his heart out over losing the illusion of a united family, he turned to an examination of the loss of his toe. This came out in the following way on January 4.

Dr. Albert was silent at first and then told me how frustrated he felt: "I don't seem to be able to generate a deep love for Jane, but I care for her. This brings to mind one of my past difficulties: Can I really love a woman? Except, of course, I love my daughter. I thought I was in love with Caroline. I had a bell-ringing, joyous feeling with her, but looking back, I can see I didn't really know her; it was a matter of being fascinated. Now Jane is my life. But you know I have conflicts about having a woman in my life, even such a fantastic sex partner as Jane. I still, after all this work with you, see women in terms of black and white: I always compare the pros and cons about each one. In spite of this, I now allow Jane literally to reorganize my entire house, change the furniture around . . . "

After seeming lost in silence for a few moments, he reported that lying alongside Jane during the night, he had had "a great time" thinking of me. "But I couldn't conjure up any mental image of you. I made love to her without fear, as I had a new image of myself." He had thought in bed of Dvořák's music and its calm periods broken by the sudden clash of cymbals. "Analysis is like that," he said. He had been wearing a fire-engine red suit of underwear Jane had given him to help him develop a new and more colorful image. Aware that his mothe liked red, he worried lest in wearing red he might be contaminating himself with his mother. It was as though he wanted to put love, sex, and aggression together. Lying next to Jane, his head full of Dvořák's music, thoughts of analysis, and flashes of bright color, he wanted to have "a good dream" with which to start the new year by a new start in his analysis, "like christening a ship."

As the hour wore on, he spoke of how Jane had brought to his house on the previous night a belt-like gadget worn by patients with cardiac arrhythmias (a Holter monitor). One of her clients needed it. She placed it on her chest and secured it there with a bandage. Dr. Albert wondered how she would look if she were pregnant. He asked if he could take a picture of her wearing the gadget, and when she agreed, it gave him "a sense of trust." I said, "Let us be curious about what it was you wanted to have a pictorial record of." At first he thought he was repeating something in relation to "the pregnant mother," but the symbol of the pregnant mother referred to loss, the loss of a mother's love to a new sibling.

Wearing the gadget, Jane had looked to Dr. Albert like an android with nice breasts, a figure in a futuristic film, while he had worn red underwear against a background of blue sheets. Dr. Albert was fascinated by the bandages that kept the gadget on her chest; she had, he said, "a bandaged body." Asked to associate to this phrase, he recalled that about twelve years earlier, he had had a thyroidectomy and had had his chest bandaged in like fashion. The anesthetics used had suppressed his ability to urinate after the surgery, and he had needed help from an orderly, feeling as though he had lost control of his penis. After he went home, he felt an urge "to screw Mamie as many times as I could," he said, remembering that he had felt relief upon doing so. I pointed out that even though he had at first been bandaged, he had come to realize that he could use his penis. He agreed, saying, "Yes! I can still use my penis although I lost a toe." He seemed ready to psychologically separate the phallic symbolism invested in his toe from the reality of his toe *qua* toe. At the time of the "accident" to his toe, he had been taken to an operating room for surgical repair. A spinal anesthesia given then had made him feel that his whole leg had "fallen off the table." His red underwear, worn between blue bed sheets, now reminded him of red blood (associated with red anger and the dangerous red mother) pouring out onto blue surgical sheets. The surgeon had not permitted him to watch the procedure, but his mind had been clear enough for him to remember, "They took *pictures* before and after." Suddenly connecting this with his urge to photograph Jane's bandaged body, he said, "That's very interesting!" He went on to tell me that he had never seen the picture of his toe, but he could remember a colorful flash of light. I reminded him of his thinking of colorful lights the previous night and interpreted that the happenings of that night were an external reenactment of his loss of his toe (penis) and his realization now that what he had lost was but a symbol and not the real thing.

Speaking of Mamie, Sabrina, and Caroline, he declared, "They are not mine. They belong to others." Because he considered himself monogamous with Jane, Dr. Albert said, "Monogamy appears on the surface as something less than macho. But that doesn't bother me now that I am alone with Jane. She and I alone, we are exceptionally good." Then he asked me if he had gotten out of his system his need to "collect pussies." I thought that this was more a statement than a question, so I said nothing. After being silent for a while, he reported a peculiar sensation, a feeling that his lips and hands, in fact his whole body, was enlarging. I said, "You are having an erection with your whole body as though it were your penis. You want to show yourself and me that your self-inflicted and surgical mutilations did not cause the loss of your penis. Your sensation is your way of expressing the intactness of your penis."

He agreed but added, "Even now I am not 100 percent comfortable." I responded that I thought this was due to his fear that his new image—with an erection—might still face what his old image had undergone—castration. As he remained silent, I thought he was assimilating what I had just told him. The session ended.

A Carnation

January 5 to Late January

Dr. Albert began his session on January 5 with snuffling sounds and a conjecture about having an allergy or a cold. On the previous day, he had heard from his mother about the death of an 80-year-old man named Clyde, someone I could not recall his having previously mentioned, but a man who had, it turned out, helped my analysand to get a scholarship when he was still a student. Clyde had been close to Dr. Albert and had become Pamela's godfather. It occurred to me that fate was playing a trick on Dr. Albert, since on the very day he had tried to "erect" his whole body before me, Clyde, a father figure, died. It was as though he had to kill a "father" in order to be a man. I thought he was responding to this unconscious process by punishing himself with one of his allergy attacks.

Dr. Albert knew that he had liked Clyde, and he searched within himself for appropriate feelings about Clyde's death. But he found none. As he told me this, however, he snuffled. I told him that his body was crying, since, if I were to close my eyes, I would mistake the sounds he made for those of weeping. It seemed that the death of a father figure induced in him a fear of retaliation from another such figure. He said that he was wearing his red underwear but that when he went to urinate before coming to my office, he noticed that he had put it on backwards so there was no opening in front. Recalling his dream of underwear with holes, and his desire for new ones, I suggested that he wanted to protect himself from me and the possibility that the father/analyst might castrate him, retaliating at the time of Clyde's death.

His old friend's death also increased his anger at women. I felt that this was a defense against the possibility of obtaining an oedipal triumph subsequent to Clyde's death; this would in turn make him vulnerable, since the imagined rival, the father, would strike him down from his triumphant position. Also, even if the rival were permanently disposed of, it would still seem dangerous to be with a woman because of his pull to become her slave. During this session he wondered why he felt so negative toward Jane and why he was preoccupied with competitive strivings against the husband from whom she had been divorced for many months. "I like Jane so much, but why do I feel negative toward her today?" he wondered. He noted that, although he accepted her accent and her bad grammar, he should perhaps tell her to "fuck off and get lost." But he mellowed after a brief silence and asked, "Is Jane really like my mother, or do I make her like my mother?" I replied that I was glad to hear his verbalization of his dilemma, and I suggested again that at the time of a father figure's death he might be inclined to contaminate his woman with the image of his mother and that of the mother/analyst who speaks with an accent and has occasional difficulty with English grammar.

He declared that he did not want to go home to Clyde's funeral. "What's a funeral for?" he asked. "To bury somebody or show respect. But it's too late then to give any message to the one who is dead. My father died before I could give him my message."

Since Dr. Albert was unable to say what that message might have been, I told him it might have been an expression of desire to be close to him, that he had been so busy trying to figure out the unfinished business he had with his mother that he had had no time or energy to be close to his father. When Dr. Albert came to his session on Monday, he reported that he had not gone to the funeral, which had taken place on the weekend, and that he had not grieved. I thought, nevertheless, that he was responding to the death when he reported that he felt numb. After saying cautiously that he felt close to Jane, he seemed to spend the rest of the session in an effort to identify with the dead father figure. He said, "I feel like I am being lowered into a well" and lay as motionless as a corpse on the couch. I told him that his attempt to identify with the dead was probably defensive, a kind of self-castration; he was "killing" himself in order to avoid being killed by others.

Dr. Albert missed his hour the next day. In a sense, his hour was "killed" because his car broke down. At the next session, he told how he was saving the life of one of his very sick patients by an *aggressive* treatment that he thought might bring down the wrath of his superiors. I thought that he was declaring that he was saving lives, however "aggressively," and thus we would never consider that he had a death wish for others (father figures) or that he had "killed" others. Toward the close of the session, after my gentle confrontations, his voice dropped. Angrily he said to me, "Lust for my mother, fear of my father! Volkan, I know you will return to these again and tell me about my fear of reprisal. Okay, Volkan, I feel guilty that I didn't go to Clyde's funeral!" Gently I replied, "You knew you were going to feel guilty when you didn't attend the funeral." His reply to this was, "Yes, yes. I knew it was going to happen. I was breaking an obligation!"

He then began mumbling about his father's funeral, and Danny's, recalling an image of the minister eulogizing Danny. Then he cried out suddenly, as though addressing one of the dead people from his past; "You are dead! You are dead!" Then his voice dropped, and he added, "Unless there is reincarnation!" He fell silent. I suggested that as he seemed anxious we might explore the reason. He talked then about how his mother perceived him as an extension of Daddy Doc but at the same time considered him second-best. He seemed regressed and confused. "Daddy Doc is someone I didn't know," he explained. "My mother did not know her background. Reincarnation does not relate to the genes. I don't believe in it!" Suddenly he asked me if Turks believe in reincarnation. I suggested that we examine this question and try to find out what it would mean to him if the answer were yes or no. He said he wanted to know who would come back to haunt him. I told him that we do not really kill anyone, that the dead may live on in our memory. "I suggest," I said, "that Clyde's death brought to your mind the relationship you had with other important persons who died, such as your father."

Dr. Albert then recalled having heard his father quote a black preacher who had intoned at a funeral, "You know Terry. I know Terry. Let's bury Terry." He seemed to want to bury Clyde, Danny, and his father as quickly and magically as these words suggested, so that the unfinished business connected with their images would no longer disturb him. I said, "The dead are still in your memory, in your mind. The conflict you had with them is now between you and you. So, if you will, let's not bury them yet, so that a resolution of the conflicts can be found." I added that in missing his hour on the previous day he was symbolically killing me or failing to attend a funeral. The conflict between him and the images of the dead was still strong enough to influence his actions, as it had done in the case of his skipping an hour with me. "Oh yes! Yes!" he replied. "I am trying to find out more about my conflict. I wish I had more of those fucking dreams."

On January 11, Dr. Albert again brought his reaction to Clyde's death to his hour, at the start of which he talked about his wish to save Jane from a dandelion fate and improve her. I summarized aloud that he had recently recalled his childhood incestuous wishes rather openly and was now better able to tolerate the feeling associated with them. Thus he was making efforts to develop a new sense of self and was competing with Jane's other men, including her ex-husband, Kenny. In the middle of this, a father figure had died and left him alone with a woman, Jane this time, whom he needed to save and make better lest she smother him. At the same time, he felt that the dead man would return and retaliate for his having a woman. He responded by talking about his father's funeral and how he had glimpsed "from a distance" his father lying in his coffin. His mother had tried to force him to take a closer look, but he could not, and his refusal upset his mother greatly. Mother and son had "almost had a confrontation" at the casket.

I suggested that his refusal to view his father in the casket had been in the service of denying his death. "That is true," he screamed. I told him that people have different reactions to death, depending on whether they have unresolved conflicts with the one who has died. I suggested that as his conflicts about his father's image were resolved, he might "let him lie in peace." Then, as though he wanted to convey that he did indeed have unfinished business with his father's image and that he feared retaliation, he reported his fantasy of breaking his neck skiing on the weekend. This trip would be the first time he had gone skiing in twelve years. Jane, more extroverted than he, had persuaded him to go. She was becoming an external influence to encourage him to take "risks," psychological as well as physical.

He reported at his Monday hour that he had fallen down often on the ski slope. Obviously, the expected "castration" of breaking his neck had not occurred. Indeed, the risk he had taken had been beneficial; he was now able to tell me that the work of his analysis was "changing my predetermined self-images. . . . I feel more comfortable with myself," he said, "and I seem to have more friends now. My roll [the fat around his belly] still bothers me, but I am less self-conscious about it. Paradoxically, it is easier for me now to work on getting rid of it." He went on to say that his getting fat was "a seal of approval of my mother's cooking."

Dr. Albert told me that, at his suggestion, Joe and Caroline had been invited on the skiing outing. He seemed to want to test himself; he still considered Caroline a rose, but he had his own woman on the outing, and suddenly he felt no longer jealous of Joe. Even Joe's superior skill at skiing did not bother him. But when Jane told him that she planned to go skiing with her ex-husband, Dr. Albert had fantasies of a bloody assault on him. He expressed his dilemma on the couch: "If I tell Jane not to see Kenny any more, if I become assertive, then she may decide to tell me to 'fuck off.' Or she might decide to stay with me all the time, and I'm not sure which outcome I would prefer yet!" He reported having been unable, after learning of Jane's plans with Kenny, to "get a hard on." He spoke of this as "expressing my anger passively!"

"You, Volkan, tell me how to be more active," he cried. I told him that I was hearing him as conflicted about being assertive with women and as expecting in return rejection and retaliation. On the other hand, I pointed out, he did not seem to want his assertiveness to succeed for fear of having a woman around his neck, smothering him forever.

After a talk with him that night, Jane decided not to go skiing with Kenny after all. But since Dr. Albert could not commit himself to her, the couple came to an agreement to continue to be lovers but to date others as well. He told me at this point that a friend had suggested that a woman from one of "the first families of Virginia" might enjoy a date with him. He was, predictably, fascinated with the idea of this new "rose." But it turned out that when a date with him had been proposed to her, she had asked to see his picture before consenting. This had infuriated him, making him feel like a dandelion. "Someone is asking for my credentials!" he declared. Indicating that he now had a stronger image of himself, he refused to send his picture. Nonetheless, he felt threatened. "My weak image still exists," he said, and toward the end of the hour, he demanded to know why I had taken him as a patient. He asked whether I wanted patients who are intelligent. I told him that he was wondering whether he had the proper credentials to be my patient. In that he had checked my credentials before deciding on me as his analyst, I asked him if my being a rose made him a dandelion.

Jane did not spend the night with him one night in the third week of January but dated instead an old boyfriend who was visiting in town. I got the impression that Jane was responding to his vacillation about committing himself to her and that she might be angry with him, as was suggested when one night she could not reach climax during intercourse with Dr. Albert. I think it was in response to her dating another man that he dropped Pamela (representing Jane or women in general) on her head while he played with her as Jane looked on. He later "dissociated" this aggressive behavior from his conscious mind, and when Jane told him what he had actually done, he felt depressed and disgusted. His bowling skill fell off, and he declared on the couch that he felt as though Pandora's box had been opened, and spoke of "infidelity." He thought of Jane as his wife, and he thought of her having intercourse with her boyfriend as infidelity. Stories about Mamie and her presumptive lover poured out, and he displayed anger, concluding his outburst with a description of his mental picture of Jane in the arms of her boyfriend! With some hesitation he said, "on the couch" and then fell silent.

"The couch," I repeated. This phrase brought up memories of his mother asleep on a couch. I thought his reference to a couch might involve the transference aspect of the story since he lay on my couch. Since he was now unrepressing newly uncovered memories, I had no need to bring the transference into the open and allowed him to talk without interference. He had seen his mother asleep on the couch when he rose early and had thought that she had not slept with his father and was thus available to him. Such thoughts led to feelings of oedipal guilt. I understood now that he was punishing himself when he pushed Jane toward her boyfriend; this was in a sense retaliation for his childhood guilt. The guilt he felt for oedipal triumph had been rekindled when he was 10 and a neighborhood child called him names and jeered, "You are probably fucking your mother and sister!" He had reported this to his mother, who was not embarrassed. She talked about what fun "fucking" was. As the hour ended, it suddenly occurred to him that his father might have had an affair shortly before his death. Since the hour was at an end, there was no opportunity to explore this notion further.

The next session began with a silence, after which he reported having gone to a basketball game with Jane, who had pointed out her boyfriend in the audience. He was younger than Dr. Albert and had a beard. Dr. Albert, who sported only a mustache, had thought that the bearded young man looked more masculine than he. After reporting this, Dr. Albert fell silent, and then announced, "I am fond of Jane. But I still keep thinking of finding my dream girl some day." He seemed to be in the mood to take stock. "Yesterday I was sorting out my feelings about men and women. These have a lot to do with my childhood." He went on to say that although psychoanalysis had been changing his personality, he could not yet see the results fully. He wanted to see the face of Jane's boyfriend. After he had been pointed out, he had only a moment of anxiety and then was able to lose himself in the game. As he spoke, I thought that whereas Jane's boyfriend was contaminated with the oedipal father, the basketball game was associated with a good father in his mind.

"Psychoanalysis is not like mowing the lawn, cutting the grass, sprucing up the lawn," he said. "You can't see the the change as easily in psychoanalysis as you can in gardening." Reminding him that he had cut off his toe while mowing, I suggested that he might want psychoanalysis to repair his toe.

"I have a sense of doing something," he said. "Writing a publishable paper, rewriting it over and over. I want to watch it take shape." I suggested that he and I were recalling and recalling and reworking and reworking his conflictual issues. He seemed relaxed and remained silent before asking me, "Why is it important that I want a mate? I like to have a sense of completeness, a sense of normalcy. Things are not worked out all the way yet." I reminded him of saying the day before that his feelings about women and men were contaminated with feelings from his childhood and suggesting as the hour ended that his father had had an affair.

"I have a sense of anxiety now," he said, going on to recall how, years ago, everyone in his home had had to be quiet when his father came home from work to let him unwind. His father would sit down, read his paper, and have a drink, and no one was allowed to bother him.

Dr. Albert kept alternating between imagining a cold, formidable father and an affectionate one. "But he and mother would hold hands and walk in the orchard," he said, recalling the Sunday afternoon drives during which his mother snuggled up to her husband and all the children laughed and giggled. But the father, who had an I.Q. of 165, never finished anything, never held a steady job, and during his 40s and 50s became an angry, bitter, defeated man who died at the age of 55, just when his son became a physician. The father had worked in a local motel during his last years, and Dr. Albert thought that he might have been attracted to a woman working in the same place whom Dr. Albert never met. He described his father's fight against death: "no whimpering!"

Suddenly Dr. Albert began talking about having seen his brother years earlier. His brother had been drunk and had talked about his connections with the CIA and the underworld. Dr. Albert knew that these claims were false, and now, as he suddenly recalled his brother's story of having accidentally killed a man in Belgium, he wondered if that tale might not be false also. He began to yawn. I told him that the story of his brother's killing someone was important to him because it showed that aggression could kill and that there was aggression in the family. If he could convince himself that he had not killed his father, he would be in a better position to put his different images of him together and would be able to recall him realistically. Upon hearing this, he spoke sadly about how it had taken his father three months to die and about how stressful this period had been for the whole family. For him, the three months had been like three years.

Dr. Albert dwelled again on his family background, speaking of how his parents' pride was too great to let them beg support from Brownie, who outlived his father by five years and died only five years before Dr. Albert became my patient. She had been *The Boss*. Although she had grown up surrounded by servants, with changing times she had become like "a rich little kid choosing to live in a cabin, making her own bread, her own raspberry jam, and hash." Dr. Albert now observed how his mother, always in search of glory, had developed Brownie's character traits after the older woman died. It was his mother more than anyone else who had wanted to keep the fantasied glories of the past alive. Dr. Albert's search for his "dream girl" referred to keeping just such a past alive because, he recalled, his mother had kept telling him, "This is good for you; this is not good for you." "Now," he said, "I am caught between halfway agreeing with my mother and halfway knowing and respecting the real and practical issues."

On a visit to town, Mamie called him that night and claimed that she needed money. Dr. Albert did not become her savior at once, but clung to his "real and practical aspect." At first he had the vindictive thought that she deserved her misery, but he was troubled. "I am in the middle, holding a pyramid," he said. "I am like a cheerleader, holding a human pyramid." It was, he said, an upsidedown pyramid with three corners, at two of which stood his parents, and at the third of which stood Daddy Doc and Brownie. He seemed very sad.

On Monday, January 29, he reported having gone to church the day before. This was another change for him; although he had not become religious, he now seemed to enjoy the social aspect of occasional church attendance. Dr. Albert spoke of the minister's sermon, which had dealt with expectation, anticipation, and reality. It reminded him of his analysis, which he kept thinking about, and which stimulated him. He had dreamed that night of being in bed in the morning in an apartment in a big city. "It was bright and open," he said. He dreamed that Pamela entered the room to say that breakfast was ready, that the two had a coversation about a Dr. Hans, Pamela telling him that she would rather have Dr. Hans rear her than her father. He felt hurt by this.

Dr. Albert said that Pamela was deserting him in this dream; but more important was that he was examining the different facets of his personality. He observed that Dr. Hans represented a condensation of himself (with a mustache, a divorce) and me (with an accent). Mamie's recent request for money had led him to reevaluate his relationship with her and with Pamela. He accordingly had had a long talk with Pamela about the circumstances of the divorce and his relationship with Jane. As a consequence, Pamela seemed more relaxed, and, indeed, had taken coffee to her father and Jane in his bedroom, as if she found Jane's presence more acceptable than before. Dr. Albert had been recently irritated with his daughter and no longer thought of himself as her "super savior." Their discussion, he said, "seems to have redefined our lives." I replied that he could now even feel free to complain about her as he had complained about Mamie on the previous day. He seemed happy about this, and said laughingly, "Physically, there are limits to what I can do." I remarked that he was less omnipotent. "I'll say," he replied delightedly.

He let me know that he would like to take a few weeks off for skiing with Jane but that he felt tied down by Pamela. "And also by me," I added. He seemed to have no anxiety over complaining.

His dream about Dr. Hans seemed to have more day residue. On the previous Saturday, I had taken my children to the opening performance of a very popular film about a comic superhero. As we left the crowded theater, I was greeted by an acquaintance, a newsman assigned to a story about popular reaction to the film. When he asked how I had enjoyed it, I responded positively, and added something about how enjoyable it is to project one's own childhood fantasies of omnipotence onto the screen. The Sunday paper carried a story on the showing of the film, mentioned my being at the showing with my children, and also mentioned my remarks on childhood fantasies of omnipotence. Dr. Albert had "felt very funny" when he read this. "It was as if I were reading something about myself in the paper," he remarked, referring to our merging in the dream. "Furthermore," he added, "I now had concrete evidence that you are a family man. I always thought you had a family, but now with this evidence I am redefining you!"

He went on to say that he was "redefining" many things. On a visit from Joe and Caroline on Sunday night he had perceived Caroline, the rose, as being too thin. Although I had an accent, evidence of my dandelion aspect, I could be a better father than he was. When Kenny, Dr. Albert's rival for Jane, had called her recently, he had confided, according to her, that he had a drug problem.

On Sunday night before having his dream about Dr. Hans, he had awakened with a salivation attack. "I had to spit out about two cupfuls of saliva," he said. He then had sweated and had a bout of diarrhea. He kept thinking that he was making psychosomatic response to stress, although the response was not full-blown. Dr. Albert pictured himself as a child, holding his breath until he turned blue. Then he recalled that just before going to sleep, he had touched his face and found a small scar on his *left* eyebrow. It was the scar left by his accident with the knife when he was 4, but he suddenly realized that he had displaced the scar to his right eyebrow in his adult mind. He was amazed, saying, "My past, and its appearance in the present time, is coming to me from every direction. I can't seem to keep track, but although I am in a sense overwhelmed, I am not blown out."

Dr. Albert went on to say that as an adult he acted like someone who had stuck his finger in a hole in a dike, trying to pretend that everything was all right and that he could do everything. "Your omnipotence is leaving you," I said. "Your omnipotent acts, now being as it were projected onto a screen, are perceived as memories, but you know now they aren't based on fact." He began to laugh, saying, "Ya! Ya! Ya! My life, instead of getting more predictable, is becoming more complex." I responded in reference to the obsessional characteristics he had previously displayed, "Once you were too predictable." He kept laughing in a friendly way. I felt friendly toward him, too, and in retrospect I can see that, as his dream had suggested, we were "merging."

Dr. Albert went on. "I feel like a drop of oil on water with detergent. The oil gets dispersed in the end, becoming one with the other elements. The detergent is the psychoanalysis. It is because of it that the oil and water can meet and become one." Then he added, "You know, I am talking about dandelions and roses." He stopped, gave a hearty laugh, and then suddenly cried, "A carnation! If you cross a dandelion and a rose you get a carnation!" He then laughingly described how useful the carnation was for so many occasions. He remembered seeing the head coach of a famous basketball team wearing a carnation in his lapel at a critical game aired on television. "Wearing a carnation is a gesture," he concluded. "A gesture of celebration! It marks an important event and a time of sadness also."

I commented, "I am glad you realize that the merging of a dandelion with a rose is a time of sadness as well as a celebration of achievement, since when you find a carnation you will face loss and will miss the rose as well as the dandelion." "That's a bummer!" he cried, all smiles.

When he came in the next day, the last day of January, Dr. Albert was sniffling and reported having bowled badly the night before. He said he had read a *newspaper* article entitled "What Price Glory?" I knew that he was referring to having found the carnation the day before and to his unreadiness to accept his new self-image. He spoke of some people prominent in politics who were divorced and commented that he did not want to get married now. Then he gave another version of his oil-and-water analogy, saying that he was an object on the water's surface, and he was not floating upon it, but sinking. Did he really want to sink (from a rose to a carnation)?

Then Dr. Albert asked aloud, "Where do I belong on the social scale?" and referred to death and the Four Horsemen of the Apocalypse. Was he a David or a Goliath? What is it to be in between, in a "grey zone"? "I never thought of myself as a 'middle type,'" he said. "Yes, it is mediocre." He went on to confide that Mamie, who had once seemed to him a rose, had been reduced to waitressing in another town to earn money. He had mixed feelings about his rose turning into a dandelion. I told him that the aim of analysis was not to turn him into a mediocrity, but to give him more than two extremes from which to fashion a life for himself.

In the past he had thought that he was able to do anything, that nothing could really touch him. But he now had so many responsibilities meeting his taxes, caring for and renting Daddy Doc's house, looking after the property he had purchased, writing professional papers and grant proposals, caring for Pamela, living with Jane, and worrying about Mamie. "I am doing a lot and I get no credit," he said, adding, "No, no, I am all right. People know how hard I work on the job!"

Dr. Albert proceeded to speak, in what I saw as another analogy of how he was putting together opposing aspects of himself, of how he had recently helped "integrate" a black woman into his professional setting. "I don't notice changes in me," he noted. "But people have kept telling me recently how changed I am. I take care of myself. I don't want to be aggressive. I want to be *assertive.*"

Giving the Finger

The First Two Weeks of February

Dr. Albert began his session on February 1 by saying that he and Jane had invited friends to his house to watch a telecast of a game played by the basketball team of the local university. When the game was over, all four had begun to talk about their childhood while drinking beer. The woman guest recalled how afraid she had been as a child that something lurked under her bed at night. Although everyone laughed, Dr. Albert confessed to having had the same fear as a child. I could see that his childhood black panther had lost its power over him since he could talk naturally in a social gathering about what had terrified him as a child.

As he lay on the couch, he recalled childhood rituals he had practiced, such as pulling the covers up to his chin to protect him from the hand he expected to snatch at him from beneath the bed. He acknowledged having had rituals of this general sort all his life and noted that even now he dressed in a ritualistic way, putting on his right sock before his left, and so on. Mamie had commented that it would be easy to assassinate him since he could be counted on to repeat the same patterns of behavior day after day. He demonstrated for me a secret ritual he carried out on the couch by moving his arms in a special way. The removal of his lenses was, of course, another ritual he had developed as his analysis progressed. Through such rituals he defensively attempted to magically control the situation, especially to control the derivatives of his aggressive drives toward others and aspects of aggression that would in turn be directed at him from other people. He said that although he felt able now to surrender some or all of his rituals, he continued to feel anxious lest something dreadful, like the massacre committed by the Manson family, overtake him.

On his way to my office that day, Dr. Albert had seen a passing woman driver draw dangerously close to his car, and he had responded with a gesture not characteristic of him. He had given her "the finger." "I shot the birdie," he said. "I gestured 'fuck you' to her." He went on, "Why do I feel aggressive lately? As if I'm trying new things—without planning—just spontaneously. But I still feel some anxiety when I vent my aggression."

I told him he might fear that if he were aggressive he would meet the fate of Danny, through whose actions his aggression could be vicariously vented, and from whom he might have wanted to learn how to be aggressive. He responded by saying, "My restraints are not there any more. I used to keep everything locked up. For so many years I did not express myself; no yelling, no screaming—and no real anxiety." I suggested that his rituals kept his anxiety down. "Yes!" he agreed. "But now my pattern is breaking up. I am like an Alka-Seltzer tablet in the water. Bubble and sparkle!"

He fell silent and noticed that his body became tense. Then he offered another analogy. "I am molten lava with bubbles, a burning volcano that may kill people." "Who is a volcano?" I asked, to his surprise. He noted didactically that there are no volcanoes in our part of the country, but I asked, "What is my name?" Surprised, he talked now about his desire to be like me and to be more aggressive, but with the hope that I would not be like Danny. But if I were more aggressive than Danny, and he became aggressive after identifying with me, he could kill people as a volcano (Volkan) does. He feared retaliation for any such expression of his aggressive drives.

Dr. Albert had been an aggressive little boy, often involved in fights. He recalled the last fight he had had, when he was 10. He made the spontaneous discovery then that a playmate's jeer, accusing him of "fucking" his sister and his mother, had turned him to passivity. "Thus," I remarked, "it was the verbalization of your incestuous sexuality that made you fear retaliation by your father and change your behavior pattern." At puberty he had learned to use his brains instead of his muscles. "I could drive the girls to tears with my brains," he recalled. In reference to his hand gesture to the woman who drove too close he noted, "That's the first time *since puberty* that I ever shot the birdie!"

Stopping suddenly, he asked me anxiously, "Do analysts ever fail?" I replied, "Do you suppose you are wondering if I would stop seeing you if you 'shot the birdie' before me?" Relaxing, he spoke about the threatening hand he had imagined under his bed when he was a child, explaining that it was not the black hand in his dream that had crushed the knobs, but a different kind of hand, with long nails ("maybe like a panther's," I suggested) and black in color. The one in his dream had been a fist like George Foreman's or Muhammed Ali's. He explained that the hand under the bed was *bluish* black, the "color of a starling." "Starlings are the dandelions of the bird world," he said. "It was my mother with her black hair that I was afraid of!" He remained motionless and finished the hour by telling me a science-fiction tale from television in which a woman had turned into a ten-foot-long black cat (panther).

Dr. Albert opened his next hour with the question, "How will I know when I reach the end of my analysis?" I suggested that we become curious about this inquiry. He indicated that he had been reviewing many things about the important people in his life and that he was allowing himself to experience new things that violated his rituals. Although on one day he would be elated by noticing many changes in himself, on another he would revisit his fear of the black panther. He said he had asked his question mainly because he still could not handle Jane's wanting to date other men. By dating others she was exerting pressure on him for commitment. She would comply with his wishes if a commitment were forthcoming or if he forbade her to date other men. "Intellectually" he wanted her to keep on dating so he would not feel smothered by her, but "emotionally" he wanted to keep her for himself. "I have been integrating many things recently," he said, "but I can't seem to integrate the way I feel about Jane. My analysis has not caught up with this issue yet!" Jane was apparently going out with another man that night, having assured him that her date involved no more than a platonic relationship. "She is torn, too," he said, able to see her dilemma. "But she wants commitment from me."

Dr. Albert was able to express his fear that she would find a younger man. He was ten years older than she, and she had remarked, "Now that you are 36, you may not get it up as much!" I told him that once upon a time, *he* had been the younger man in a competition for the love of his mother. My remark brought to his mind the image of his father as an athlete, and he spoke again, in great detail, of his father's athletic prowess. A well-rounded athlete, his father had excelled not only in basketball, but also in tennis, boxing, high jumping, and other sports. He had been 28 at the time of Dr. Albert's birth, so the son knew of his athletic accomplishments largely by hearsay. As a child, Dr. Albert had played horseshoes with his father and had always lost. He would be so frustrated over never winning that when his mother watched the two, she would ask her husband to let the boy win occasionally.

Dr. Albert recalled other activities, including fishing, which they had done together. They had always competed. At this point in his account, he seemed frustrated, and he cried out, "I don't want to lose now in anything!" Again he reviewed, with considerable emotion, how the competition with his father had driven him back to his mother. He had even learned to cook well as a child in order to win praise. "Horseshoes have numbers," he said. "You know how many horseshoes there are and how many you throw successfully and how many you miss. No numbers in cooking. With cooking you can't compete!"

He fell into an angry silence and then noted that he had no knowledge of his father's sexual prowess. "I don't know how often they had intercourse," he said. But he knew that when his father fell ill, his mother had six months of sexual frustration. Apparently she had confided this to Dr. Albert's sister, who in turn had told him. When his silence lengthened, I suggested, "You may be trying to tell me something by your silence." He complained of a stomach ache, which he ascribed to "anxiety about competition."

During his next session, Dr. Albert feverishly continued his examination of his childhood relationship with his father, mother, and important other people, but this time he had a more observing ego. I felt as though he were taking stock, defining and redefining the images of others and the corresponding images of himself. On February 9, he detailed how his mother had clung to certain objects of Daddy Doc's and had made them almost magical. I have published extensively my observations on the phenomenon of clinging to some object to magically evoke a departed person. People who cannot progress through the normal mourning process need to keep, sometimes forever, an exaggerated relationship with the images of the lost one, and thus they "create" the unique function of such objects in order to continue a symbolic link between the survivor and the lost one. I named such objects, "linking objects." Dr. Albert's mother had kept the watch, ring, and other items that had been Daddy Doc's and saw to it that they were given to her son, Chris, when he was in high school. There were no such keepsakes for his brother. Dr. Albert pondered how he had been "the chosen one" to keep Daddy Doc's memory and glory alive for his mother. He was his mother's link, a living linking object to his grandfather.

When Dr. Albert's father died, however, his brother had been the one to get all the keepsakes, including a shotgun Dr. Albert had wanted for himself. Chosen as a link to his grandfather, "It seems I couldn't compete with my brother to have and keep something of my father's," he explained. A few days later, an event took place that symbolically could overcome his mother's interference with his relationship with his father. As he was getting ready for his early morning session with me, Jane, who had spent the night with him, asked to be taken to her apartment because she was coming down with a cold and felt that she needed rest. He thus found himself "between a woman and a man." If he said no to Jane, he risked being rejected by her, or so he thought. He finally chose to come to his session with me, after explaining to Jane that he would drive her home when it was over.

Dr. Albert seemed busy protecting the good father image in me and seemed to feel very positive about me. He tried to create such images outside his analytic hours also. For example, when one of his favorite university basketball players, who was, I believe, contaminated with the image of his good father, failed to receive an award, he wanted to write to the local newspaper in protest.

As his attempts to find a strong oedipal father increased, it seemed to him that the only way to succeed was to break away from woman/ mother. Once again he spoke of Jane as his "sacrificial lamb." I interpreted to him what he was experiencing, and how Jane's image was being contaminated with that of the mother who interfered with his having gotten to know his father. With these issues, we came to the end of his second year of analysis.

The Third Year

A Step into the Sun

Mid-February to the End of April

When we started our third year together, in mid-February, I felt uneasy with the knowledge that I would be leaving Dr. Albert for three weeks early in March. My connection with the medical school gave me academic responsibilities that sometimes interfered with my analytic work, and now it was necessary for me to go overseas on a project for the medical school. I knew that a new and rather long unexpected separation might bewilder Dr. Albert and interfere with the flow of the analytic process. Anticipating that he would react to the proposed separation, I tried to observe his response and to interpret its unconscious aspects aloud.

When I told him in mid-February that I would be unavailable to him during the first three weeks of March, I pondered whether to share with him the reason for the separation. I decided not to because I thought that an explanation might seem apologetic and interfere with his fantasies about my unavailability. He himself said that he would not ask why I was going to be unavailable, that he knew I would not answer such a question directly. He was clearly upset and angry, and I felt a measure of fleeting guilt, but once I had made my announcement I sat back to observe his reactions.

Dr. Albert's main arena of "retreat" was the controlling (anal) mechanism of his obsessional character structure. He had on many occasions left the anal level after his psychoanalytic work began and had "gone up" to face oedipal issues until they became charged, when he would regress to the anal or oral level before returning to the oedipal. Now the shock of the impending separation sent him back to the anal level. The hour was full of angry silences (he kept his words to himself, like a stubborn child retaining feces rather than accede to his parents' wishes that he move his bowels) and memories of his sitting on the potty as a child without results. In spite of my attempts to interpret what was going on, he was too angry, symbolically rather than openly, to listen. He even spoke of quitting psychoanalysis altogether. Although I was aware of feeling a certain guilt for "failing" him, I felt at the same time angry at him for reacting in this way. But I was careful not to overwhelm him.

At the last hour before our separation, he brought in a venomous attack on psychoanalysis that recently had been published in a medical journal. Lying on the couch, Dr. Albert brandished the article as though it were a flag of aggression, and without turning his head to face me he demanded that I take it. I took it, glanced at it, and put it on the ottoman near the couch, saying, "I've been aware that since I am about to leave you, you want to tell me to go and fuck myself!"

Smirking, Dr. Albert fell silent. Then his expression softened, and playing out the typical balancing act of the obsessional, he began to speak of another but favorable article on psychoanalysis. But the emotions that he expressed only indirectly in action were too charged to be handled by a balancing act. He insisted on "narrowing the margin of error" in determining intellectually whether psychoanalysis is a good thing. As he spoke of "the margin of error," he did something most unusual: he rose from the couch, only to lie down again on it at a greater distance from me. I felt that he had done this in a dissociated state—that is to say, in a different state of consciousness—and that he was unaware of having done it. I observed that this action represented an attempt to widen "the margin" between us. He even extended one of his arms behind his head, and I felt that his moving beyond touching range was a defense against the aggressive feelings toward me that he could not verbalize. I told him what he was doing and that I understood it as protecting himself from a desire to hit me while at the same time protecting himself from retaliation from me. He listened without replying. I had the feeling that he had put me at a great distance and could hear me but could not process what I said.

As he was about to leave at the hour's end, Dr. Albert made no move to pick up the article that attacked psychoanalysis. I commented that I did not know what he wanted me to do with it, that he had brought it because of his discomfort over my going away. I suggested that he take it back, because if I kept it, I might be helping him to express himself in action instead of talking about his feelings, and interfering with any fantasies he might develop. He recalled that on the first Christmas in our association he had spoken about wanting to bring me a box of candy as a gift, but that I had told him that I would prefer *talking* about his wish to give me something. He picked up the paper, and with a friendly look that turned sad, left my office.

We had our first hour together after my overseas trip on March 27. Dr. Albert opened the session by saying that he had spent the three weeks of my absence "recounting," going over the changes in him since the start of his analysis. He now noted more and more grey areas in himself and in Jane as well. Much to his surprise, this aspect had led him to a deeper relationship with her and to greater "tolerance about others' behavior." "I also understand how others feel," he said. I told him that he was partly glad to see me back and that I appreciated his tolerance of the analyst who had left him unexpectedly in the middle of our analytic work. In response, he indicated that he was aware of "the positive aspects" of his reaction to the separation; he had, indeed, finished writing a chapter for publication. But he wondered about reactions of "an aggressive nature"; he felt aggressive and thought he might have waited for my return before unleashing negative feelings, which, if not controlled, might have caused my death and precluded my return!

"I wish I were like Frankenstein," he said. "Then I could unscrew my head so all the things inside me could come out all at once!" He then went on to say that during the first week of our separation he had kept smashing his hand and accidentally cutting his fingers.

On the following day, Dr. Albert had returned to an anal-retentive state, holding his anger in and sulking. It was on March 29 that he unscrewed the head of Frankenstein. That session began when Dr. Albert recalled a Tarzan film he had seen as a child. It had pictured a *volcanic* underground lake into which a careless person might readily fall. I noticed the play on my name, and I had an odd intuition that the lake also stood for a toilet bowl. I listened in silence for the time being.

The volcanic lake was full of alligators or piranhas, and some evil natives were pulling people with ropes toward the lake. The victims were terrified, since they knew that the natives planned to cut the ropes and give them to the predators below. Again I had the image of feces separating from the body, being gulped down by the flushing water in a toilet bowl. But Tarzan arrived and saved the people from their peril.

Dr. Albert recalled that although he was pleased at seeing the people saved, he continued to feel the terror the scene had aroused.

He was ready to connect this image with our recent separation, his anger over it, and his terror that I might retaliate for his anger. I was the volcanic lake with alligators and piranhas. But I was also, in good image, Tarzan. He could not directly express his anger toward me for leaving him, because if I found him ungrateful, I could let him drop into the dangerous water. He also felt himself to be rejected, bad, dirty, and unworthy, like excrement.

As we discussed the possible meaning of the Tarzan film, I noted that he was giving me the finger, slyly, so that it looked as though he were simply scratching. Since I thought he was not conscious of doing this, I decided to bring it to his attention, showing him once again that I could see his anger and I could tolerate it. After this, he confided that Jane had left him recently to attend a meeting and that he had felt anxiety. He had "lost" her telephone number and so could not call her. Although he had pretended to be above feeling anxious about the separation, when he found that she was actually out of touch by telephone, he was flooded with anxiety and with fantasies of her being courted by men richer and more handsome than he (roses). "I'm the grasshopper who never reaches the wall," he said. As the hour closed, I gave him a brief summary of my observations of him since the resumption of our work. He put in his lenses, which he still removed at the start of each session with me, and left.

On April 3, Dr. Albert began his hour by saying how much simpler "it" would be if he left his lenses in place while he lay on the couch. He then reported having dreamed of standing in a mountain lodge, looking down into a dark valley full of trees with a musty smell. He thought there was something fearful—some "it"—in this valley. Along with a man standing nearby, he began to shoot into the valley at the frightening presence. As he peered into the valley, he could see only a dark cloud rising toward the lodge, enveloping and then entering it. Although it was like a *black* mist, Dr. Albert at this point in his dream felt no anxiety. The dream ended.

During the evening before he had this dream, he and Jane had sprayed paint over some wallpaper, and he suggested that the act of spraying, with its sexual connotations, might have influenced the content of his dream. He was a tomcat spraying his girl friend; they made love over and over when the painting was done and experimented with different positions. Once they made love side by side, face to face, and it had occurred to him that that was how an old man might make love. Recalling his fantasies about "roses" being his rivals for Jane, I observed that he had been trying to identify himself with an older man. Nonetheless I sensed in the dream an attempt to be a tomcat; the black cloud in the valley probably represented the vagina, and its appearance made him less anxious than he had been when confronted by a black panther. As I pondered the dream with him, he began giving me his own associations. The blackness in the dream was associated, he said, with a black man who was his neighbor. The day before he had had this dream, Dr. Albert had noticed on arriving home that a tree in his yard had been cut down by someone unknown. It had stood at the boundary of his yard and his black neighbor's, and he thought that the black man had cut down his tree (castrated him). He felt helpless at first, but then rallied enough to knock on the door of his black neighbor, who was apparently not at home. He had left a note for him about the tree.

As Dr. Albert spoke of his assertiveness, I noted that he lowered his voice, and I sensed some hesitancy about letting me know that he had tried to assert himself. I then reminded him of what he had said at the start of the session: "It would be simpler if I did not have to remove my lenses, but kept them in while I lie on the couch." Paraphrasing this, I told him that it would be simpler if he could express freely how he would not accept passively the loss of his tree and made assertive efforts to deal with it. He responded with relief. He said that he knew he could not get his tree restored, but he was determined at least to have the wood. He then stated, with bravado, that he had asserted himself in another area recently but had kept this from me until now: when a paper of his had been published in the wrong section of a journal, as though it were the editor's intention to devalue it, he had called the editor and had received an apology, along with a promise that an apology would appear in the next issue. "I found out that I couldn't erase all the damage done to me, but at least I could do something about an injury! But why do I hesitate to tell you that I am beginning to assert myself?"

When he returned home and sat at dinner, his black neighbor came to see him. Dr. Albert was angry at the interruption to his meal. He insisted that the tree had been his, but his neighbor was so pleasant and so quick to admit his mistake that he calmed down at once. After the neighbor left, however, his unexpressed anger returned and turned against himself, leaving him depressed. At his session on the following day, he showed considerable insight in telling me what had happened. He also noted spontaneously that he now realized how he had confused aggression and assertiveness and that he had not wanted others to know that he could assert himself lest he lose their love.

He made an association between his penis and the cut tree. When making love to Jane that night, he had been impotent. Earlier in the evening he had spent some time cleaning his house, aware that he was becoming a "good little boy" and that Jane was becoming his mother. But strangely, she was *not* his mother since she failed to appreciate his being a "good little boy." His bafflement was "another reason for my depression today," he explained. During the rest of the session, he alternated between trying to assert himself with very macho language and taking refuge in helplessness. At this time, he got Jane to give up wearing a necklace given to her by her ex-husband. This represented the symbolic expunging of the other man's mark on her, a triumph over the competition. He also learned at this time, from overhearing Pamela on the telephone, that Mamie had secured a job as hostess in a restaurant about to open in a nearby town. He made reservations for Jane and himself for the opening night of the restaurant, in a clearly assertive exercise. In a sense, he was telling Mamie, "Look, I am leaving you for good. I have my own woman now." With what seemed to me a total failure to appreciate the feelings of either woman, he appeared at the restaurant with Jane, wearing a new three-piece suit, designed to indicate, especially to Mamie, that he was a "rose." He held Jane's hand during dinner. He was so absorbed in his own internal processes that he did not consciously perceive how he was using "his women."

Jane invited him to visit her family in Kentucky in the near future. He agreed to go, but only on the condition that they occupy the same bed. Jane disagreed, but he insisted. As he described this, he blurted out, "D'you want to bet?" (in reference to his sleeping with Jane in Kentucky). I suggested that we follow up this question, and Dr. Albert recalled the bet he had had with Danny (who had been his externalized aggression and assertion), and whose bet had foretold his death. Dr. Albert began to weep, and I told him that he was now internally trying to assert himself, to repair the damage to his body, and that, although he was pleased to be assertive, I thought he might still be anxious that he might be killed, like Danny, if he asserted himself too much and seemed committed to a woman. He sobbed until the end of the session.

In retrospect, the session on Friday, April 6, was a milestone; it was the first time he had given up his custom of removing his lenses. He was fully aware of what he was doing and told me that he had a little jar in his pocket in case he needed to remove his lenses. He left them in, however, and began to talk about having gone around his house naked and having been seen by Pamela. At my urging, he associated this with his incestuous thoughts about his mother. Thus Dr. Albert was talking openly about incestuous wishes in a non-castrated position (with his contacts in place), asserting himself and anxiously testing me to see if I would blind (castrate) him. His boisterous voice and behavior suggested that he was prepared to fight if I attacked him. We now would embark on an analysis with his newly developed self-image, one in which his eyes (penis) were attached to his body! He kept his lenses in during his subsequent hours.

On Monday, Dr. Albert brought in a dream that, I believe, summarized his original fixation at the anal level (contaminated as it was by oral issues, which reappeared whenever oedipal issues became too hot and induced castration anxiety). On Friday, he had presented himself as a boy with a penis, one thus vulnerable to castration. Now, on Monday, he was regressing to earlier levels, at which there is no perceived castration danger. In his dream, Dr. Albert was taking a psychological *test* when he became aware of a "U-shaped bedpan." Someone said that his test results would demonstrate that he was very schizoid, but someone else declared that he was worse than that, a schizophrenic. He relaxed completely as soon as he reported this dream. He then spoke of the sound made by the heater in my office. He felt good thinking about warm vapor. He was seeing me as a good, caring mother, and he was becoming my sick (schizophrenic) child, whom I had to protect from danger.

I interpreted to him that the test in the dream represented our previous hour, during which he had not removed his lenses. He had asserted himself, but he was paying for his assertiveness by turning into a sick, dependent child. He indicated that he was aware of what he was doing, but pointed out that going back to his mother's care had its own dangers. Only the day before, he continued, he had found his house dark on his return, the lightbulbs blown out. The darkness had made him anxious, and he had, at least fleetingly, thought of black, dangerous things such as black hands. I told him that I thought the *U* in the dream was in fact *You*, the analyst, and that he wanted to defecate on me as a representative of the blinding father or the smothering mother.

As soon as he entered my office on April 11, Dr. Albert ostentatiously blew his nose into a large white handkerchief, which he waved at me before taking his place on the couch. I wondered if the gesture stood for "surrender" and it was a substitute for removing his lenses ("plucking out his eyes"). On the couch, he presented himself as helpless and complained about being out of breath. It turned out that he had climbed the stairway to my office with a Miss Ann, a young woman employed in the office complex next to mine and therefore, in a sense, "my woman." Although he had been aware of her for some time, today had been their first encounter. I could see an oedipal situation developing between us, with a focus on Miss Ann; he was asserting himself but at the same time surrendering himself to me. I chose not to interpret this to him since I wanted to see how the rest of the hour would unfold.

After a moment's silence, Dr. Albert reported feeling that he was tied by a rope to something. I sensed that this might be his further defensive regression (to being tied to his mother by the umbilical cord) to take him away from the oedipal issue. I said nothing, and he reported a news item he had seen on television the previous evening. It concerned a man who had won the Nobel Prize thirty years earlier, but who was now being threatened with litigation for having used human subjects in his medical experiments. I asked him to associate to this news item and to the reason for its coming into his mind while he lay on the couch. After he recalled his favorite daydream of becoming a Nobel Prize winner, I asked him what he had done thirty years ago that might be catching up with him now. After a long silence, he began to speak of "human experiments" that had been practiced on him when he was a child, that is, the radiation treatment for his thymus gland. This recital was confused in his mind with an account of his having been infatuated at age 6 (exactly thirty years earlier) with a little girl in kindergarten. His infatuation had continued as they grew up and attended high school together. The "human experimentation" that punished him thus seemed connected with his sexual desires in his unconscious fantasy. He was not the only one who was tormented; he noted defensively that even a Nobel Prize winner could not escape justice. He then told me that Daddy Doc had once cut the ear off a corpse and carried it in his pocket. Daddy Doc was the potential castrator. When, as a child, Dr. Albert had cut off his toe, I recalled, he had wanted to put the toe in a pickle jar and carry it around with him, but a minister buried it.

This session was profitable since Dr. Albert was again integrating and consolidating events from his childhood and his perception of them as they affected his unconscious fantasy life, his character, and his symptom formation. He stated that all he was learning in analysis made sense to him, but he nevertheless continued to deny the knowledge. As he stood up to leave my office, his attention was caught by flowers blooming on the balcony outside. With a smile he turned to me and asked, "carnations?" Although I did not reply, I understood that he was symbolically telling me that we were still putting roses and dandelions together, and mending them. (The flowers on the balcony were really geraniums, and I felt that on one level he recognized that they were not carnations.)

On the following day, Dr. Albert began his session with references to the flowers' red color. He said that he had always supposed that if one crossed a rose with a dandelion, the result would be a yellow flower. He now saw, he said, that if the "carnations" on my balcony were red (he still associated the color red with the idealized red rose and the devalued carmine mother), "averageness" could also take different colors; this intuition excited and surprised him. He wanted to get up and examine the flowers on my balcony closely to see what I really had there, but he could not. He spoke about feeling "like a horse with blinders." When I asked his associations to this image, he spoke about Danny's funeral, to which he had taken a dozen red flowers and at which others had supplied many carnations.

Before his friend's death, and at his urgent recommendation, he had bought a derringer, but he had found that it had a short range—like the short-sightedness that kept him from seeing my balcony clearly. Recalling that one barrel of the derringer had not worked, Dr. Albert laughed nervously and joked that he now understood his need to castrate elements of himself in order to live without the anxiety of being castrated by others.

The next session came on a Friday the thirteenth, an ominous sign. The previous night, he had bowled poorly; in other words, he castrated himself so that I would not injure him on Friday the thirteenth. The thought occurred to him at the bowling alley that he had psychologically amputated his toe by his poor bowling performance, so he toasted me silently as an interpreter when he drank beer after playing, thus acknowledging his appreciation of the truth of my interpretations. Everything had gone well for him after this, and on his way to my office, he had noticed tulips and other "average flowers" on the approach to my building. On the couch, a humorous notion came into his mind: "Why don't I put all these flowers together and make a blend?"

Dr. Albert had decided to tell his mother that she could not take Pamela driving with her when she came to visit. He considered her a poor driver and worried that she might cause his daughter's death in an accident. Forbidding her was an act of self-assertion, but it had a deeper meaning as well. It happened that on the day of this session, a widely publicized All-American high school basketball player was in town to be recruited for the local university's team. It became evident that he represented Dr. Albert's aggressive, athletic father as well as the aggressive Danny. The death of each of these men had been caused, psychologically speaking, by his wife. Now Dr. Albert was asserting himself and saying no to his mother's dangerousness in order that his manhood survive. I told him so and reminded him of when his mother had seemed to have life-and-death control over him as a child and that it was quite an achievement for him to assert himself against her.

His desire for association with sportsmen held dangers of competition, and Dr. Albert continued to bowl poorly and to "feel shitty." He had an image of a beautiful sunny day on one occasion, but it made him feel sad. I explained that although a sunny day might mean enjoyment to most people, sunshine without the protection of his straw hat still made him anxious. His having said no to his mother and having abandoned this protection had failed to cure his anxiety about being in the sun. "I am like a little boy sitting on the potty and suffering," he said. "But I think I'll never produce (be well). You see me suffer and you suffer, too. You want to be healing, but at the same time you punish me. You are like the cough medicine I was given as a child. It was given to help me, but I perceived it as punishment." He then went on about improving his condition; he would permit me to heal him if I were sure to make him perfect. He felt that psychoanalysis should be as precise as computer science. I told him that he wanted to be completely sure that if he were ready to step into the sunlight without his protective straw hat, the risk would be worthwhile.

He came to his next session huffing and puffing and declared, as he took his place on the couch, that he had either the flu or a muscle spasm. It soon became clear that Dr. Albert was concentrating on his skin above his waist, which felt as though he had a *sunburn*. He recalled having had a similar feeling before—but when? On the previous night, the thought had occurred to him that he had felt like this after his radiation treatments. Late that night, he had gotten Jane to take care of him, to bring him aspirin, and so forth. "I feel shitty and vulnerable," he lamented. "It is so bad to be sick; it is springtime outside!"

He spoke of having gone to an Easter dinner with Jane a few days earlier. Everyone there had spoken of death and dying. His mind was full of thoughts of exotic illnesses, and he kept mumbling to himself on the couch as though I were not in the room. I kept seeing him as a little boy alone in bed, with horrible worries and fantasies that his little mind could not sort out. I felt sympathy for him, but I did not interfere. He was revisiting this scared little boy who still lived within him. When he remarked that his muscles hurt "like a son-of-a-bitch," I remarked that that was a peculiar way to refer to his muscles. Beginning to laugh nervously, he commented, "At least my mother was married when I was born!"

Dr. Albert wondered whether his mother had been Jewish and susceptible to certain diseases. Then he lamented, "Hurt, hurt, it hurts so much!" As his unregressed observations interfered, he would say, "Don't be so fucking stupid! Your muscles don't hurt that much. My muscles hurt because I pushed my car this morning to get it started." Then he regressed again, his chest heaving, reporting spasms of pain. Again, his observing ego appeared: "Fuck off, fuck off! I don't need this," he said. "I can take dreams any day to work out my problems."

Easter represented death and rebirth, so in visiting his anxieties about mutilation and death he could still hope for recovery. Suddenly he said, after a spell of silence, "When I stopped running a fever, I got fat." I understood that he was telling me that he was so dependent on his mother that he could separate from her only by retaining her as fat tissue in his body. Also, he was enlarging himself by oral means to protect himself from being annihilated (eaten) by his smothering mother. Since he was in the midst of a regressive experience, I did not convey this to him. Now in referring to childhood experience he used the present tense. He mumbled, obviously referring to the straw hat, "If I don't wear it, the sun may hurt me!"

Then he recalled, in a fragmentary way, being wheeled into an operating room for a tonsillectomy. His hands pressed down on his trousers as he recalled how he had insisted that his penis and his bottom be covered on the way to surgery. His eyes watered, and he rubbed them feverishly. The session came to an end.

On the following day, Dr. Albert told me that he could recall the previous day only hazily. He was slow, as though he were "recuperating" from an illness. He reported that he had just painted a room at home yellow and only now realized that he had copied the color of my office. It reminded him of the yellow brick road in *The Wizard of Oz*. He recalled that the actor who had played the role of the lion in *The Wizard* had recently died. The cowardly lion had found courage as he traveled this road. Dr. Albert associated him with Danny, and he felt that he himself was the Tin Man. He had been so rusty that only with difficulty had he been able to step onto the yellow brick road (his analysis). Now he thought that the Witch in *The Wizard* resembled his mother. He himself would melt in the sunlight. I felt that he wanted the sun to melt his "bad" mother instead, or he wished she would melt under water. Once more I told him that he was perceiving his individuation from her as an act of aggression, feeling guilt or fear of retaliation, as though the Witch would have to die if he were to reach the end of the yellow brick road.

He spent most of his hours in April assimilating what he was now able to understand in his analysis. Dr. Albert had a dream in which someone told him to clean the mud off his house. Suddenly his house disappeared, and he was in the country looking at a cinderblock foundation full of mud. He associated mud with feces, and recalling his stubbornness at the potty as a child, he stated that he now realized that he should take the responsibility of "cleaning up his own shit."

Dr. Albert reported that his sense of smell was returning. He was no longer taking antihistamines for his "allergy." He had not been able to smell very well for years, but now he was smelling the scents of spring. He also began to exercise his sense of vision and regarded various items in the room as though he were seeing them for the first time. All his experiences of "new" sensations were accompanied by pleasant memories of his father.

Who Really Wore
the Straw Hat?

The Beginning of May though the Third Week in May

As May began, Dr. Albert worked feverishly to master the dangers threatening him, and to modify the behavior that he had once developed to deal with his internal conflicts. He had come to his analysis with obsessional characteristics and depressive symptoms. The former reflected regression from oedipal conflicts, and as I learned more about him, I came to appreciate keenly the role of conflicts from earlier phases of his life that had made the oedipal phase so hard for him to work through. Behind his obessional character structure I had for some time seen his inability to bring together his self-concept and corresponding concepts of persons important to him. He perceived whatever he was emotionally involved in as absolutes, as in his analogy of roses and dandelions. In technical terms, it could be said that behind his higher-level (obsessional) character structure, he had a personality organization of a lower level, the main operation of which was to split self-images and the images of objects (other persons). He had what are called "object-relations conflicts" that arose from the attempt to mix black and white to make grey—and from the dread of doing this. Making grey would mean the disappearance of all that was all black, but it would also mean the disappearance of everything white, idealized, and valuable.

Dr. Albert's reference to producing a carnation when he crossed a rose and a dandelion alluded to his attempt to mend his splitting. Early in May, I found him working hard on this, "visiting" opposing aspects of himself and important others, examining them piecemeal, letting them go or letting them come together, allowing himself to discard those no longer useful. The loss of anything, even of internal images, involves a mourning. As Dr. Albert mended his personality organization, he mourned primarily his father.

Dr. Albert opened the session on May 2 by telling me that he "chose" not to invest time in bowling any more. His associations indicated that bowling was a link to his dandelion-redneck aspect. He went on to say that a patient he was then treating in his hospital was politically powerful (definitely a rose); the allusion was to "contamination by a rose person." This patient was a candidate for high office. His supporters, equally powerful men, were to send representatives to Dr. Albert's office to learn whether the sick candidate was physically able to undertake the office for which he was being proposed. In a sense, then, the future of this rose person depended on Dr. Albert's statement.

He was, he said, treating this patient "*aggressively,* with a controversial method." In other words, although he was caring for this man and trying to cure him, he was being aggressive toward him and using a controversial and perhaps dangerous method of treating him. His associations on the couch that day related to his guilt over his father's death. He wished he had found a cure for cancer. His opposing thoughts about his father came forward, and on the following day he reported that he now "had a different image of him." This hour was filled with memories of his father's illness, death, and funeral. Dr. Albert sobbed and grieved during the whole hour, as though his father's death *had just occurred.* His grief spilled over into the next session.

When Dr. Albert and Jane went to a nearby city for a medical convention, his mother arrived to stay with Pamela. When he came to his session on May 8, I noticed a large bruise on his left forearm, which, he explained later, he had sustained when he hit his hand by accident while playing racquet ball. He began this session by reporting that he had again asked his mother about the realities of his childhood. But this time he had had a big surprise. Although it was true that he had had radiation therapy as a child—his mother recalled that he had been about four months old—it was not he who had been required to wear a straw hat for protection against the sun, but his *brother,* who had also undergone radiation therapy. Moreover, his mother told him that she had had no miscarriage before his birth but had had several after his birth and before his brother's. I was able to tell him how angry and disappointed he may have been about his mother's pregnancies and the birth of a brother, and that one way of handling this may have been to identify with his brother's symptoms. Through identification with a "sick" brother, he could get his mother's attention again. I sensed that he had already figured this out. He seemed amazed at the power of the unconscious mind.

Dr. Albert then spoke of his mother's having "a medical fixation." He recalled that when he and his brother had gone sledding together, each had bruised his legs badly. (Here I pointed out that he had come to this session with a bruised forearm.) On one occasion, his mother had taken them to a physician, whom, through a slip of the tongue, Dr. Albert called Dr. Sibling. (It was this doctor who later removed a mole from Dr. Albert's penis.) The "sibling" rivalry itself was condensed in his expectation of punishments through castration!

In the middle of this session, he told me for the first time that he and Jane had been talking about marriage. I said nothing, and he fell into a preoccupation about whether he was a rose or a dandelion.

While on a short trip out of town with Jane, Dr. Albert got into an argument with a threatening-looking *black* taxi driver over the small matter of 40 cents. He knew that it was his inner psychological processes that had been stirred up in his analysis that made him "assert himself" against this "dangerous" man in the presence of his woman. He sensed that this act of assertion was connected to his asserting himself when he rose to speak before a group at the meeting. This group was considered elite in professional circles, and its members were referred to as the "Young Turks." Thus, transference implications were involved, the group representing the oedipal analyst/father. One of the Young Turks was a physician friend he had always considered his superior, but now Dr. Albert felt able to compete with him openly, to hold his own in his assertiveness, and even to consider himself the better man professionally.

Assertiveness against the black, dangerous, Turkish, oedipal father was paralleled by his assertiveness against the smothering, eating, biting mother—the black panther. Dr. Albert went to the zoo "to see the dangerous lions and tigers," but he reported that all he saw was a "puny lion." I interpreted his attempts to be assertive and their transference implications, and he fell silent. Then he reported that a rhyme had popped into his head; it was a variation of the Ogden Nash quotation, and ran, "Incest is best; bad liquor is quicker!" This led to a discussion of the possibility that his taking a glass or two of whiskey at night was to repress his incestuous desires. At the end of the hour, he responded by telling me that his need to search for an idealized mother might have arisen from his having been traumatized when his brother was born and his mother became unavailable to him. Thus he had kept an idealized image of her and had kept searching all his life for her. He compared Jane with a fantasied ideal woman. It was a good insight. When he wondered aloud how Pamela would feel if he were to marry Jane and have a baby, I told him that he was still concerned about his feelings about the birth of his brother.

Before coming into my office the next day, Dr. Albert stopped to talk to a woman working at a desk nearby. He had never done this before. She had just returned from maternity leave and provided Dr. Albert a point of departure for reliving the childhood trauma caused by his mother's pregnancy and his brother's birth. I thought that this woman was either the oedipal mother impregnated by the oedipal father-analyst or my extension as the pregnant mother of his earlier years. On a few occasions, Dr. Albert had seen me talk to her. Although he had never mentioned her pregnancy during the past months, he could scarcely have been unaware of it. Nonetheless, as he came into my office, he spoke of having stopped to ask her if she had had her baby yet. Since she was seated behind a desk, he could not see that her figure was no longer swollen.

When Dr. Albert came for his next session, he whimpered and exhibited another bruise, this one on his elbow. He had had another accident playing racquet ball. While bowling was not a "rose" sport, racquet ball was. I interpreted his presenting himself to me as hurt, saying that because he expected punishment for his sibling rivalry, he was presenting himself as already injured. The self-inflicted injury removed the threat of castration. He was no longer vulnerable to castration since he was imperfect!

On the previous night, Dr. Albert had had a fright lasting for a few seconds when he had gone downstairs in the middle of the night, naked, and had felt the presence of a bogeyman, a *black,* ape-like monster. He had trembled lest it seize him by the penis, leg, or throat.

Jane later told him *her* dream, of the same night in which penises were detachable. Dr. Albert spent the session considering ways of making her "a better woman"; he wished, for instance, she had longer hair, since with short hair, she "looked like a turtle." I asked him to associate to the turtle, and his associations indicated that he was still afraid of phallic women, who might seize a man's penis in their vagina, or "snap it off" as a turtle might. He could now recall having had conscious *vagina dentata* fantasies as a teenager. I felt that Dr. Albert entertained two opposing but balancing images of women, one idealized, one castrating. As he grew less afraid of being "snapped" at by a woman, he would also have less need of an idealized image. The two extremes needed to be brought toward a middle ground in his perception of Jane. Dr. Albert was aware of the physical characteristics of his idealized woman and said that she would have his mother's height, eye and hair color. He saw the (hair) color black in this connection as soft and nice, not the threatening black of the fog in his dream, associated as it was with the frightening, murky image of his mother's genitals. I told him that his fear of seeing her genitals made him perceive them through a fog.

I had to cancel the following two sessions because of a speaking engagement. The next time we met, Dr. Albert described a dream about a woman with "a space" over her abdomen. (This image might have been a reference to the "space" of my absence. I was like the mother who had left him to have a child!)

On the following day he began the session with a dream "like a surrealistic painting, probably taking place in New York." He had lived in New York with Mamie at the time of Pamela's birth, and in his dream he and Mamie were living in an apartment building, the steps of which he was climbing when he turned a corner and saw some people sitting with a small baby. It occurred to him that the infant would enjoy being tossed into the air, so he snatched it and threw it upwards. The baby fell on its head and got an enormous bump. The blanket in which the baby was wrapped opened up, and Dr. Albert could see the baby's insides— liver, spleen, guts, and all—but no blood. The baby was made of plastic. It occurred to him that he had injured the baby more grievously than he had supposed; when he turned it over, he noticed that it had split open. He felt very guilty and anxious and had Mamie call the hospital (where, in reality, she had given birth to Pamela).

Dr. Albert's first association to all this was a recollection of having once dropped Pamela on her head, when he was either drunk or in a dissociated state. He recalled that at the time of Pamela's birth, he had been having an extramarital affair, about which he had felt very guilty. When Pamela was born, he had said to himself, "I will repay you for what I have done." The plastic quality of the baby's insides in the dream reminded him of plastic Saran Wrap, from which he associated to "Sirhan Sirhan," the assassin.

Dr. Albert now realized that his murderous feelings about his pregnant mother—and about the analyst who had put a "space" in the analytic process—had been transferred to pregnant Mamie, and that it had been because of these feelings that he had become involved in an extramarital affair. The murderous feelings he had had toward his brother had been transferred to Pamela, whom he would compensate for his aggressive feelings. He had decided to mother her himself, not for any altruistic reason but because he did not want to compete with her for the love of a mother/wife. He now realized that unconsciously he had pushed Mamie away because of his desire to mother their daughter himself!

The word *cleaved,* which he had used in describing the split infant in his dream, reminded him of the story of King Solomon's judgment. Recounting it, Dr. Albert kept repeating, "Who is the real mother?" He then said that his mother, Mamie, he himself, and now Jane were respectively "the mother" and that he was also Sirhan Sirhan. As to the bump on the head of the baby in the dream, he remembered that once, as a child, he had lowered some venetian blinds on his head to raise a bump: "I was fixing up my own punishment," he said.

The surrealistic quality of the dream reminded Dr. Albert of the television show "Saturday Night Live," on which appeared a character named "Mr. Bill," whom everyone seems to treat cruelly. Dr. Albert noted, "I am Mr. Bill as well as those who punish him" Then he said that it was not the time for him to discuss marriage with Jane, in that he was still working on the problems of women from his childhood, and Jane might become contaminated with their images. He wanted to postpone any decision about marrying her until he could better understand his feelings for Jane herself, *qua* Jane, untainted by the images of these other woman.

When the hour was nearly over, I noted that I had said literally nothing during the entire session, and I was delighted to see how much work my analysand had been able to do by himself. At the end, he told me that he had made arrangements to go fishing with his brother on the coming weekend, as though to convey that he was sublimating his childhood murderous rage at his brother by becoming his friend. But it was not clear to me whether this were a truly sublimated gesture or whether it included elements of obligation and compensation.

Dr. Albert began the next session with another dream, one in which his mother gave him a haircut that made him look like someone in a comic strip, Dick Tracy, or, perhaps, Dick Tracy's son. He told how his mother had prepared him for a haircut as a child by tying a cloth around his neck—at this point Dr. Albert had an attack of sneezing—and how his father had then cut his hair. He always checked whether bits of his ears had fallen away along with the chunks of his hair. (It should be recalled that Daddy Doc had carried the dried ear of a dead man about with him.) During his marriage to Mamie, she had cut his hair, and after she had left, he had begun cutting it himself. It was only during the previous week that he had spoken of his decision to go to a barber to overcome his anxiety about barbershops. When he did go, the shop felt "foreign" to him (Turkish?).

According to Dr. Albert's dream, in the Dick Tracy comic strip, the wife of Dick's son, a lady from the moon, was blown up by a bomb intended for her husband. Here was the dream wish for the gratification of Dr. Albert's aggressive drive. He wanted to kill all women when they represented his bad mother. Associating further to the dream, he told me that he had seen the film *Hair,* in which he perceived the character George as a dandelion. George had gone to New York, where many rose types made fun of him. Toward the end of the film, he got a haircut when he joined the Army in place of a friend. He was sent to Vietnam by mistake and killed. I interpreted to Dr. Albert that he was like George: dying in place of another; that through an unconscious identification with his brother, he had thought of himself as under a death sentence and obliged to wear a straw hat if he hoped to stay alive. He had put himself in the shoes of a condemned man because he felt guilt over his murderous feelings for his brother. We then discussed how he had transferred some of these feelings onto his daughter.

The Reenactment of Childhood Injuries

The End of May through Labor Day

Toward the end of May, I sensed that Jane was exerting pressure, consciously or not, on Dr. Albert for a commitment about their future together. When he told me that he needed more time to decide about marrying her, I agreed, although I did not convey my approval directly. But I believe that Dr. Albert sensed it. Kenny, Jane's ex-husband, now began calling her frequently at Dr. Albert's house, possibly with her encouragement. Although this irritated Dr. Albert, he was determined to go slowly in making up his mind. But he did entertain the idea of taking Jane to meet his family and in turn visiting hers (his mother, of course, had already met Jane). The prospect made him anxious. He fantasied that Jane might see his relatives, expecially his brother and his brother's family, as dandelions. On the other hand, he could not make up his mind what to expect from Jane's family: roses or dandelions, or, to use a new analogy of his, butter or margarine.

Dr. Albert seemed almost overwhelmed by the combination of the material related to his childhood and the pressure to deal with present situations. He reported feeling disorganized. I tried to help him by suggesting that disorganization is usually followed by new, and often improved organization.

Dr. Albert came to his hour on May 29 feeling very negative about me. His associations indicated that I might be like Jane's father, who, in his fantasy, would devalue him and perceive him as a dandelion. "Oh, yes!" he lamented. "I am accepting many things about my background, but at the same time I feel angry and sad giving up the idealized aspects of my family!" I thought he was mourning, and he did indeed report that his eyes were watering. I thought he was unready to grieve openly when he explained that his eyes were irritated by my cigar smoke. (I had not smoked in my office for some time, and fresh air was pouring in from an open window. When the lens in his left eye began to bother him, he sat up to take it out but dropped it. He had trouble finding it, and for more than five minutes moved his hands over the couch, trying to find it with his fingertips. Then he knelt by the couch and ran his hands over the carpet. Neither of us spoke while this was going on. I felt awkward in my silence, because I had seen the lens land on the carpet next to my feet. I thought that my discomfort came from the challenge that I gratify my analysand's wishes actively. Although I wanted to help him, my help would mean, I thought, giving him back his eyesight, uncastrating him. (It will be remembered that in October of his second year of analysis he had fantasied losing his lens during a session and my joining him in a search for it.) But as the hour was ending, and he seemed unable to find the lens, I picked it up and gave it to him, saying that an event unusual for both of us had taken place in this session. I said that I had no way of knowing how he would perceive my retrieving his lens and that I was sure that the meaning of this event was something we should examine in subsequent sessions.

As soon as he lay down on the couch for the next session, on May 30, Dr. Albert complained that his eyes were hurting. He had been unable to wear his lenses the previous night and thus had come to his hour wearing his glasses. His thoughts seemed disorganized at the outset of the hour, and he began talking about competition between Pamela and the daughter of friends over their musical ability. The other girl's parents had been good to him and to Pamela. Speaking of this competition reminded him of the competition between himself and his brother: "I remember never losing to him in any contest," he said, "except once when I lost a Pepsi bottle to him." I told him that he had in fact lost to his brother in regard to something else; he may have felt that he had lost his mother to him. I added that one way he had been able to be first in his mother's regard was to be sickly or injured and that this accounted for his identifying with his brother and punishing himself in reponse to the guilt he felt for his jealousy of his sibling.

Dr. Albert replied that he really did not know when his eye injury had occurred. "I was 4, 5, 6, or 7," he guessed. I thought to myself that this response, which related the eye injury to an indeterminate period of four years, might reflect how he had used this injury to deal with psychosexual issues of many years, including issues from the oedipal age.

Now Dr. Albert was as though in a trance while he gave the details of his eye injury. "I recall being next to the tree and thinking or even making some noises. I don't exactly remember. It seems I was studying the tree and trying to loosen its bark with a kitchen knife. Was it the kitchen knife or a loose piece of bark that hurt my eye? I don't remember. But I do remember the blood. I remember also my frightened mother. Now I have a mental image of her; she is running as though before a wind, and her clothes and her hair are streaming out behind her. I remember her picking me up and running again. My mother says; 'Oh! Oh! My goodness!' She thinks I lost my eye." At this point in his recital, Dr. Albert had a short "allergy attack" and sneezed and snuffled. After collecting himself, he continued, "The mental image of my mother is returning. She is wearing a dress made of thin nylon. It is white or pale blue."

Suddenly he stopped to tell me that what he recalled could not be true since as far as he knew his mother never liked to wear blue. Now the image of the mother and the color of her dress reminded him of someone under a floodlight. He recalled being taken to a doctor's office and remembered the doctor's floodlight. I told him that he might have been so anxious at the time that his memory connected the anxious mother and the flash of light from the doctor's headband. He recalled that the physician had tried to calm his mother and relieve her anxiety.

After making this report, Dr. Albert seemed ready to project onto me different images of the original people of the drama—the mother, the child, and the helpful physician. Recalling that the previous day he had lost his left lens (it had been his left eye that was injured), he shouted, "You just sit there. Just like not answering my questions! I would never have found my lens with one eye!" When I had picked up the lens and given it to him he had been surprised, and he had thought that I might squeeze and break the lens. He said that he had not been able to put in his lenses the previous night, because the lens that had fallen on my carpet had become dirty and irritating. "It had *foreign* material on it," he cried, and suddenly seeing the humor in this, he added, with a nervous laugh, "No, I don't mean foreign, Turkish material." His humor was fleeting. I interpreted his ambivalence about me without referring to the possibility that he had sexualized putting the foreign material in his eye.

Dr. Albert reported feeling negative and irritated, "just like sitting on a potty!" He said, 'I have better things to do than coming here or having fantasies and dreams. I just won't do it. I just won't tell you fantasies or dreams. I have an image of sitting on the john. I don't read books or take time on the john in real day-to-day life. I am the fastest shit in the west!" This last remark reminded him of competing with a childhood friend to see which defecated the faster. The concept of competition allowed me to repeat reference to his competition with the "bad" aspects of Daddy Doc and his brother and his assuming their "bad" characteristics. He could win over his brother only by punishing himself—by injuring his eye—for his murderous anger over his brother's birth.

The next day Dr. Albert reenacted the theme of the mother with two sons, repeating stories about Jane, himself, and Kenny, telling how he had acted "sickly" to draw Jane's attention from Kenny, who was still calling her on the telephone. I interpreted to him the possible unconscious motive behind his getting me to find and return his lens while he was acting helpless in my office. Another reason underlay that symbolic reenactment of the accident to his left eye. I was planning a two-week vacation at the start of June and an additional holiday in August. At the time he dropped his lens he had known that, like a pregnant woman taking maternity leave, I would be separating from him.

When I returned from my June vacation, I moved into a new office. This was a less drastic change than the earlier one, involving only removal to adjoining quarters that had previously been unoccupied. The area had been newly renovated as the permanent office of the hospital's medical director. Both my analysand and I had observed the men working over several months to change my quarters into something more comfortable and spacious. Like the office I was vacating, it had been part of a sunporch and had a balcony. I used the same furniture, including the couch. My analysand faced a wall, with bookshelves and an ink drawing of a mulberry tree, the glass over which reflected the out-of-doors. I had had the yellow-flowering plants, some in Turkish copper pots, brought in from my first office, and they stood against the walls; a handsome polished desk, too big for the other office, completed the decor. When Dr. Albert began seeing me in this more spacious place, it reminded him of the "cave" of a panther. However, this preoccupation lasted only briefly, and we both adjusted quickly to the change. He now seemed ready to give attention to another incident of self-castration, the amputation of his toe.

Early in July, Dr. Albert reported a dream about hurting his leg. To his surprise, in his dream he found that he could remove his leg at will, and he took it off, walked about, and replaced it. Then he dreamed of stepping on something and, on looking down, seeing blood all over his shoe. There was a piece of glass under his shoe, and he pulled it out. This made more blood gush from his foot and fill his shoe. He walked to a hospital and looked for male surgeons whom he knew in real life, but a woman doctor tried to get someone to help him.

When he awakened and recalled his dream, it occurred to him that he had cut his foot because he felt superior to other physicians in his specialty. It was like losing his toe after being elected class president. He had recently read about the sewing back of a severed leg, and he wished that his toe could be sewn back on to "uncastrate" him. The detachable leg in the dream let him have his leg when he wanted and remove it (castrate himself) when he felt anxious.

The shoes he wore in the dream reminded him of some he had bought during his last year in high school. That year he had worked in a cement plant, often in places so high that when he dropped a sack of cement he could count to six before it hit the ground. It was dangerous and frightening work so high up (symbolically higher than others or than the oedipal father). He was both fascinated and frightened by going to the edge of a high platform.

His preoccupation with the question of whether he should castrate himself or regain his penis was connected with two issues. One was Jane's departure for the summer to stay with her parents. Symbolically, she was a rejecting mother, and this symbolism was enhanced for a while when Jane thought she might be pregnant. Thus a pregnant mother was leaving him, and he was repeating the role of the injured child to regain her attention. But the more important issue was Jane's invitation that he go home with her and meet her parents. The prospect of facing a new father figure (Jane's father) reactivated his fear of his real father. Should he assert himself against this man or "self-castrate" himself as a protection? He still insisted that he would visit Jane's family on the condition that he and Jane slept together. He fantasied that Jane's father would oppose such an arrangement, and he fought him in his mind. It was during this time that he dreamed of having a gun in his hand and facing another man similarly armed. He was going to shoot his adversary but was afraid that he would be shot himself. It looked like an oedipal shoot-out! Since the dream images appeared to him against a background which had the same color as the rug in my office, the gunfight had a transference implication. The name of this color was also the name of a physician who had once "stolen" some of Dr. Albert's research material—as his father had stolen his mother, or as Jane's father would steal Jane.

When Jane called him on July 11 to say that her father had consented that the pair occupy the same room, Dr. Albert felt as though a rug had been pulled out from under him. Jane's father would not in reality fit the oedipal father in his fantasy world!

Dr. Albert brought to his next session a dream in which he had gone to his daughter's bedroom. There the air conditioner was running, although the window was open. He thought that electricity was being wasted. The window in his dream was in a different place from where the window really was in Pamela's room—at her feet as she lay in bed. In the dream, it was behind the head of the bed, and Dr. Albert closed it by turning a handle, which turned like "screwing something in." This dream's day residue came from his having made a hole in the wall of Pamela's room for the installation of air conditioning. His concern over wasting electricity reminded him of his father's objections to spending money for electricity and therefore denying the family a television set until Chris was 12. In the dream, Dr. Albert felt as though he were violating his father's orders by wasting electricity with an air conditioner.

I told him that I thought this dream was concerned with Jane's father having given permission for him to sleep with Jane at her family home. Jane's room was displaced to his daughter's, where he was doing (or was about to do) something (sexual) that he thought his father would forbid. There was further concealment of his sexual wish for the woman in his displacing the window (the opening, the female genitalia) from the legs to the head of the one who would sleep in the bed. In the dream, his sexual wish materialized in his "screwing" the window shut and thereby pleasing the father who hated to waste electricity.

During his next hour, Dr. Albert seemed to be preparing himself for a visit to Jane's family. It was still uncertain whether Jane was pregnant. Dr. Albert dreamed of a hairless rat that his associations implied represented a fetus (also his brother), and he injected something into the rat's veins to "put it to sleep." Then the dream became vague, and the dreamer found himself "sleeping," identifying in a symbolic way with the rat he wanted to kill, even as he identified with the sickly aspect of the new brother.

In another dream, a uterus was represented by a lobster; as I explained to him, its red color represented blood. By bleeding, the uterus was evacuating the fetus! The dreamer kept putting cheese into the lobster's mouth; his associations suggested that this reminded him of Jane's inserting a diaphragm.

Finally, in reality, Jane called to tell him that she was *not* pregnant. This issue, psychologically connected to his mother's pregnancy, now settled, Dr. Albert returned to consider how he would face Jane's (oedipal) father. Early in August, he sent Pamela to stay with her mother, in preparation for his trip. At this time, he removed his right shoe while sitting on the couch in my office, complaining that something irritated his foot: "There are colossal boulders in my shoe." I thought he wanted to check with me before the impending visit that his toe was all right, but I said nothing. He did find two pebbles in his shoe, and after removing them, he put his shoe back on and lay down. It occurred to him that the two "colossal boulders" were associated with his mother's breasts; he had wanted "to exorcise the tits."

A childhood memory of his mother's hair being caught in an old-fashioned wringer-washer came to his mind. As a child, he had feared that she might be pulled all the way into the machine and be flattened. Thinking of his mother's "bad" image activated a like image of Mamie, and he recalled that after they had become officially engaged, Mamie had called him from a nearby city to ask his permission to sleep with a man she had just met. He had objected and over the years had felt a silent fury whenever he remembered her request. I suggested that he might want to get rid of "bad" images of women before visiting Jane's home. He then said that "boulders" also reminded him of a diamond. He said that he wanted to buy Jane a diamond ring but was hesitant because he did not want her to think that he was trying to buy her love.

Dr. Albert was having sleepless nights in anticipation of the visit, counting sheep in his efforts to get some rest. I did not interfere now by stating my observations. A cameo ring he bought for Jane reflected his ambivalence; it stood for an engagement ring, but he felt guilty over not having bought the conventional, and more expensive, diamond.

A few days before the visit, Jane called him to say that a previous engagement would make it impossible for her mother to accompany Dr. Albert and Jane to dinner one night of the long weekend, but that she, her father, and Dr. Albert would dine out that evening alone. This triangular situation made him anxious, and I told him that to him it represented competition with another man for Jane, who was very fond of her father. It recalled his competing with his own father for his mother and disturbed him accordingly.

Two days before the visit Jane called again and told Dr. Albert that although her father knew about the proposed sleeping arrangements, her mother did not. This reawakened his fantasies about an oedipal confrontation. I recall feeling that he looked like a soldier going off to battle. Somehow I sensed that he was ready for it and that he would protect himself. I felt warmly toward him. He was very excited and anxious. As this, the final hour before the visit, came to an end, he rose from the couch and turned an anxious smile on me, saying that when he returned, he would have much to tell me. I was careful to offer neither discouragement or encouragement as he went off "to battle."

Dr. Albert came back from the visit like a triumphant Roman conqueror. The trip had been a great success. He had slept with Jane and had gotten along well with her family. He had had a good time and met none of the dangers he had fantasied. His sessions were now full of accounts of his success in every aspect of his daily life. I began to hear that there was no further need for psychoanalysis, that he had passed his oedipal test and no longer needed me. In a kind of confrontation with me in transference, similar to that he had recently had with Jane's father, he kept pushing me to agree with him that his analysis was completed. I said nothing. Frustrated, he pushed harder. I simply stated that he seemed elated over an experience in which a father had not proved dangerous, as he had anticipated, and that he was celebrating. I further suggested that this might not be the best time in which to discuss terminating his analysis, that a mood of celebration was perhaps not the best in which to take such an important step as setting a date would involve. He agreed to discuss the matter in a calmer moment.

One day soon thereafter Dr. Albert was suddenly deflated; he had called Jane at her family home but had learned that she was not there. His fantasy of her returning to her ex-husband came back (although, as it turned out, Jane had only been shopping). Moreover, this (fantasied) rejection coincided with the real rejection of a paper he had submitted to the journal of the Young Turks of his specialty. Although he therefore felt inferior, he began behaving in his old, narcissistic, defensive way, suggesting that he was above hurt and was "secretly" better than the Young Turks themselves.

When, toward the end of August, I took the second installment of my summer vacation (for a week), Dr. Albert for the first time was open in reporting that the separation had been "brutal." He brought himself to say that he did not want me to leave. He recalled the way he had felt as his father lay dying, when he had been unable to save him. We did not see one another again until the day after Labor Day.

Are You the Son of the Fellow who Sold License Plates?

The Day after Labor Day to the End of September

Dr. Albert came to the first session after my vacation with a most friendly smile and reported a dream, saying that it might relate to our reunion. On the previous night, he had dreamed of coming to my office but finding it altered; it looked like that of a psychiatrist he had seen some time before while "shopping around" for a therapist. He had had a diagnostic interview with that psychiatrist, and in his dream he felt that he had come to me for the same purpose, "as if we were starting from the beginning . . . but with all the knowledge I have gained in my analysis 'till now."

Dr. Albert had dreamed that while seated in my office, ready for an interview, he saw the door open and people entering as though a group session were about to begin. One who came looked like a policeman; another looked like one of his patients who had had an infection in his skull that had required brain surgery. There were also two women, one of whom was another physician's girlfriend, the other of whom was a woman he himself had once slept with. The dream continued as I brought up things Dr. Albert had said about different characters, as though I were conducting an episode of "This is Your Life," and that I asked him what these statements really meant. As I concluded, I said, "Let's get down to the basics" and spoke of his chief of service in his hospital, asking aloud if this man were giving Dr. Albert a hard time. I was dressed like a judge, and he had the feeling that I was sitting in judgment on him and on his relationships with the people in his life.

After describing his dream, Dr. Albert stated that the different characters stood for different images of himself and of other people important to him in his childhood: "Instead of ghosts and ghoulies, I was seeing real people in a new light, as though I have moved to a new plane in my analysis. When I awakened and recalled the dream, I felt like celebrating. The word *celebration* came into my mind, but it felt funny. Then the word *dichotomy* popped into my head." I asked, "Do you suppose your dream has to do with dividing things into two groups?" He said yes and gave the following information.

In the dream, the person who first entered the room after Dr. Albert's arrival began talking about how great psychoanalysis is. This reminded Dr. Albert of having seen in a magazine a day earlier a review of a book called *Freud and God*. On the same day, he and Jane had discussed Jane's meeting, at a professional gathering, a psychologist who compared "behavioral medicine" with psychoanalysis. Jane's praise of behavioral medicine induced Dr. Albert to praise psychoanalysis. Thus the dream had something to do with my analysand's ambivalence (dichotomy) about me, with this feelings of being rejected by my recent absence, and with his delight in having me back. The patient with the skull infection in real life regarded Dr. Albert as God, as did his whole family; who, then, was God in my office—he, me, or Dr. Freud? His associations to the statement I had made in the dream about "getting down to basics" and my question about his service chief's "giving him a hard time" made him anxious now, and he began to yawn. He could say, however, that his service chief had recently, during an absence from work, changed his appearance in some way in an effort to look younger, and his acquaintances, including Dr. Albert, had joked about this and about the possibility that the man was having an affair. The service chief had a young male relative who was in trouble with the police; and someone had recently displayed a caricature of the service chief himself conducting a band the name of which was, by coincidence, the name of the hospital in which I have my office.

The meaning of the dream began to emerge. The service chief represented the analyst, who had a woman. The chief's young kinsman, who stood for the patient, had done something criminal to embarrass the chief and was being punished. (This association had an oedipal ring, but Dr. Albert's cautious manner kept me from developing further ideas about the meaning of the dream symbols.) After a silence, he reported having written to his ex-father-in-law during my absence to tell him that he hoped they would remain friends, although the situation between them would change now that he had his own life to live. Dr. Albert said he felt sad after writing this and even felt sad talking about it on the couch. I thought that he was indeed reporting his arrival on a new plane of psychological organization; although still involved in unresolved oedipal issues and continuing to expect punishment for self-assertion, he *was* asserting himself, and I thought he might be ready to bring his oedipal struggle more into the open.

I thought that he kept figuratively flexing his muscles while on the couch during the next several sessions. Dr. Albert openly but cautiously expressed negative views toward father/analyst figures, such as his chief of service and the president of the United States. He wrote to one of the (male) leaders in his hospital, challenging the way the senior officer had handled an issue. He began to have an "allergic attack" as he told me about this. When he sneezed, I suggested that he might be using the same mechanism (succumbing to an "allergic attack") in confronting power-ful men as he had been in the habit of using when confronting separation from a powerful woman.

He began his session on September 12 by telling of a dream in which he had seen himself standing by a coffin which was placed vertically on the floor rather than horizontally. The day residue reflected his receipt of a gift from his ex-father-in-law for Pamela: a life-sized doll standing up in its box. At first glance, it had looked to him like someone in a coffin. He referred to this dream again at his next session, recalling the actual burial of someone whose instructions had required that he be buried standing up on a hilltop from which he could "look down upon" his land even in death. There was a large cross on the hill in which he was buried. This man had given Dr. Albert a pearl-handled pocketknife for being the only student graduating from his high school who planned to continue his education. Dr. Albert had carried this knife with him for a long time, but when he married, his father-in-law had given him a Swiss army knife, which was larger, and he had begun carrying that instead. Because it was so heavy, he had moved it from his pocket to his briefcase.

In his Maryland hometown, it was usual for fathers to give knives or rifles to their sons, but young Chris's mother thought a rifle too dangerous. I thought that Chris had gotten phallic symbols (knives) from other father figures, too, but that now that he was trying to be a man in his own right, he could not escape from the idea that, even in death, the father figure would be watching him.

He pursued his associations and came up with the angry announcement that it had been his mother's fear of rifles that had prevented his having a (phallic) gift from his father, and that he had denied the existence of some manly aspects of his father such as his father's athletic prowess. He could remember now that his father had brought home hams and turkeys that he had won in shooting matches and realized that his father must have been a good shot. "Because Daddy Doc was a god to my mother, I knew nothing about my father," he declared. I sensed that he wanted to identify with a strong father in spite of his fear that getting to know a strong father might be dangerous.

Dr. Albert talked again about his mother's "phobias" about cows and how this had made him afraid of cows himself until his father had reassured him. His father had been "an equalizing force." "I don't want to see my father in the shadow of my mother, in a foggy way," he said. He recalled that his mother had not permitted him to gaze upon his father in his casket, as he had wanted to do. In reference to his dream about being in my office with other people, he indicated that he wanted to see me also as a total person, just as he wanted to integrate a total image of his father. He noted that his dream made it now clear to him that he was gathering clues for and against psychoanalysis in order to gain perspective on me.

Dr. Albert then spoke of the Chinese way of celebrating death in the belief that death and rebirth are intertwined. I suggested that the integration of old images might be in the service of burying some of them in order to be free of their influence and that this might be perceived as a rebirth. "That's a nice thought," he agreed. Recalling the hill where the older friend who gave him the knife had been buried, he recalled the myth of Sisyphus, who was condemned to roll up a steep hill a stone that invariably slid back to the bottom. "I, too, am condemned to Hades," he said. "As I go up the hill, I fall back into my mother's shadow."

On September 16 he said, "I am busy trying to integrate things. It's like blending chocolate and vanilla sauces; they don't mix, but I keep trying." I did not answer, and he went on to capture different memories of his father, behaving as though these old images were alive and in the room with us. Some, such as that of the father who failed to persevere with what he undertook, were negative; others were positive images of a charming man. I learned that the father had wanted very much to become a pilot but had been tied to his wife, who would not leave the town where Brownie lived. This session ended with talk about Dr.

Albert's having seen a show about Peter Pan and his concluding that psychoanalysis was like Peter Pan. I made the interpretation that he wanted me to teach him (or at least to teach the father in him) to fly, to free him from the old bonds.

On the following day while he was climbing the stairs to my office, Dr. Albert recalled having, as a child, climbed the stairs of an old building to see an eye doctor. He spoke of his allergy as he mentioned this and went on to recall a man who had an office in that building and for whom his father had once worked. This man had subsequently become highly successful in business—had, in short, been able to "climb up." We talked about Dr. Albert's anxiety to climb up to manhood. The man above, the ophthalmologist/analyst, like the father figure buried on the hilltop, might cure his eye—or blind him. If Dr. Albert were to climb up, he would first have to have reassurance that this would not result in his needing to "pay dues" and undergo castration.

He then reported a dream in which he was "upstairs" in a bedroom. Although in reality his carport is on the right side of his bedroom, in this dream it was in front of it, just below the window. It was night, and Pamela was sleeping in his bed. Small children had climbed up onto the carport roof and were coming through the window to play with her. When Dr. Albert told them to leave, they fled to the woods. He looked after them from the window, and saw a scene of the kind featured in the film *Dr. Zhivago,* a snowy woodland bathed in moonlight. In his dream Dr. Albert got out his revolver, carefully loaded it, and began to shoot into the air to scatter the children as though it were necessary to protect Pamela from them. He had three different kinds of cartridges and had to be careful to select the right sort.

As soon as he reported this dream, Dr. Albert began spontaneously to give his associations to it, saying that its most striking feature was the bluish-green, snowy scene from the Dr. Zhivago film, in which there was both warmth and chill. He could not recall if Dr. Zhivago had been married when he fell in love with the character played by Julie Christie. When he spoke of how Dr. Zhivago and the woman he loved lost one another, and how he had died looking for her, he noticed that his hands felt ice cold. He was Doctor Zhivago, looking for an idealized woman and never possessing her for long. His daughter, lying in his bed in the dream, represented his idealized mother. Dr. Albert said that in recent days he had found himself merging his daughter, Mamie, Jane, and his mother together. He had accidentally called Jane "Mamie"; and on one occasion instead of saying Mamie he had said "mother." He also called his daughter "Jane."

He had been pondering why he kept Pamela instead of encouraging his ex-wife to take her. He felt as though he had stolen his daughter, as though she were the idealized woman representing the mother who had come to him at night, playing musical beds; and as though in getting rid of Mamie, he had rid himself of the bad mother. He noted that his possessiveness about Pamela had given way to a genuine love for her, "As if I started from A and went to B, shifting from one location to another as my carport did in the dream."

Dr. Albert spoke about how he had wanted to keep his mother when his brother came along. He kept two images of her; one, which belonged absolutely to him, was idealized, while the other had abandoned him for his brother or his father. He now thought that when he had Pamela to himself, he triumphed over his brother and his father by having absolute control of one girl. But he realized that this made him feel guilty. He also realized that one reason for his negative feelings toward Jane was that she intruded into this dyad.

Brownie had remarried after Daddy Doc's death, to a rather shadowy "second best" man to whom Dr. Albert seldom referred. The revolver in the dream was his; it did in fact take out-of-the-ordinary shells and require careful handling. Its "second best" owner represented Dr. Albert's devalued aspect, devalued in relation to the father or brother whom his mother sought out. In spite of her having gone to little Chris's bed at night, it had always been her husband's to which she returned for real, sexual love, leaving her son only a sexualized image of her for his masturbatory fantasies.

Dr. Albert now recalled that when he used the revolver in his dream he had shot into a snowbank in the woods, in a way that would bring no one harm. Doing this was like "jerking off" all by himself, but the incestuous fantasies connected with his masturbation were guilt-provoking. It was not safe for him to do more than masturbate, since actual incest would bring expected punishment. So, like Dr. Zhivago, he was fixed in his search of an idealized women, never succeeding in finding and possessing the good and idealized woman. In the dream, he had gone "upstairs," had climbed to where he wanted to be. However, he declared that he was the eternally wandering Jew, like Zhivago in his search for the ideal. His continuing search was a defensive adaptation that promised safety, but at the same time kept him from doing better in the real world. He arrived at these formulations by himself with little help from me.

Dr. Albert continued to interpret the images he had of his father and to examine the evolution of his relationship to him. He began his hour on September 19 by confessing that he was still a little nervous at having heard nothing in reply from the medical authority to whom he had written a critical letter. After a few moments' silence, he reported that recently while driving he had stopped at a stoplight alongside a van on which a cemetery scene was painted. Recalling an old cemetery in which he had played with friends as a child, he said, "Cemeteries are neat places." His mother had warned him not to stand on the graves because it was improper. He fell silent, but I told him that I thought he wanted to speak of the influence of some dead persons on him, and that if he did, it might be like standing on their graves. Was he wondering if I would consider that improper? He replied that he was thinking of a stillborn baby brother. He himself had been 17 when his mother's belly began to swell, and his parents had seemed worried. He recalled how on her return from a visit to the docotr, his mother had said that she did not, after all, have a tumor; the swelling was a baby. His friends teased him, saying, "Your old man forgot to use rubbers!" It was hard for him to think of his parents "screwing"; he had never though of their "doing that sort of thing." Although his mother's belated pregnancy awakened his feelings abouth her earlier pregnancy with his brother (and other pregnancies that had resulted in spontaneous abortion), he had not made the connection then, simply feeling awkward about the evidence of his parents' sexuality and guilty when the baby was stillborn.

I said nothing. Dr. Albert seemed in a trance; he was reliving the funeral of Danny and that of his father.

The minister in charge had glorified the dead. "That was bullshit," he cried. Then he was overwhelmed with sadness and talked about the horrible death his father had had to face. He began to shout at me, "How many times am I going over this? How many times am I going to repeat this?" He was very close to tears. I told him that each time he reintegrated his father's images, he had a new image of him to grieve over. He said "Hmph!" and fell into a thoughtful, sad, and teary silence, which he broke by mumbling that he thought of a pot full of images of his father that he was stirring up. He spoke of his lips' feeling dry, and after being silent for a while, came up with a story that moved him greatly. I was moved also.

He and his brother had gone together to a store in their home town on a recent visit there. Dr. Albert wrote a check to cover a purchase he made, and when the storekeeper examined it he had asked, "Are you the son of the fellow who used to sell license plates?" Dr. Albert was stunned by the man's remembering his father after twenty years, and said, "Jesus, I was addressed as the son of my father and not as the son of my mother. Jesus, I felt like crying. I was caught off guard. Jesus, my father's license plate business was not a small one; he really sold a lot of license plates. People lined up to get them." His voice cracked as he felt this closeness to his father. He then told me that physically he resembled his father except that his father did not have his odd mustache. I thought that his sporting the mustache had been his defensive way of separating himself from his father.

Dr. Albert went on to say that his father had long dreamed of building a sunporch on his home, but had died before being able to do so. I now understood another reason why he had tried to build a sunporch soon after starting his analysis. I also wondered if he had been influenced by the fact that my office had a sunporch built for the use of tubercular patients; although he had never made reference to this, he may have comprehended it on one level.

His father had died without ever saying "I love you" to his son, and in turn Dr. Albert had never told his father that he loved him. He felt like apologizing for this oversight now, and seemed bewildered. At this point I told him that there are many ways of saying "I love you" and that the storekeeper's mention of his father had confirmed in him a feeling of love for his father. My words stunned him with a realization of the depth of his affection for his father, and he said no more.

He began the next day's session, on September 20, with an account of a dream in which he saw objects that lay side by side under Plexiglass, in rows like sardines or cigars. He associated this with an orderly grave-yard and his having been in touch during the previous session with his father. The more integrated his father's image became, the more easily he could let him rest in peace.

The rest of the session centered around his effort to tell me how much he appreciated me. He struggled to express himself, and I told him that his struggle to say something nice to me was like the struggle and inability to tell his father of his love for him. He explained, "You know I appreciate you, but I can't tell you this freely yet." When Jane's parents came for a visit with Dr. Albert, Jane, and Pamela, Jane's father was friendly, and as he drove to his appointment with me, Dr. Albert thought of telling me how he felt about the older man. But the thought was replaced by another: "I don't want another father. I have Volkan."

At one point Dr. Albert expressed a wish that he were Alexander the Great and could cut the Gordian knot in a second. If he were, and could in a second resolve the issues from his childhood that still influenced him, he would marry Jane at once. He wondered why he had thought of Alexander and then suggested that Gordium was probably in present-day Turkey. I told him that this was so. He vaguely recalled a story of Alexander's capturing "a greedy king" and killing him by pouring molten gold into his throat. He said he wanted to be rid of the greedy little king aspect of himself; he was greedy in his search for the perfect woman. To be no longer greedy would mean that he had abandoned the search, his "grass-is-greener elsewhere" syndrome would disappear, and he could marry Jane without difficulty. He wanted to do this with me, the Turkish analyst, in the background.

On September 26, Dr. Albert heard from the medical authority in response to his critical letter. He was upset by the reply and forgot the markedly positive feeling he had been entertaining toward me. Once again the father image became negative and he dreamed of me "wearing the robes of a judge; you were judging me!" he said, I explained the connection between his changing image of his father/me and the medical authority's nasty letter. In spite of what I said, he continued to back away from any effort at positive identification with the oedipal father and dealt instead with his wish to have his mother for himself and his jealousy of his brother. He remembered bending over his brother's crib and feeling like saying, "You lucky prick!" He ascribed his having become a "greedy little king" to his brother's birth and to his mother's bestowing on the younger child the greater share of her affection.

The Tin Man

October

As we moved into October, Dr. Albert began taking more and more liquor as a nightcap, up to five or six glasses of gin. While drinking he would think exaggeratedly about beautiful women, and he reported fantasies about them that occupied him as he drove to our sessions. He had been trying to have a positive relationship with the oedipal father/ analyst, but this had brought anxiety lest the "bad" oedipal father/ analyst punish him. Thus he regressed to his search for an idealized woman; this search had followed the fantasy he had entertained while feeling rejected and victimized by his mother's giving birth to another child. His fantasies and his drinking gratified him.

It did not occur to me at first that his exaggerated return to the idealized woman might be in the service of reviewing her, so to speak, in order to give her up. I found myself irritated by him, and apparently Jane had the same reaction, since she talked more often on the telephone to her ex-husband. I did not comment on Jane's apparent irritation with him, and I tried to conceal mine, but it surfaced in a warning that if I were his family physician instead of his analyst, I would be obliged to point out that his current drinking habits were bad for his health. Certainly my remarks were not interpretations of the problem, and I had made a technical mistake in intruding in his activities. He responded by sulking for a week and dreamed of enlarging a small tear in a coat lining to annoy the tailor who had made the coat. He was victimizing himself further in order to make the tailor—my representative—

miserable. I interpreted how he was responding to my intrusion on him, admitted my technical mistake, and said that I would prefer to explore the reason he was drinking more at bedtime. He indicated that he needed to revisit the image of his mother feeding him (the gin) and to take stock of her before coming up to deal with his relationship with his father. It appeared that his drinking and "dope" taking (marijuana) had increased after a visit home. He had not taken Jane with him, and without her he had become a target of his mother's intrusive attention, much the same kind of attention he had set me up to give him. His mother had cooked many dishes for him and even had cut the meat on his plate, gratifying him instantly so that he felt smothered and weary of her intrusions. He wanted to rid his mind of her image. I suggested, however, that his increased oral gratification showed an unconscious reluctance to surrender the mother who provided instant gratification.

Dr. Albert worked on moving away from the influence of his mother's image in the following way. I first heard on October 9 that he was thinking of making a Tin Man costume for Pamela to wear on Halloween; it was to be like the one in the film of *The Wizard of Oz*. When he asked if I had seen the film, I said, "Hm! Hm!" to encourage him to continue the flow of his remarks. He likened the Wizard of Oz to me, noting, for instance, that we had the same color of hair. He pointed out that the journey on the yellow brick road to the palace of the Wizard was like his analysis. (It will be remembered that he had used this analogy before, but at a time when he associated himself with the Tin Man.) He said that his analysis had given him almost all the pieces of a puzzle but that he needed to arrange them in their proper places. This was his first reference to the possibility of the successful completion of his analysis. In a thoughtful, stock-taking mood, he counted three areas that he said still required work: his "grass-is-greener" syndrome, which reflected his search for an idealized woman; his envy; and the occasional recurrence of his allergic symptoms.

On the following day, Dr. Albert came in in a foul mood, demonstrating by much sneezing how much work still needed to be done on his allergic symptoms. He complained of having played handball poorly the day previous. I said nothing, and after a silence he made the suggestion that after "a beautiful hour" the day before, he might be seeking to balance it by making this a bad one. He had pondered the night before how good he had felt after that day's session, until the thought, "Fuck you, Volkan," had come to him and he had kicked his dog (thinking of

his name as mine) and poured himself a drink. He had become aware of
how dependent he was on me and regretted this. He felt frustrated and
unable to understand his love or hate for me. I told him that what he felt
for me reflected his frustration about having opposing feelings about his
mother; that he did not want to be dependent on her, but that at the same
time he did not want to surrender the "instant gratification" that he
thought she would give him.

He said he was aware of reactivating the "greedy little king" in
himself, who was "shitty." He had "all the shit" to do in his daily life,
and then he had to deal with "the shit coming out" in his analysis. I told
him that he might perceive me as his feces, since I represented in this
connection the mother he knew when he was 4. Should he love and
retain me, or should he let me go? "To have or not to have the shit
Volkan," I added. "That is the question."

Dr. Albert began talking about the Tin Man costume he was making.
In the story, the Tin Man had hoped that the Wizard would give him a
heart, but he found out that this was impossible. "You, Volkan, like the
Wizard, do not have magic," he said. But in the story, the Tin Man
discovered that he did have a heart after all, since he began crying when
he had to separate from Dorothy. I told Dr. Albert that for him Dorothy
might stand for his idealized woman, his greener grass. The session
ended.

In mid-October came the anniversary of Jane's having moved, for all
practical purposes, into his house, and she wanted to surprise him by
arranging for an elaborate weekend stay in a resort. Pamela was to be
left with a babysitter at home. When he learned about the plan, Dr.
Albert's nose started to drip; he recognized spontaneously that he had
made Jane a smothering mother, as was demonstrated by his typical
allergic response. He wanted to be rid of it, but it persisted, to his
frustration. But he and Jane did go to the resort. They passed his
mother's home en route but did not stop. Dr. Albert realized how guilty
this made him feel, and his allergic reaction was so severe that on their
holiday he and Jane slept in separate beds. They both felt frustrated.

Dr. Albert gave the particulars of this incident, and his observations
concerning it, at his hour on Monday. After being silent for a while, he
told me that on his way to see me he had heard over his car radio a man
talking about the teddy bears one had in childhood, speaking of how
even as an adult one continued to be charmed by them. The speaker went
on to say that a shop specializing in repairing teddy bears was patronized

by many businessmen; one adult owner had recently even brought in his teddy bear to have its "voice" put in operation again.

At this point, Dr. Albert came up with an insight and said, "My mother is my teddy bear; she is in my head—stuck there!" He then reported an important dream that reflected my comment that the mother/analyst was like the feces that he simultaneously wanted to keep and to give up. A toilet, particularly "the U-shaped part" had featured in his dream. As he spoke of this it occurred to him that it stood for *"You,"* by which he meant his analyst, and that the dream had obvious transference implications. In it he had seen an arm reaching into the toilet and pulling something out—"not shit, but body parts like arms, hands, and legs. So there had to be a body in there. There was no blood; the body parts were green." He recalled his remarks about his mother's being a teddy bear stuck in his head. Now he was pulling the mother out of himself. The green color reminded him of the Witch in *The Wizard of Oz*. The arm was that of the Tin Man he was making. In the film, the Witch melted away when water was poured on her, but in the dream his mother's parts stayed in shape in the water like pieces of fecal material. "I had to chop her into pieces to pull her out!" he exclaimed.

Dr. Albert recalled that his mother had worn odd clothes when he was small and that once, when she was dressed all in black, a child in a department store they were visiting pointed to her, saying, "Here is a witch!" His mother recalled this incident and spoke of it later, chuckling, but he now thought that the remark might have hurt her. I sensed that he did not want to hurt his mother's feelings by thinking of her as a witch; after all, she could retaliate. But I sensed also that he empathized with her. He elaborated on why his mother's behavior was odd: after all, she was an adopted child.

He unrepressed a childhood wish that both parents be killed, chopped into pieces. He was surprised that the memory was accompanied by a feeling of glee. He declared that once a teddy bear was broken it was lost, since a repaired teddy bear would not be the same. More important, he talked about how he was putting different parts of his mother into Jane. "I am tired of all this, you know," he complained. "I now have the key (of understanding), but I can't turn it yet." Then he began playing with the word *turnkey,* which reminded him of *turncoat.* "I feel like Benedict Arnold," he said, "a traitor, for trying to give up the parts of my mother that are stuck in me."

Before his next session, Dr. Albert received a letter from his ex-father-in law, who acknowledged that things would no longer be the same between them. Thus Dr. Albert was faced with giving up a figure on whom he had projected an idealized image of his father. I now learned that the ex-father-in-law was a millionaire, although he had done little to relieve his daughter's financial problems after her divorce. Dr. Albert had entertained the expectation that, as Mamie's husband, he might inherit a substantial fortune. This hope was gone forever now, and he said he felt like an orphan, empathizing in a sense with how his mother had felt.

After a silence, he reported having read about the Turkish prime minister and fantasizing that I was related to him. I made the interpretation that it was still difficult for him to give up idealized images. Just as his mother had idealized Daddy Doc in order to deal with her hurts, he needed to keep an idealized image before him when he was on the point of giving up old images (bad as well as idealized) of his parents. He was making me important by linking me with a famous statesman. He began to laugh, then became sad. "There are no Utopias," he concluded and then said that he was integrating himself in a new way. "The Tin Man I am making is about finished," he added, and the session concluded.

Soon he learned that one of his patients was considering filing suit against him. He knew that he was not at fault and was irritated and full of "Fuck you, Volkan" thoughts. However, he soon took steps to protect himself by talking to appropriate people, including a lawyer, about the matter. He then told me that the Tin Man was finished: "All the pieces are tied together."

On October 22, Dr. Albert reported having read a book entitled *Mom Kills Kids and Self*. It was the true story of a man whose wife had killed their children before committing suicide. In his book, the husband described how he had resolved in his mind the conflicts about his tragic losses. Identifying himself with the writer, Dr. Albert told me that he felt he was in the process of resolving in his own mind the conflicts about killing different images of himself and of his parents. But in the next hour he said he was afraid that if he surrendered the idealized mother image, he might at the same time be killing some aspects of himself that he liked. He felt sad and had tears in his eyes. He spoke of marrying Jane, indicating that this would mean giving up the fantasied position of being adored by idealized women.

That night, before going to bed, he sent out for and devoured a pizza along with a considerable amount of liquor, observing how "the greedy little king" was dictating his behavior. He felt like Dr. Jekyll and Mr. Hyde, as though he could see two parts of himself and feel them struggling within his chest. He had been able to see "the greedy little king" begin to act out when Jane talked about a divorced man and spoke of his good looks. Dr. Albert knew that in his mind he had made this divorced man his brother, and Jane his mother, and this made him feel victimized and greedy. As the hour ended, his insight comforted him, and he left my office joking about his greedy part.

Dr. Albert continued having to deal with the lawsuit, and he noted changes in himself with pleasure, reporting them to me. His relationship to male authority figures had changed, he said, and this change included some of his superiors in handling the lawsuit. "I have an inner security. It is something new for me." He was able to be assertive with such figures and could struggle with them without anxiety and without fantasizing himself as above all others. Heretofore he had felt comfortable with the "rednecks" he bowled with and could be a physician as though playing a doctor's role, but at the same time keeping other professionals at a distance. Now he found himself involved in the politics of his medical institution. In the midst of this, Mamie made one of her visits to town, called him, and had some interaction with Pamela. Dr. Albert handled all this appropriately and said, "My reactions are so different! I am observing myself observing others."

Just before Halloween he said, "I have this dynamite good feeling in me!" The night before Halloween he watched with Pamela a Dr. Seuss cartoon on Halloween and was fascinated by its fantastic shapes and colors and the imagination it exhibited. It occurred to him that he contained similarly fantastic possibilities, and he said, "I can't wait for all those things to be liberated. Do you remember my telling about the puppy I had who looked like an old dog when he was just a puppy? I feel as though I missed my childhood and the exciting adventures I should have had as a teenager. I want to let my hair down. It is a dynamite feeling!" On the following night Pamela wore her Tin Man costume.

A House on Mons Pubis

Early November through Christmas

In November Dr. Albert was feverishly trying to put the pieces of the puzzle together. He seemed to be in a hurry, and in consequence he seemed extremely disorganized. I felt comfortable with his disorganization, hoping that it was a necessary antecedent to new integration. I listened to him, allowing the process to unfold with minimal intervention. He did not seem panicky and was excited at being at work, psychologically tearing down and reconstructing his inner structures according to a new order. I think Jane was puzzled by him at this point; when a boyfriend called to say that he would be in town, she agreed to have dinner with him. Dr. Albert vacillated between asserting himself toward her and being limp. I said nothing.

It seemed to me that in his sessions he rapidly covered different relationships with different images as they were transferred to me or to other symbolic parent figures such as the president. In a single hour, he would move from mocking me to idealizing me and then return to mocking. He was aware of great inner turmoil as well as turmoil in his daily life; his attempts at inner organization were echoed in new activities in his daily life. He was doing many new things; at a professional meeting in another city, for example, he found himself standing up before the assembly questioning the speaker. In doing this he felt anxious but proud—a "dynamite" feeling. He also made what he called "an important speech" at the meeting.

On returning from the trip with Jane, Dr. Albert asserted himself toward his mother, who had stayed with Pamela in his absence. He forbade her to give Pamela extra money without consulting him first. In spite of feeling good about these changes, he reported being still unable to believe in his "success" in dealing with others. "I used to be very successful—or very inferior—in my fantasies," he added. "But now I think I am becoming successful in real life situations, although I still can't accept fully the fact that I am succeeding in this way."

When his mother came for Thanksgiving, Dr. Albert could tame her intrusiveness with his newly acquired ability to say no. He took a short pleasure trip with Jane, leaving Pamela with his mother. On their return, before his mother left for home, he managed to have a talk with her about her adoption. "As if I am reaching for the answer to a puzzle," he said. "As if I've come to the end of a road and found this puzzle awaiting me there." He wanted to learn the real story behind his mother's adoption, to find the answer to the puzzle. His mother told him that for a long time now she had not minded being adopted and added that there were apparently some documents in the office of a state agency where one might possibly learn more about her adoption. She did not care to pursue the matter; Dr. Albert solemnly concluded that "her burden of being adopted had been transferred onto my shoulders."

As though he wanted to tie together all the loose ends in his life, he wanted to learn the facts of the affair Mamie was supposedly engaged in at the time of their separation. He knew the supposed lover, and kept up a peripheral relationship with him; toward the end of November he invited him to his home, where the two men "had a good time" talking about Mamie until far into the night. Dr. Albert concluded that this man had observed some odd characteristics in Mamie, that she was a dependent or at least only a pseudo-independent individual. He decided that there never had been an affair between this man and his ex-wife, but that Mamie had used him to gratify some of her dependency needs.

As Dr. Albert spoke of meeting with this man, he had another insight. The two men had spoken of Mamie in front of Jane, who was according-ly pushed to compete, at least on that occasion, with the ghost of her lover's ex-wife. When Dr. Albert realized this, he understood that he was indirectly becoming sadistic toward Jane to retaliate for her making him compete with an ex-boyfriend about to visit town, and for her making him jealous by talking to her ex-husband on the telephone. In early December, his realization of what had been going on led him to discuss with Jane their commitment to one another. He still felt that were he committed to Jane he would definitely let "the idealized woman fantasy" die. He instructed Jane not to see her ex-boyfriend and to hang up on her ex-husband's telephone calls. While I remained an observer to his struggle, he finally made a verbal commitment to Jane. On December 5, he told me that he felt that "psychoanalysis is like a parent" and that against a background of his analysis he wanted to "regulate" his life.

Telling Jane that he wanted to be the only man in her life and that she should no longer be interested in other men made him cautious and negativistic. He transferred these feelings to me the next day, when he began talking of how he did not want to be committed to Jane and how part of him did not want "to keep Jane lest she smother me." He was angrily silent and sulky for some time as he lay on the couch. I did nothing to interfere with his silence, and at the very end of the hour he told me that during his silence he was drawing mental pictures on my wall, seeing an X marked there, on one side of which he saw a man, and on the other, a woman. Then he envisioned crushing them. With this the hour ended.

Dr. Albert began his next session, on December 7, by referring to his mental image of the X on my wall. He kept playing with this image and reported rotating the shape in his mind and coming up with two cones pointing their small ends at each other, and his crushing them. His associations indicated that his recent commitment to Jane had made him anxious. I then learned that the pair had been house-hunting together. This seemed to me a further step toward cementing their relationship; his fear that she would turn into a smothering person increased. The cones he fantasied were associated with two breasts, and now he fantasied that he might find himself squeezed between the cones. At home his "nose noises" had worsened, and Jane had said that morning, "If psychoanalysis could cure your nose, I'd gladly pay for it."

After a silence, Dr. Albert reported that he wanted to make a painting of the cones as well as of the valley about which he had recently dreamed, the one with the black mist. The tall mountains on either side of this valley reminded him of the two cones. They were tree-covered, and as I prodded him he declared that the geographical image he was describing was a woman's genitalia. He noted that the trees on the mountains were cypress, which he associated with Cyprus, my homeland. His realization that his description of "female genitalia" included a reference to me made him anxious, and he remarked that the house he and Jane had looked at on the previous day had been made of cypress. I suggested that although he seemed to be strengthening his commitment to Jane, he might still be contaminating her with his mother's image, and including me in the picture as his father. He then became anxious that we were competing for the same woman.

Dr. Albert responded by recalling how once, while he and Mamie were out driving, a passerby had made a sexual remark about her. Mamie had wanted him to stop the car, get out, and fight but he had been afraid. "I had become a chicken as soon as I began wearing glasses. I was afraid this man might hit me in the eye and injure my cornea." I told him that his search for a house to share with Jane might be perceived as a competition with me in which he could be injured.

Over the weekend and before his Monday session, he put in a bid for a house to which they had been taken for the first time but which excited him. It was not completely finished, although the exterior had been completed. It was in the country and reminded him, he said, of places where he had roomed as a child. As the session went on, however, he realized that what had made him bid for this house was the fact that it and the surrounding area reminded him of the house and the valley in his dream, which my interpretation had led him to recognize as representing his mother's dangerous genitalia; it was on a hill, with a balcony overlooking a valley. He joked that he was going to live on Mons Pubis, and he realized that his excitement was due to his symbolic "conquering" of his fear of the female genitalia.

He learned that someone else was bidding for the house. He called several people who might encourage the owner to accept his bid and who could influence the outcome of the competition. The house was built on several acres and was in a considerably more prestigious location than Dr. Albert's current house. "I have the neatest feeling," he said. "I never imagined doing anything like this before, even if I knew I had enough money to do it. I am leaving my 'rednecks' behind. The new neighborhood is one of other physicians, engineers, and lawyers." He said further that, even more important, he had at the last minute decided to buy the house with his own money instead of making it a joint purchase with Jane. "If Jane decides to stay with me there will be no bribery, no strings attached," he said. He felt more committed to Jane, and she agreed to move into the new house with him and Pamela as soon as it was completed in April. Once again Dr. Albert had told her, "No more phone calls to or from your ex-husband!" and she had agreed. He felt so elated and "well" that at the close of the session he began talking about the possible termination of his analysis. I made no comment.

Dr. Albert began his next session in a somber mood and he said that Pamela was anxious about leaving their present home, changing schools, and the like. He readily stated that he, too, was having "separation anxiety." I said only "Hm! Hm!", and he fell silent. He then said that the word *conflict* popped into his mind. When I asked for associations, he reported that his dog had been sick the previous night, and it had occurred to him that a change of houses would be accompanied by the dog's death. It was as though he had to "kill" the old before trying something new. When he had awakened in the morning, the radio brought news of a murder that had taken place in his neighborhood. I thought to myself that this was quite a coincidence, since few murders take place in our town, and one in his neighborhood was quite extraordinary. The news of the murder made him anxious. "It is as though someone has to die in order for you to succeed and move up to a better neighborhood and live on Mons Pubis," I said.

Dr. Albert grew thoughtful and told me that he could not recall having shared good feelings with his father. "I was afraid of him," he said, recalling the beatings he had suffered at his father's hands. Once again he fell silent. He smiled, and his eyes sparkled. "What is in your mind?" I asked. He replied that he was thinking of how he had once done something to short-circuit the electrical system in their family home, causing a blackout while his father was working on his tax return. Young Chris had been afraid that his father would be furious, but he had not been. "It is an unusual memory. It amuses me," he commented.

Nonetheless the image of a benign father soon gave way to that of someone who might castrate him since he was about to "conquer" his mother's genitalia. The notion of self-castration as defense against an attack reappeared, and he talked about hearing about someone who cut his own head off by accident while using a chainsaw; the idea made him feel sick. I interpreted that he was reacting with thoughts of self-castration to his fantasy that I might hurt him because of his success. "Is my old habit of 'paying dues' coming back?" he asked. "I have come to understand the meaning of it, and I am really surprised to see it again in my associations," he added. "It is so fucking stupid." Then, instead of remaining anxious and self-castrating, as he would have been in the past, he reported that he was very close to proposing marriage to Jane.

In mid-December, Pamela had a letter from Mamie, who was traveling in Europe. The letter was a general announcement that she might be marrying a European and would not be returning to this country to be with her daughter. Dr. Albert noted that for the first time, Pamela expressed hostility toward her mother. His response to the news was to drink considerably more than usual that night and to have short-lived fantasies of finding an idealized woman. When he met Caroline at a party, he no longer saw her as the symbol of his idealized woman, but felt even closer to Jane than before. He decided to talk privately with Pamela about her disappointment about her mother's absence. When he did, Pamela in turn was able to tell him her fantasies about her mother's death. He understood her anger and was supportive toward her in a gentle way.

Dr. Albert was sad when he awakened on December 18. He could recall no dream, but a thought occurred to him that he had had a similar feeling at the time of his father's death, the tenth anniversary of which would occur in a few days. In reporting his mood to me that day he said, "I don't want to die. In my analysis I am between A and B. I know A is the starting point. Sometimes I think I am very close to B, but I really don't know where B is. I don't want to die before I work things out."

In the following session, he reviewed the memories of his father's death. Again, he wept and mourned, but he also held hope for his future. He spoke of how greatly he felt he had improved and expressed warmth and affection for me. "I feel close to you," he said. "I don't even feel irritation because we are going to be separated for the Christmas vacation."

The Wish for
a Hydroelectric Generator

The End of December through February 8

During the Christmas and New Year break in his analysis, Dr. Albert asked Jane to marry him, and she accepted. Although they told Pamela, Jane's parents, and their friends about this, Jane soon had second thoughts and told Dr. Albert that it would be better if they postponed a definite decision about marrying. Dr. Albert told me about this in our session on January 2 without anger, giving as an explanation his belief that Jane was waiting for "a knight in shining armor" to appear. This remark seemed to convey the notion that in fact she was like him in believing that somewhere, somehow, an unquestionably ideal partner would be found.

Dr. Albert went on to speak of changes in himself, saying that he was leaving his "redneck" self behind and was coming close to being the knight in shining armor Jane wanted. He seemed certain of being ultimately successful with her. After being silent for a while, he reported having thought that I should see Jane in my role as analyst, since she might need to work on her attempts to hold onto idealized images. I suggested that we examine this notion. It then occurred to him that introducing Jane to me in that connection was like his bringing me the candy that I had "refused." He recalled having proudly taken some mudpies to his father, expecting admiration, only to have his father step on his productions and wound his feelings. I told him that I understood his desire and that I appreciated his recent successes and his choice of Jane as a future wife as well as his dread that I might be like his father in showing disapproval or indifference. He then said that he still had opposing images of his father, just as he had of his mother. One father he saw as harsh toward him and without appreciation, but the other he continued to idealize.

He was flooded by different and opposing images of his father that night, and when he came to his session the next day he began it by reporting these positive and negative images. Halfway through this account his thoughts were blocked, and he fell silent, imagining the sight of a very high tombstone on which the sun shone. Then he saw himself, an inch tall, standing by it. "I'm a midget and my idealized father is a giant," he said. "I wish now I knew both of the giants of my childhood— my father and Daddy Doc."

All at once Dr. Albert had an image of his father repairing something young Chris had broken. He began sobbing and reached for the box of tissues. He had shed tears before but had always avoided this kind of intense display and had never needed to use tissues. As he wept, he described seeing one black and one white wall. "I am keeping the images of my father apart," he said. "But now the walls are becoming liquid, like my imagination. They are turning into oceans, one white and one black. Moses is walking between them, splitting the white water from the black. I want to put my father together, but I feel so sad."

His weeping increased. When he stopped he spoke of wanting to have a son with Jane and asked if it would rob Pamela of his love were he to have a son and love him deeply. I answered his question with another: "If you come close to your father do you think that you would then need to stop loving your mother or that she would stop loving you?" He spoke of how difficult it had been for him to say, "I love you" or to end a letter to anybody with the phrase "With love." "'I love you' was reserved for my mother; I could not say that to my father." His tears continued.

At the next day's session he reported a dream. "I saw a hallway as wide as your office. The floor was shining, like a hospital floor. I saw the figure of a man. It was Dr. Lawrence (a physician who, in reality, had been a father figure for most doctors in Dr. Albert's institution, before his recent death from cardiac arrest). He walked gently before me and went through a swinging door. In my dream I knew he was dead. It was as though he had come back to pick up something and then went away again through the door."

As he had awakened, he felt as he had felt in the dream, and he connected this feeling with his father's death. It was as though he were visiting with his father and "killing" him again, symbolically, by dreaming about someone who had been fatherly toward him. I told him that his declaration to Jane came at a time when he was busy integrating his father's image and that he wanted to know his father's reactions to his choice.

He began crying again, very hard, and reported a feeling of resolution about his father's death. He was sad because he wished his father were alive to know Pamela, whom he would love. It occurred to me that he would give Pamela to his father in order to gain his permission to have Jane, but I did not speak of this to him, feeling that it would be improper to do so while he was in the middle of an emotional experience. "My father is not bad; my father is not good. He is just my father," he whispered. Memories of his father poured out once again.

After being silent for a while, Dr. Albert again began crying. It seemed that I was now contaminated with the image of the father. On the previous day, he had seen Caroline and Joe and had told them he was feeling very comfortable with himself and that he thought he was getting ready to terminate his analysis. This involved recognition of the fact that he would have to give me up. Sadness arising from the idea of this prospective separation seemed to be condensed with his integration of his father and his "burying" him. Meanwhile, he was himself becoming "a man." He reported a visit to his chief of service on the previous day and noted that he had negotiated for an improved salary "without guilt and palpitations." "I feel optimistic," he added.

While driving to his January 9 session through snow, he fantasied skidding into a snowbank and calling me to help him and to tow his car. His associations pertained to a day when he and Danny had been driving in the snow. Young Chris had been at the wheel. As he had since discovered in his analysis, Danny was the person he had regarded as being the one to "teach me to be a man." But Danny had died, like his father, and I was now the one who should extricate him from the sticky relationship with his mother so he could choose his own woman and marry her. At this point, he disclosed that Jane had given up her idea of waiting for a knight in shining armor and that on the previous night the couple had begun to plan for a summer wedding. They had planned to the point of deciding that they should buy an oriental rug. Suddenly Dr. Albert realized that the rug had something to do with me. "It will be a Turkish rug, the Volkan rug, I guess," he said. "I want to keep part of you with me all the time!" Then he began showing an active interest in the furnishings of my office and said he had no anxiety in doing so. It was as though he wanted to know me as I exist in the real world. Before I saw him again on January 10, he had bought an oriental rug.

On January 10, he reported an incident that showed how much previously unconscious material was now available to him. A woman who had for some time been his assistant in his laboratory had a baby, and he took Pamela's outgrown crib to her for the new infant. Jane and Pamela went with him. In his laboratory assistant's house, he felt uncomfortable at the sight of the baby, and his on-the-spot self-analysis indicated to him that the newborn baby reminded him of his experiences at the time of his brother's birth. The discomfort he experienced was the reactivation of his childhood jealousy.

Driving home, he had run over an animal that had jumped across the road in the dark. He thought that it was a cat, and it occurred to him that this was the "black panther" mother who had just had a baby. He thought of this all the way home, and when he arrived there he had had an urge to drink. Since he had symbolically just "killed" the bad mother, he wanted to merge with the orally gratifying "good" one!

He continued making his own "interpretations" during the next hours. He seemed happy and was able to skip around among the memories of his very early childhood. He counted his recent successes, the changes he recognized in himself, and talked about his wedding plans. He had friendly feelings toward me and thought that I might now want him to sit face to face with me instead of lying on the couch. His associations to this idea brought the termination of his analysis into consideration more directly than before. Suddenly words from a song came into his mind: "Who, who are you?" and he said, "I am thinking of finishing my analysis, but I don't really know who you are. You are my father, brother, mother. No, no, you are my analyst!"

He said very little during the hours that followed.. When I spoke of this, he associated his silences with a possible symbolic message to me that he had finished with analysis. Instead of telling him whether I agreed, I suggested that he might want now to take stock of where we were in our work. His response seemed to me to demonstrate considerable ability to use the insight he had gained in analysis. For example, when he and Jane went skiing again, he found that he still did not ski well, and so he created in his mind an idealized skiing partner for Jane and began mentally competing with him; the "idealized man" turned out to be only a 15-year-old youngster. He also began looking for an idealized woman to soothe his narcissistic hurts. Suddenly realizing what he was doing, he stopped this fantasying and began simply to enjoy himself with Jane.

After reporting this and speaking about how his new insights helped him to avoid his old ways, he thanked me and began showing me more direct attention, as though he wanted to know me as I am and not as a transference figure representing people who had been important to him in his childhood. Nonetheless, certain symbols connected with me or my room recalled images of his past, and he wanted to examine such "links" between me and his old images. For example, he said that two fire sprinklers on the ceiling above the couch were perceived by him as "tits"; he had, in fact, thought of them as a gimmicky representation of nipples. He apparently perceived a picture on the wall as more masculine; at least, it represented my anger toward him, and in it, an abstract design, he had seen a "bursting volcano." The bookshelf across the room from the couch was perceived in an ambiguous way, with sexual symbolism that might refer to a vagina if it were seen as receding into the wall, or as a penis, if it were seen as protruding from the wall. He could not decide. He seemed a child at play, toying with different aspects of the room in order to learn the truth about us through play.

At this point, Dr. Albert professed to be fascinated with such unconscious processes as those responsible for slips of the tongue. For example, on January 17, he noted as he began his hour that there was no telephone in the elevator he used in getting to my office floor. He then went on to say that he would be unable to keep his appointments with me during the following week because he was going to an out-of-town meeting. Suddenly stopping, he said that the unconscious reason for his telling me of the absence of a telephone in the elevator might have been the lapse of communication in prospect for us during the next week. He seemed to take pleasure in finding such connections rather than being engulfed with anxiety about the impending separation.

On my way to my office the next day my car stalled; it needed a minor repair that would take only a short time at a nearby service station. Dr. Albert was my first scheduled patient, so I phoned him that I would be twenty minutes late, explained the reason for my tardiness, but assured him that we would have a full-length session as soon as I arrived. He began this hour with the remark, "You don't know much about the mechanics of a car. (His perception was accurate). I used to idealize you so much that I thought you knew everything. But I feel comfortable now bringing you down to human size." Recalling that I had called him "Dr. Albert" on the phone, he said, "That was formal. I felt strange that after so many years we still refer to each other with formality." I made no comment.

Dr. Albert then told of having made a speech to a group on the previous day. He had felt a tightness in his chest at first, but it disappeared as soon as he began speaking. His speech was generally well received, although he noted that some colleagues "took some swings at me." "I handled that okay," he said. "I gave them the same." He laughed. "Nobody chopped off my head, and I didn't chop off anybody else's." He then returned to his direct curiosity about me, asking if I were married and where I lived. I knew that he realized I would not answer such questions, and his tone was humorous and friendly. He told me that his brother was to visit him that night and that they planned to watch a basketball game together.

It was January 29 before we got back together again. He came to his hour with three bandages on one hand. Half laughing, half frustrated, he said that on the last day of our separation he had managed to cut or mash his fingers. He had been aware of irritation that day, and he knew that his "accident" had some relation to his trying to tell me something about the separation. He had mutilated himself to get attention from the mother/analyst. But what was more important, at his meeting he had triumphed further over the "Young Turks"; his "self-castration" pattern had returned in a modest way to ward off retaliation from the Turkish analyst.

As he thought about his new house, into which he expected to move within a few months, a mental image of the stream bordering the property kept coming to his attention. He wanted to dam it and generate electricity by means of a hydroelectric generator. He seemed obsessed with this plan. "I don't know why," he said, "but thinking about generating my own electricity reminds me of a kid trying to learn to walk." I told him I understood his desire to be self-reliant and indicated that this wish might in fact have been reactivated by the recent separation between us.

Dr. Albert gave exaggerated attention during his next hour to his observation of his psychic processes. For example, when on his way home from a skiing excursion on which he had performed well, he saw a police car. The sight gave him palpitations briefly, until it occurred to him that he was expecting punishment (a ticket) for his success. He could now find this reaction amusing.

He spoke of how his divorce was the best thing that had ever happened to him and wanted me to attend his wedding as the ghost of his father. He had taken from his mother's basement a desk his paternal grandfather had made and planned to put it in his new house. "I feel proud of my father's background now. Taking the desk is an attempt to integrate my father's background into my life. There are pencil marks in one of the drawers, and I am not going to erase them," he said.

In spite of his feeling so well and continuing to speak of terminating his analysis, Dr. Albert told me at the end of the session that although he did feel really well during the day and in the evening, when it came to be 10:30 or 11 at night, he would recall that it was at this time that his mother had played "musical beds." "The greedy little king takes over," he said, and he confided that it was then he felt the need for a drink. I interpreted that he still seemed to need a link to his mother by drinking, just in case he needed to retreat to her.

Early in February, he bought a diamond for Jane and called his mother to tell her about it. Her remark that "your father never bought me a diamond" gave him "a twinge in my heart." The thought of going out and buying his mother a diamond also occurred to him. He was aware that this was connected with his fear of her retaliation for leaving her. He reported that he had been invited to apply for a job opening in another city. This had produced "a peculiar feeling of freedom," and he said, "In my analysis I built a model airplane; now I want to take it out and see if it will fly." Associations to this analogy once more disclosed that although his father had wanted to become a pilot and leave the small town in which the family lived, Dr. Albert's mother had kept her husband there. The possibility of a new position in a large city apparently reactivated in Dr. Albert's mind the drama his parents had played out. The peculiar feeling he had reminded him of how he had felt in his dream about Dr. Lawrence. He now knew that this dream had something to do with his bringing back his dead father, integrating him in his mind, and then letting him die again. "The hallway in which Dr. Lawrence was walking now reminds me of a wind tunnel," he added. "As if I built a model airplane and tested it in the tunnel to see if it would fly." He went on, "I want to get out from under the domination of my mother. I want to be strong. I am really asking you, 'Is my eye going to be okay?' 'Can I give a speech at a big meeting?' 'Can I tell people things I know will piss them off?'" Since I said nothing, he answered his own questions in the affirmative.

After a brief silence, he spoke of his anxiety about surpassing his father, being "unlike him, able to leave the little town and my mother's influence." He went on, "Partly I know it is all right to surpass my father and fall short of my mother's ideals, but I partly believe that more analytic work needs to be done on this." He fell silent and then began to show interest again in my room, my furniture, my painting. He then reported feeling as though he were putting together a jigsaw puzzle and approaching completion of the task.

On February 6, he reported calling on the phone a woman who owned the property on the other side of the creek from his new building site. He asked Mrs. Noble (whose name made her symbolically powerful) if he could buy an acre adjoining the creek and if she would allow him to dam the creek for a pond. Her reply, generally negative, seemed rude to him. "Here is a woman fending me off!" he cried. His wish to acquire a hydroelectric generator according to his plan not only seemed to symbolize self-reliance to him but also identification with the good, athletic father. He kept imagining fishing in the pond as he had done with his father and ice skating on it in the winter. I told him that he was reliving the experience of being prevented by women (his mother/Mrs. Noble) from identifying with his father, who went fishing and ice skating and always seemed so strong. My words made him very sad. He kept saying, "Yeah! yeah!" and was as motionless as though he were hypnotized before reporting daydreams of revenge against Mrs. Noble. He fantasied hiring a lawyer and taking her to court, for example. I said nothing, and in his fury at Mrs. Noble he blurted out that he suddenly felt irritated with me. I was like a certain ski instructor who failed to give practical instructions. I told him that he wanted me to be a strong father who would help him to tame "noble women" like the Duchess of Windsor or the daughter of a Spanish nobleman his mother was once thought to be.

Screaming, he referred to powerful women: "If you get angry, they don't like you. You pay dues every time you get angry. I have so much anger toward this—this—*lady*!" He spat out the final word. There was a reaction formation in his suddenly making this woman a "lady." "A lady?" I asked, and he shouted back, "A bitch! A bitch!"

He said that Mrs. Noble owned hundreds of acres next to his property. He felt like David facing Goliath. "But David won!" I exclaimed. "He had a gimmick, a slingshot," he replied. He suddenly felt that his slingshot (his penis) had been taken away; his toe was cut off. His body became flaccid on the couch, and he reported a fantasy of breaking his leg while skiing. Throughout this experience he was able, however, to observe that he was feeling castrated (or self-castrated) before a powerful woman. He whispered that he no longer needed to feel castrated, and the session came to a close.

Dr. Albert reported in beginning his next hour that Dr. Sanders, one of his superiors, had regarded with favor one of his requests for more professional equipment. He added, "I had nothing to drink last night!" Then he asked, "What do people do when they get mad?" I felt that he might be telling me that by refraining from drink he was separating himself from the image of the mother of his childhood and that it was possible to be angry at it. Instead of drinking on the previous night, he had kept playing with a fantasy about Mrs. Noble in which he was a wealthy man at an auction where she was bidding for a picture. In his fantasy he overbid her, took the picture, and then threw it on a bonfire. "My getting even with her in my fantasy was an eye-for-an-eye thing," he said. I repeated, "eye-for-an-eye thing" and he cried "I knew you would catch that!" He went on to describe how, in a prison riot recently in the news, some prisoners cut out the eyes as well as the genitals of their opponents. Somehow, genitals and eyes were linked; he was, in a sense, desirous of recovering his eye/penis from a powerful woman. He continued with his association and talked about how some primitive people poked out the eyes of the dead so they would not be followed by their gaze. It seemed to me that his fantasy included elements of being protected from his dead father.

In his fantasy, after buying the painting he went up to Mrs. Noble and reported his purchase to hurt her for refusing to let him make his pond. Then he took out his pocket knife, shredded the picture, and burned the shreds. I reminded him that the injury to his eye (brow) at the age of 4 possibly had been accomplished with a pocket knife. I asked him if he were telling me that if a powerful woman tried to cut off his balls, he would do the same to her, as his fantasy indicated. He said "Yes!" with glee and went on about how the picture was a dark one with an ornate, nicked frame. He was describing a "super vagina."

In reality, in his basement at home he had a copy of an El Greco painting of a red-robed prelate of Madrid holding out one hand as though expecting a gift. Someone had once said that Dr. Albert resembled the subject of this painting, save for his odd mustache, and he secretly cherished the idea of having some association with the Spaniard. The painting he bought in his fantasy had some connection with this picture; perhaps it was the same. I urged him to associate to his desire in his fantasy to be rid of the painting while watching the frustration on

Mrs. Noble's face. "I think Mrs. Noble is a Spanish noblewoman in my mind," he said. "By fostering the myth that she was the daughter of a Spanish duke, my mother gave me this nobility crap. I guess in my fantasy I am rebelling against it."

Dr. Albert fell silent and then said that the hydroelectric generator he wanted for his pond—if he ever built it—was "the nearest thing to a perpetual motion machine." He went into detail about how water goes through a tube and then works on certain movable parts to create pressure and energy. "I'll put it on my side of the creek," he cried. "It is like a pulse. I will make noise and disturb Mrs. Noble!" I felt he was describing a big, self-reliant, self-sufficient penis. "Mrs. Noble will come to see what is making the noise. She will see my machine, but it is on my side of the creek so she can't do a thing about it!. I'll fuck her!"

He thought silently for a moment. "I am as obsessed with building this pond as Don Quixote was with his windmills," he commented and then referred again to Mrs. Noble's first name, which he considered rather regal. He called her "a queen." "The queen has power, but the king has power, too," he observed.

His mind turned to a film called *The King of Hearts,* in which the hero hid from the enemy in an asylum, only to realize when the time came for him to leave that people on the outside were insane, while inmates of the asylum were not. This realization led him back to the institution. "I am getting out now and looking around, finding out that people are people with their own faults and weaknesses. But even I know that I feel the lack of an instrument to deal with the powerful," he declared. I suggested that he was again presenting himself as one castrated. At this, he told me that he had again seen Dr. Sanders embrace a young woman in his office. There had been rumors of an extramarital relationship between this man and his laboratory assistant, who had been working at the time for Dr. Albert also, during the maternity leave of his regular assistant. What Dr. Albert had seen confirmed his suspicions. "He's fucking around with the laboratory assistant," he screamed. "What can I do about it?" I asked. "A man and a woman are making love, and the little boy doesn't know what to make of it." Dr. Albert laughed nervously at this and went on, "If I tell my superior that I know what is going on, then he can cut off the money coming to me!" Quickly he caught himself. "*Cut off!* Good old term!" His nervous laughter increased. When he finished, he added that he wanted me to know that he was learning to protect himself. He reminded me that he had recently bypassed the superior who had once intimidated him, going to one even higher in the hospital hierarchy to discuss his salary.

Dr. Albert spoke of how another laboratory assistant had once told him that as small children she and her siblings had secretly watched their parents having sexual intercourse. He kept talking about sexual organs, how they had been great mysteries to him as a child, although he might have known more about them than he realized since his perceptions of them had appeared in a picture frame of his fantasy as a "super vagina."

When on the following day he attended a lecture on psychosomatic disorders, he thought about his own somatic responses, to psychological situations, especially his allergies. He wanted me to know that he felt his allergies were gone. "I am not taking any more allergy pills, you know!" he insisted.

The next day he played mental games while driving to my office. He began wondering about the sex of the driver in the car just behind his, deciding that if it were a woman he would not be anxious. He was not afraid of a woman who might "sneak up on him," but if it were a man he might be anxious. Then he wondered why a male driver would awaken anxiety in him. He then associated a male driver with his superior who was allegedly having an affair, or with the one with whom he had discussed his salary. They were father figures. It occurred to him that they were after him to learn his secret, which was his four-times-weekly rendezvous with me. He thought that he and I were having a secret affair that would be revealed. The notion of a sexual connection between us, and his speaking of such a possibility, embarrassed him. I said that what had come to his mind was a new version of his childhood fantasies and expectations. He was having a "secret affair" with his mother when she came to his bed at night; he feared lest his father find out about his "secret"—one like the secret he had wanted to find out from the parental bedroom—and had found out about in the office of Dr. Sanders. When he remained silent for some time, I thought he was busy assimilating what we had just discussed.

Dr. Albert then said that an image of a telephone book had come into his mind. This reminded him of household addresses, and he said he still had no idea where I lived, but he could find out "my secret" by looking into the telephone book. Reference to his interest in looking into "my territory" made him very anxious, and he changed the subject quickly, displacing my image onto another psychiatrist, not one of the field's best representatives, whom he had encountered at a meeting, sensing his inferior quality. When he belittled this man, I told him that he seemed to be interested in different Goliaths and their strength. Even an opponent he considered weak seemed to him a possible danger.

The telephone book in his mind's eye was now an old Sears, Roebuck catalogue, in which there was a device for gelding boars. He went on to tell how a boar's legs are caught and held before the testicles are removed. "Gelding makes the pig *fatter*," he said, emphasizing the word to remind me that he had been a fat child. "I thought you would like to hear that," he added between laughter and anxiety. "I am castrated by Mrs. Noble!" Then he flexed his muscles and mumbled, "Old bitch, Mrs. Noble!"

Dr. Albert fell into a long silence. I noticed that his mood was somber. "Today is my father's birthday," he declared, "and he is dead." He went on to describe in detail one night when he and his sister had sat up all night discussing their childhood, with particular reference to their father. He had realized then how much more his sister could recall and to what an extent he had repressed his own memories. "There are ways of remembering," I commented. He agreed and said that he had learned much about his childhood during his analysis. Since the greedy small king still appeared at night, he said that "I still have a dissociated core. In some respects I am still Dr. Jekyll and Mr. Hyde. I have learned so much, but I still don't take the full responsibility of integrating fully all that I'm learning."

He fell silent again. The memory of his father's death reminded him of the burial of his toe, and he went into great detail once again about this childhood accident. He recalled that because of the spinal block given while his toe was being treated, he could not keep his foot from sliding off the table; nor could he feel it. "I felt as though my body were cut in two," he said. His voice fell to a murmur, as though he were reliving the event. He remembered that on his return from the hospital, a minister had told him that it was God's will that his toe be buried. He never found out where it had been buried, and he kept a mental image that the minister had buried it "in our back yard, like the dogs I buried there."

Listening to him speak of his "dissociated core" and his recollection of his body feeling "cut in two," I told him that he had been dividing himself into a daytime self, one already damaged and castrated, and into a pre-castrated self—the greedy little king trying to achieve union with his mother by oral means. I acknowledged that he had been trying to change all this in recent months. My remarks made a great impression on him, and he reported feeling as though a weight had been lifted from his shoulders.

He said something about George Washington's supposedly wooden teeth, about which he had seen something on television, and I suggested that the thought of detachable teeth had come to mind because as a child he may have thought of eyes and penises (and, later, toes) as detachable. I repeated my interpretation, more completely this time. I emphasized that he could divide himself and, for example, behave during the day as though his body parts were already removed and their loss no longer an imminent threat. Nonetheless, he could secretly fantasize the retrieval of his eye, his penis, and his toe when he regressed from confronting the castrating father to the presence of the nurturing mother (as when he drank in the evening). He agreed. "This may be so, because when I drink I make love better; I am more potent." To this I said, "You activate the fantasy, and act as though you had secretly recovered your detachable penis." He looked thoughtful and replied, "The next thing you'll tell me is that I can be as potent when I don't drink as when I do." He smiled broadly. "That will be neat," he commented.

Forming a Neurocrest

The Week of February 11

After the session of February 8, Dr. Albert seemed ready to move toward further integration of himself and to surrender the fantasy of a detachable penis in favor of possessing a penis permanently, one that could stand up to any threat of castration. On the night of February 9, a Saturday, he had a dream he reported to me on Monday. Some of the dream's day residue referred to his concern over some sagging plaster in the ceiling of his basement. "In my dream, I saw a white ceiling with a big bulge," he said. "It was a very pronounced bulge, producing a concavity. I knew that something like a wood stove was in it." He recalled how Brownie's house had had wood-burning stoves with something primitive about them. He said that he thought that the dream represented something primitive and earthy, "something coming out of my primordial mud." Before having this dream, he had attended a conference at the local university on *The Origins of the Earth,* which had included a geologist, a physicist, and a nuclear biologist on the panel. They had spoken of how primal elements form and had referred to the forming of a flower, for example. He had thought of dandelions and roses as he listened to them, and then of carnations and of a daisy. He felt as though he were experimenting with new flowers, enlarging his world. In his musings he thought of how, in Shaw's play *My Fair Lady,* Henry Higgins turned the flowerseller, Liza Doolittle, into a lady. It seemed I was Henry Higgins, he was Liza, and the psychoanalysis was bringing about the transformation.

After the conference, Dr. Albert had gone with Jane to a restaurant, where the sight of an older couple led him to wonder if they might be Mr. and Mrs. Noble, whom he had never actually met. He felt angry at them and then sensed a separation from them. After all, he could still build his pond without help from Mrs. Noble. His associations indicated that the couple represented me; he had wanted me to give him many things—advice, for example—just as he wanted Mrs. Noble to give him the opportunity to buy part of her land. He was irritated with me because I gave him no answers but left things open-ended and made him work to discover things and take the responsibility for his acts. It occurred to him that the boundary between his land and Mrs. Noble's was clear and that this really meant he was separated from the powerful woman.

Dr. Albert told me that the bulge he had seen in his dream reminded him of a pregnant woman's belly. As he lay on the couch, he gazed at the ceiling. Although the surface was not smooth, in his dream he had seen a ceiling as smooth and white as the skin of a pregnant woman. The shape of the bulge and the stove-like object it contained reminded him of pictures in an embryology textbook. The conference on the earth's origin had stimulated him to dream about "the formation of a neurocrest." He reminded me that in an embryo it is the neurocrest that becomes the spinal cord: he was giving birth to his backbone. When he realized this, he felt pain in his spine and said, half jokingly, "My forming neurocrest is hurting me." I joined in his delight by suggesting that he was having growing pains, thinking to myself that the dream marked another milestone in his analysis.

After being silent for a while, he reported that he was wondering about inviting Mamie's mother to his wedding. "I decided *not* to invite her, but separating myself from a powerful woman from whom I used to want something is a hard thing to do." He spoke of fantasies of getting money from his ex-mother-in-law, property from Mrs. Noble, or advice from the woman/analyst. "I am back to square one. I see that I need a strong father image to help me separate from powerful women. I have been involved in this illusion for a long time now, but now I see it clearly. I see that it is my responsibility to find a solution to it."

Dr. Albert symbolically conveyed to me at the start of his next session, on February 12, that he was working on his solution. If he were to identify with a strong father/analyst and make his functions his own, he could then conduct himself in the world depending on his own backbone. He seemed very animated at this session. As soon as he lay on the couch, he said that he wanted to report a dream which in turn reminded him of another he had dreamt earlier the same night. Both were connected with his bulge-in-the-ceiling dream, and he realized now that all three were set in the same geographical location. In the first two dreams, he saw houses built near water, and he knew that the ceiling in his third dream had some connection with them. It was as though he had seen nothing but a ceiling at first but was now, in his dreams, engaged in building whole houses. The geographical site reminded him of what he had seen in the French Quarter in New Orleans, but he knew that the houses were in some foreign country, perhaps on an island.

His first dream featured a festival like Mardi Gras. He passed through streets lined with houses of adobe, covered with plaster painted white. They seemed Spanish or Oriental. Jane was with him. He looked for a shoe store, and although he always tried a number of shoes before buying in real life, in the dream he knew exactly what he wanted. But he was presented with nothing that suited him; the shoes were odd looking and the wrong size. When a pair of the correct size was finally brought, the shoes had high heels, higher than those on a woman's shoe. The shoe was made of fuzzy cloth, and even while dreaming, Dr. Albert sensed that it represented half-male and half-female genitalia. The salesman assured Dr. Albert that he would be comfortable with these shoes and should try them on. As he did so, he remembered how it had felt to be a small boy trying on his mother's shoes and walking in them. He thought he would look silly in the shoes, but Jane and the salesman offered reassurance. He felt, however, that high heels were bad for the wearer and was uneasy about their green and blue color. He decided to ask for Hush Puppies instead, but the dream ended.

After recounting this, Dr. Albert related the dream he had had earlier, in which he also had seen a large number of painted adobe houses built around a bay. He and Jane were renovating one, and he thought in his dream that he had built a "white city." He felt happy about the house he was working on with Jane; it was spacious, many-windowed, and full of sunshine, ideal for their life together. He declared that all three of his dreams were connected and dealt with whiteness, airiness, sunshine, and the feel of a foreign place. While dreaming them, he had had a keen awareness of everything around him.

The sun was shining in my office as he spoke. Part of the couch was in direct sunlight. Both Dr. Albert and his father had worked to build (or rebuild) a sun porch; it will be remembered that during our first separation after he began analysis, my patient had spent much time repairing Daddy Doc's sun porch, and had, indeed, dreamed about this activity. At the time he reported this dream, the interpretation of it focused on his attempt to "undo" and "redo" his inner world (represented by the family sun porch) without help from his analyst. It had always interested me that my new offices had been contrived from sun porches, but he had never connected this circumstance with any psychological significance until now, when he connected my ample and sunny office with the houses in his dream. "I am in a sunny room, and you are a foreigner and an islander," he commented. The notion that the houses in the dream were Spanish connected with his mother's story of being of noble Spanish blood. But now he thought of the houses as Turkish or Cypriot, since he (correctly) imagined my homeland as a sunny place with many white houses. Just as the shoe had been half female and half male, the houses were half mother and half me. He felt embarrassed to realize this. "The color of the shoes reminded me of Turkish rugs," he said, going on to declare that he was developing a neurocrest, a backbone, a penis, but that he was still neither fully of one sex nor the other, but had a sexual organ halfway between a clitoris and a penis. He had rejected the sexually ambiguous shoes offered him in his dream, demanding Hush Puppies instead, as though he were keeping his maleness "hush-hush" in order not to invite castration or danger. His association with *puppy* later would become clear when he recalled the dog he had had in childhood who had eaten his feces.

Dr. Albert would identify more with me in order to tame the mother within himself, but I was a foreigner and he still had uncomfortable feelings about foreigners. He could disclose for the first time now, he said, that he had secretly been a bigot and a hypocrite. I told him that he wanted to change a terrible Turk to a sunny one but needed to trust me more.

He continued telling me that his dreams might represent new integration and inner comfort, in spite of his embarrassment that his shoes were not yet fully male shoes. The prevailing whiteness in his dreams unrepressed memories of dreams he had had as a very small child, dreams of infinite white plains on which pinkish balls rolled toward him. These had been terrifying, repeating dreams. I interpreted that it was likely that the white plains had represented his mother's bosom as he lay nursing on her lap, looking up. I suggested that the pinkish balls were her nipples. He seemed to have had some anxiety at nursing; as an older child, he had dreamed of being crushed by one of his mother's nipples whenever his relationship with her became strained. This interpretation made sense to him, and he said, "In my early childhood, the white plains were so flat." Then he added, "But in my new dream, I made the whiteness three-dimensional. I am so enthusiastic, creating sunshine, and openness, and new forms!"

After being silent for a while, Dr. Albert offered more associations to the bulge in the ceiling. The stove in it had ashes that reminded him of feces; the bulge now resembled a toilet bowl. Once more he recalled his mother's scolding the dog who ate Chris's feces. He had a mental image of himself as he was then, standing by a bedpost and scarcely reaching the height of the counterpane. He felt that his mother was reprimanding him, too, rejecting his "production" as she did. Now he was making a similar "production" in the bulge to see what I would do with it.

He was still cautious, however, about trying to put things together. One association to the houses in his dreams referred to the film *Black Orpheus*. In one scene of the film, someone was climbing up a stairwell while a festival was celebrated in the streets outside. He thought he was "climbing up" to the top, i.e., he had been called by Dick, a man important in his profession, to inquire if he would be interested in a position as director of the division of his medical specialty in another city, a position that would mean professional advancement. In *Black Orpheus,* however, the end had been death. Dr. Albert asked himself if he would be castrated if he went to the top; would his newly developed neurocrest be destroyed? Why didn't I tell him what would happen? Would I give him guarantees?

Dr. Albert suddenly began thinking about the successful conclusion of his analysis and the possibility of moving away, saying, "This still puts me in a bad mood. The idea of separation still disturbs me. Even Jane can see changes in me whenever you and I are separated, even briefly." He insisted that I tell him when his analysis would terminate, crying, "When the fuck will I finish my analysis? Aren't all these changes in me enough? What do you expect me to do—actually grow a penis or develop wings?"

He fell silent and then commented that the Turks and Greeks were still fighting in Cyprus. "There is hostility there," he commented. "After all, I may still be a terrible Turk," I remarked. "No, you are not," he said. "But you have the potential of being one." He then spoke of my position as director of the hospital where my office is located: "You are the director here, so you must be doing some nasty things." I asked him to explain, and he told me that when Dick called to speak of the possibility of giving him a directorship, he had said that if Dr. Albert became the director, he would have to "cut down a few people." Dr. Albert wanted to identify with me and tame the mother he retained in himself, but such identification might mean that he had to be aggressive, and displays of aggression could invite retaliation. His body became flaccid, and I noted this. This pose was his way of castrating himself; it was a familiar maneuver that he could observe, understand, feel—and even change. The session ended.

Dr. Albert opened the next hour with a new dream. "I had a scar on one of my fingers," he said. "As if a nail had been drilled through it and then removed. The wound healed; the hole was sealed. Then suddenly my finger began to bleed from the scar tissue." His association was to feminizing himself defensively and to the other occasions when he had bled from injuries to his eye and toe. It was as though in his youth he had been crucified, and now this wound reopened in analysis. During the last few days, something had been going on; he had seemed to be reviewing old conflicts and old symptoms. His eyes had been feeling sticky, and he had even had a sneezing attack.

On the previous day, while shopping in a department store, he had come upon a display of small, fuzzy, toy black panthers, and he wondered now if he were responding to these black panthers as well as to his dreams and associations of the previous day. Growing up would still mean that he would need to be able to express aggression and to deal with expectations of retaliation. The Mardi Gras part of one of his dreams now reminded him of his dream of the black hand that had killed a man with a karate chop, and the placing of the dead body in a coffin. He was about to have another talk with his chief of service, and he was determined to be very assertive in this interview.

After a moment's silence, Dr. Albert asked if I were married. I did not reply. "I know you are a director here," he said. "And I see your award for teaching. I used to think you would sail me through psychoanalysis, but I don't know you." I said nothing. "Sometimes," he went on, "I think you see things I don't see even when they are right in front of me. Where am I? Tell me what is in front of me that I don't see." I told him he was behaving as though he were blind in order to keep me as his caretaking mother and at the same time making me his father to keep from confronting him. Perhaps he was not really blind to what was *in front* of him. "Oh Christ! My penis!" he said as the hour ended.

During the last session of the week, Dr. Albert began the hour with an account of a conflict with a "foreign physician" on staff in his hospital. He had asked this man for some medical data, but the foreigner acted "as though he were paranoid." "He actually thought," said Dr. Albert, "that I was going to steal his research data and use it as though it were my own." Then Dr. Albert asked if I were paranoid. I told him he wanted me to be a strong father with whom he could identify, and I suggested that he might perceive identification with me as robbing me of something—something like my penis—and that this might be making him anxious. I told him he was behaving as though it were possible for only one of us in the office to have a penis, as though there were no possibility that each of us could have one. I told him moreover that there was no requirement that his new neurocrest should become an aggressive Turkish saber, and at this he relaxed.

After a silence, Dr. Albert said that his mistrust of foreigners really should derive from his mistrust of his mother. Referring to the family myth about her birth, he said, "After all, my mother is the *original* foreigner," and went on to say that he wanted to visit the state agency that filed birth records to see if he could learn the truth about his mother's background. "I don't need to have windmills around," he added.

The Fourth Year

A Volcano Burns a House

Mid-February through February 23

The fourth year of Dr. Albert's analysis began with a bang. There was, in reality, a big fire, and this further ignited his psychological insights and hastened his working through of conflicts.

By mid-February, his interest in me as a person, a Turk uncontaminated with and untarnished by parental images, continued in an exaggerated way. He wanted to identify with me, but he needed to sort me out so that, unconsciously, he identified only with selected aspects of me. He seemed now to be more separated from the different representations of his mother and better able to face his oedipal father, even to compete with him. His old defenses still appeared, but he was able readily to observe and even alter his responses to anxiety.

On Monday, February 19, he missed his appointment with me, sending word that he could not come; the house in southern Maryland that had been Daddy Doc's and that Dr. Albert had renovated after beginning analysis was on fire. His message was that he had to go there to assess the damage to the building, part of which had been rented. At his next hour, Dr. Albert said nothing about the fire or the broken appointment but complained as he lay down on the couch that his trousers were too tight; they should have been size 38 but seemed to be size 36. I wondered if he were telling me that he was getting "too big for his britches" (with a bigger penis) or that he was getting fatter (feminizing himself), or sending both messages at once. But he gave no more attention to this subject and went on to report a dream about his need to deliver some urgent message. (It was an urgent message he had sent via Jane to account for missing his Monday hour). He dreamed that he was looking for a woman to deliver this message, and that he found one swimming in a lake, into which he jumped after shedding his clothes. He and the woman swam back to shore, and they went together into a bathhouse. While he dressed, he turned his back on the woman, leaning over to pull up his socks. When she asked him if he were pregnant, he replied, "I'm a boy!"

He identified the woman in the dream as Marietta Hartley, the actress then appearing in television commercials as the actor James Garner's girlfriend or wife. Dr. Albert had read recently that Garner's car had been struck by a car driven by a black man who beat him up in spite of the fact that the actor weighed 230 pounds and his assailant was small and puny. As Dr. Albert spoke of this, he recalled again the dream from his first year of analysis of a black hand smashing the knobs of drawers. He had then been renovating Daddy Doc's sun porch and his preoccupation with this enterprise had been interpreted to him as evidence of his resistance to analysis.

The lake in this dream reminded Dr. Albert of his later dream of building a "white city" of adobe houses on a lake shore. He said he was building a city for himself but that meanwhile his own house, formerly Daddy Doc's, had in reality been damaged by fire. This was his first reference to the fire, and he laughed nervously, recalling that I had long ago told him that in renovating this house he was expressing an attempt to do his own analysis instead of working with me on it.

His mother had called at 7 a.m. on Monday to give him the news of the fire. He had started crying because of his investment in this house, but he claimed that he had had a premonition that one day the house would burn. By the time he arrived on the scene some hours later, the fire had been extinguished, but on the drive there he had thought of himself as "waiting for the axe to fall"—the fire to occur—and felt that the worst had indeed happened and that it was all over. He thought on the couch about his father, who had been a volunteer firefighter; as a child awakened by the sound of fire sirens, he had been anxious when his father got up and dressed to go to a fire.

Dr. Albert had found the burned house seemingly standing in a lake because of the amount of water the firemen had used, and this recalled the lake in his dream. The fire had started in the attic and had shot so high into the sky at the entrance to the widow's walk on the roof that it had been seen fifteen miles away; it had looked like a volcano. At this point, Dr. Albert commented that, of course, I (Volkan) was the volcano. He emphasized that the widow's walk had not been destroyed in spite of the fierce fire; contrary to his expectation of the worst possible case, "The axe had fallen without causing too much damage" and without killing anyone. He felt that a "prophecy" had been fulfilled; he had spent his energy on the house during his first analytic year instead of spending it on his analysis, and I, the volcano, was getting even with him by my burning it. His feelings about this were mixed. He was irritated that I had burned his house, but he felt also that the fire had been a cleansing of his conflicts.

The image of the fire reminded Dr. Albert of a character in an episode of *Star Trek*, Gar, the fiery-eyed computer who governed the planet on which people had no gender, never aged, and lived without aggression. They were obliged, in what seemed to me to represent preoedipal childhood, to pay homage to and feed Gar if they wanted to continue in their benign state. The *Star Trek* story showed people from the starship *Enterprise* landing on Gar's planet and helping the natives to conquer the evil computer character. As soon as Gar was stripped of his powers, the people could develop gender, have sex, and display aggression—but at the same time to grow older. It should be remembered that one of the good characters in the series, Dr. Spock, came from the planet Vulcan (Volkan). It would seem that in identifying with the good analyst, my patient could tame the bad one!

I noted that *Gar* was the first part of the name *Garner,* and suggested that he was putting Gar, Garner, volcano, and Volkan together. Furthermore, I said that I, Garner, and Gar had power on the surface. If, as he thought, I had retaliated for his failure to invest in his analysis by burning his house down, he nonetheless was experiencing a feeling of relief. I told him that on a lower level he could tame Gar. A puny assailant could beat a strong man, as Garner's assailant had beaten him; and human beings can tame a powerful computer. I told him that this was his dream wish. He gets his punishment, but, on a lower level, he also triumphs over powerful figures. Recalling our recent talk about his "backbone," he said that he knew he had the backbone to stand up to Garner or Volkan.

It seemed to me that the fire, which Dr. Albert fantasied I had been responsible for, represented on one level parental intercourse. The volcano had shot up through an opening in the roof onto the widow's walk without causing great damage there. As the father I appeared ferocious, but I really did not cause irreparable harm, and I did not kill anyone. Certainly, the fire represented the fury of the analyst/father, the oedipal threat materialized; but now it was all over and he could handle the threat, survive confrontation with the oedipal father. Also, his oedipal wish to kill the father was gratified. The mother now was a "widow."

After moments of silence, Dr. Albert expressed curiosity about me, asking again if I were married, had children, etc. Receiving my noncommital answer, he stated that he now understood that his dream was suggesting that adversity was giving way to something better. Lead was turning into gold; although his house had been partly burned, he now knew that it would be better than before, better insulated and heated and structurally more sound. Likewise, he had been divorced but now anticipated a good marriage with Jane. He felt like a mushroom (a phallic symbol) springing up out of the mud, and this remark led him to tell me that Daddy Doc's wife *Brownie* had lived until her death in the house that ultimately became his, and that in his dream the lake was brown and muddy; he spoke of "coming out of the mud" and was reminded of how in his dream about the bathhouse he had not been embarrassed to declare himself "a boy." He was now being born as a boy, shedding his identification with his mother (the rejecting pregnant woman who was also his own "fat self"). He then recalled a male teacher who was fat enough to have seemed pregnant; he associated his own "fatness" with the image of this teacher.

Dr. Albert spoke rapidly during this hour, animated about grasping what his dream meant. He spoke of "running his mouth without stopping," and this reminded him of the sprinklers on my office ceiling. I felt that he was identifying with the sprinkler/analyst who can quench fires, and I told him so.

He began his session the next day with a dream in which he had been in Washington, D.C., pushing his little car by a concrete wall that was six by ten feet. (The couch is next to a concrete wall in my office.) He left his car there, and when he returned, he found a ticket charging him $89 for a long list of infractions spelled out on what looked like an IBM card. Surprised, he looked at the ticket a second time, only to see that he had been fined $892. A nearby policeman explained that his fine had been increased hour by hour. This seemed a reference to his analytic hours.

Dr. Albert's associations were that he might be getting retaliation for something he had done. Washington represents the Department of Justice, but it is not without corruption. The tenant in his burned house moved out because of the fire, and although he was sorry for the inconvenience this caused her, and for the loss of some of her belongings in the fire, he felt that he had not been to blame.

At this point, he stopped associating directly to the dream, and, pointing at some papers on my desk, asked if I were writing a book. He went on to say that a scientific paper of his had been published in a medical journal recently and that he had received a copy of the publication the previous day. The initials of his real name had been given incorrectly in the attribution, in a way that made his name suggest a horse. He said, "They made me a horse's ass." He then spoke of the mounted policemen in Washington, the locale of his dream; he had been told the horses wore some kind of diaper to contain their manure, and he commented that it would be quite a job to change those diapers. After a brief silence he returned to his dream and told me that the wall he saw in it reminded him of the Secretary of the United Nations, Kurt Waldheim, whom he associated with me. He then spoke of having run into the "foreign physician," who still thought Dr. Albert had designs on his research material, and of reassuring him that this was far from the truth.

Dr. Albert then began talking about the ticket he had been given in his dream, and that resembled an IBM punchcard. On the previous day he had in reality looked for his insurance cards, learning that he had misplaced some that resembled IBM cards. He thought that unless he found them he might not be able to get reimbursement for the fire's damage from his insurance company. He then spoke of the policeman in his dream, noting that he had been a short man with no resemblance to his analyst. However, he had kept *writing* tickets. At this point I reminded him that the foreign physician had suspected him of trying to steal the data he had gathered for his writings.

Dr. Albert told me that the policeman in the dream had definitely been black, and emphasized that his short stature and black complexion clearly differentiated him from the analyst. This reminded him of a presidential candidate's recently publicized ethnic joke and led him to insist that one should not have prejudice. He then became thoughtful and pondered whether he himself still held any prejudice about me, or about black people. He then noted that one should not have prejudice against the poor, and this reminded him of his recent increase in salary and led him to wonder if he made more money than I did. I told him then that he seemed to want to compare our situations, although the idea seemed to make him anxious. I suggested that he carry this discussion further.

Dr. Albert then began to speak of how he had been noticing that he attributed power to others. This led him to speak of the computer, Gar, and how a less powerful person might be able to win out in the end. He considered the number 892, noting that if the number 8 is turned around, it looks like two breasts. The number 9 is a penis with a bow. He could find no meaning for 2, but I suggested that it also might be breasts. Toward the end of the hour, after considerable give and take, I could summarize in the following schematic way what I understood had been going on between us: I had burned his house because he had given attention to it instead of to me; he had overcome Gar (the analyst) and was about to build a better house, in a sense saying, "I can now have my own backbone and I can stand up to you"; I was retaliating, and thus the foreigner, the black policeman, was making him a horse's ass; he defecates, saying that I should change his diapers; and the cycle continues as he expects further retaliation.

After I made these remarks, he shifted on the couch, placed his hands on his chest and looked like one dead. I referred to this, and he realized what he was doing. What came into his mind was a flood in a certain part of the country where people had been drowned. He disclosed that the flood had occurred in the place where he had recently been asked by "Dick" to be a candidate for director of a medical division, a proposal he was still considering. Again, the possibility of success was balanced with self-castration—lying as one dead. Realization of this made him say that he was aware of what he had done, but was also aware that he had a backbone.

Dr. Albert was a few minutes late for his next appointment, which fell on February 23. Since this was very unusual for him, I felt it might have something to do with his toying with the idea of being independent, but I did not speak of this to him. He reported feeling that he had mentally reconstructed and gazed at his "white city," which seemed formless now, as though he were seeing many bright colors in something like a revolving barber pole, multicolored and transparent. This visual image reminded him of going as a child to the barbershop in his home town and being embarrassed because his mother insisted on going with him. He had wanted his mother to leave him alone in a man's world, but he was afraid of the barber's cutting off his ear. This recollection made him uneasy, and his body shook a bit on the couch. Then he became calm and went into a silence that he broke by referring to his laboratory assistant. She recently had had a baby and was on maternity leave. (It will be recalled that his first sight of her infant had reminded him of the birth of his brother.) He now told me that on the night before he had the 892 dream, he had gone to see his laboratory assistant and her baby again, taking Jane and Pamela along. He thought the dream might have something to do with the newborn, and kept repeating, "8-9-2, 8-9-2" until he burst out, "Ate . . . mine . . . too!"

Becoming very anxious, Dr. Albert described an incident that had taken place when he was in college. He had been eating in a cafeteria with a glass of milk before him when a friend reached over, seized the glass, and drank the milk. This had made him furious. He was completely beside himself, although he could not understand why he was so angry. The milk was gone and would not come back. This was associated with his visit to the laboratory assistant, during which she had excused herself to breastfeed her infant. I told him that "ate mine, too" represented his feelings about his brother's birth. His brother had taken his milk away, and this had awakened murderous thoughts in him, led him to feel guilty, and to identify with his brother's sickliness to win his mother back, while at the same time he expected retaliation from his father. I suggested that he was now reviewing important events of his life in a way that we could easily see.

It no longer seemed to make Dr. Albert anxious to bring into his conscious awareness previously hidden conflicts and unacceptable impulses. He became very animated and said that he must really have identified with his brother's sickliness. He remembered rubbing the clinical thermometer on the bedding to elevate the reading so his mother would devote herself to him. He had begun doing this when his brother started nursery school and his mother would come to Chris's side if he were "sick." He confessed to having had a fleeting "death wish" for Jane and Pamela after visiting his laboratory assistant. Now he could easily understand that this was targeted at the baby, but momentarily had been transferred to his fiancee and his daughter.

The Basketball Games

February 25 to March 29

An ardent basketball fan, Dr. Albert attended every home game of the university team whose recent successes united the community in jubilance or whose losses united it in grief. I sensed that his fascination with the sport went considerably beyond the usual boosterism and indicated an interest in keeping alive the image of a strong father, a man who had been a basketball star himself.

The end of February found our team in a favorable position to compete in the three-day, out-of-town regional championship that followed the regular conference schedule. Dr. Albert brought to his session on February 25 two dreams about basketball games. In the first, he was a player, shooting baskets and scoring. His team was behind but was catching up. Although in his dream he did not consider himself as graceful as some players, he felt that he was doing his best. In his second dream, he was dressing in a bedroom to go to the game as a spectator when he found that his trousers were too big for him, and his socks were so enormous that they came up to his hips. (In due time I told him that the fact that his clothes were too large for him probably reflected unfinished business from his childhood, when adult clothes would have been outsized for him.) The next scene of this dream found him on a train, traveling to the game. Dr. Sanders and his wife were also on the train; according to his associations, they represented his parents. (It should be recalled that Dr. Albert had, seen Dr. Sanders in a compromising situation with a laboratory assistant some time earlier. He had mixed feelings about the older man, usually seeing him not as a strong, good father figure, but as an oedipal father who might retaliate against him.) In the dream, Dr. Albert was sitting next to a most beautiful woman, a figure that corresponded to the ideal woman in every way save for having one *black* tooth. He kissed her while the train rocked and shook.

Dr. Albert's remarks implied that these two dreams were in a sort of balance. In the first, he identified with a strong father and became successfully active, in a reflection of what he was trying at the time to do with his life; but in the second, he regressed to a time in his childhood when a frightening oedipal father still lurked. He had once again created his idealized woman, and he kissed her while the train rocked and shook in sexual symbolism, nonetheless merging her with an aspect of his frightening mother—her black tooth. This caused him to recall the black panther image of his mother, but he noted that the presence of *one* black tooth was much better than total contamination with blackness. He poured out memories of his early fear of trains; this fear dated from when he was 5. He spoke of his anxiety lest a villain like Charles Manson push him into the path of an oncoming train.

When we resumed our schedule after an interruption that permitted my attendance at a meeting, Dr. Albert fantasied that my absence had been due to attendance at the regional basketball championship games. "Only rich doctors go to championship games," he commented. As he often fell silent, I became aware of his envy and anger over being left behind like a rejected child. I did not tell him where I had gone, but waited to see what would develop. I recognized how much he had wanted to see the championship games, and how much he might feel left out if he truly thought I had seen them; he would feel once again like a child left at home by adults engaging in grownup sports. He sulked throughout the session.

At the next session, I heard that during my absence, he had visited his mother's house and found a box full of his high school mementoes and pictures of himself and his parents. Going over these, he had been particularly impressed with pictures of his father taken at a picnic; these pictures awakened warm feelings. I sensed that during my absence Dr. Albert had actively sought a representation of a strong father to compensate for my "rejection" of him.

When he came to his appointment on March 5, Dr. Albert could see me through the open door of my office, talking on the telephone. He entered and lay on the couch as I finished my conversation, watching me closely. When I sat in the chair behind the couch he then occupied, he reported a "weird thought"—the notion that his coming upon me engaged in this way was like coming upon his parents having sexual intercourse in their bedroom. "I'm not really upset," he explained quickly. "In fact, I feel that what I did—watching you standing up with a phone in your hand instead of sitting unseen behind the couch—is therapeutic." He went on to associate my holding a telephone in my hand with the father of his childhood, who had been in the habit of toying in a concentrated way with a curious item on his desk, a small wooden coffin in which there was the wooden figure of a man with a large penis and glans penis painted red; when the coffin was stood on end, the little man exhibited an erection.

As Dr. Albert spoke of this, I was reminded of his tale of the man buried on a hill, standing up, who represented a father figure able to watch over him in death. Dr. Albert's present association to his account, however, was his "discovery" that his father had disclosed an interest in sex by his preoccupation with the little wooden image. "Discovering this is somehow not scary now," he noted. "In fact, it has a therapeutic impact on me." He recalled again his mother's confiding in his sister her sexual hunger after she was widowed. His real "discovery" seemed to be that parents do have sex, after all, and that they belonged to each other. This insight helped to free him further to find his own woman and to possess her without fear, since his father had had his own and would not compete with him.

"I have recently come to understand," he added, "that sexuality is more than fucking. Holding hands, kissing, and cuddling are part of it." He told me delightedly that one night he and Jane took off their clothes and rolled in the snow in the privacy of their backyard. "I am allowing myself to do this, to hold hands with her, to be playful, and to have warmth in our lovemaking," he noted. "These are the fringe benefits of psychoanalysis." He went on to say that Jane had recently called her former husband to tell him she was getting married. Dr. Albert felt that she had by now completely severed this old relationship; he need no longer consider himself in competition with her ex-husband.

Dr. Albert spoke again of the possible termination of his analysis. As though fearful that I would announce the completion of his analysis, he quickly noted that during my recent absence from town he had felt it necessary every night to have a nightcap, that what he regarded as symptomatic still persisted. In discussing this, I used the term "bridge" in comparing his late-evening drinking with regression, or seeking a bridge with the mother of his childhood. As the session ended, he reported having an image of a "curved bridge." "It is breast-shaped, of course," he joked, "and surrounded by black fog." Quickly growing somber, he told me that he had taken his dog for a walk on the previous night and had been alarmed by a sound that suggested a black panther in his driveway. I knew that instead of insisting on my response about the termination of his analysis, he was answering himself by reporting the persistence of conflicts and their symptoms.

That night he saw me at a basketball game in which the university team would compete in a preliminary contest of the National Invitation Tournament. Although there were some 8,000 people in attendance, by some coincidence Dr. Albert, accompanied by two young girls I took to be Pamela and a friend, was seated almost directly in front of my family group. At our next session, he spoke of having seen me walking in the aisle before the game with a small boy he (correctly) took to be my son, although I did not confirm his assumption. He then had realized that I would no doubt be sitting directly behind him, and that I might be accompanied by my wife, but he could not bring himself to look back at where we were seated. "Do you have a wife?" he asked. "Why don't you tell me about yourself?" When I made no reply, he went on to report that seeing me at the game had reminded him of his father's having played basketball and that his image of a "curved bridge" reminded him of the persistence of his wish to keep up regressive contact with his mother.

Dr. Albert accused me of being "passive" when I failed to answer his personal questions. "I know something about you," he challenged. "I know, for example, that you are from Sicily!" I made the interpretation that his glimpse of me at the game had reactivated his oedipal fears, because of which he spoke of my birthplace as Sicily rather than Cyprus since Sicily suggested a frightening member of the Mafia. I also told him that he was displacing his own passivity onto me in his accusation. Indeed, it was his turning me into a bad, frightening father figure that made him passive and unable to look to see if I had a woman with me at the game.

The night following this session he took no nightcap but went to bed with visions of a bridge—a breast-shaped bridge. At the following session, he kept talking about finding out that Dr. Sanders had taken the laboratory assistant they still shared to another city on the excuse that the trip was required by a business meeting. Dr. Albert wondered at his preoccupation with this couple. He reported that his superior had failed to answer questions about a medical matter, and I called to his attention that he himself had used the same words on the previous day to accuse me of failing to communicate with him. He confided that it was still hard for him to be curious about me directly. After falling into a silence, he suddenly cried out, "What do you want me to say? Do you want me to make up stories? Tell you about ghosts and ghoulies *bumping in the night?*" I asked him to associate to "ghosts and ghoulies." "All right," he cried, "I am remembering and repeating my feelings about my mother and thoughts about her and my father and where I stand."

After a silence, Dr. Albert asked if I had tickets for the next basketball game soon to take place in our town. When I made no reply, he went on to say that he was interested in learning if I had a wife. It then became apparent that his anxiety about my marital status stemmed from the fact that he planned to take Jane to the game and felt I might steal her away from him if I had no wife. He seemed regressed. His voice changed, and his speech was slow as he reported feeling like a little child who wanted to possess his mother. He pictured his father with a cigarette in his mouth. Since his father had in reality died from lung cancer, I sensed that Dr. Albert was regressing not only to the longing to possess his mother, but to a reactivation of the death wish for his father.

Suddenly his mood altered, and he seemed very melancholic. In a choking voice, he recalled a Christmas morning of his childhood spent in a warm room with a hearth fire and Christmas presents. His father promised to buy him a sled if he would stop sucking his thumb. "I must have been between 6 and 8, and I was still sucking my thumb!" he said. "My father reached out to me and told me to be *active* and to leave my mother (my thumb-sucking) alone. Leaving off my thumb-sucking was the first thing I ever determined to do, and it was my father who directed me to do this. He bought me the sled."

I understood him to be saying that if the oedipal father were to put limits in a benign and loving way, he himself would at this point be able to stop "bridging" himself with his mother, and to stop competing for her with his father. His further associations indicated that he now wanted to be friendly with his father and even to identify with his good aspects. Memories of his father waxing Chris's sled and of Chris riding on it began to pour out. He spoke about wanting to repair the sled, which he thought was still in the basement of his mother's house; he wanted to take it to his new house and use it with his daughter. He wanted to do with her the enjoyable activities he and his father had shared. Then he began to speak of his growing ability to ski well. "From sledding to skiing," he mused. Since his father had not known how to ski, he felt on one hand that he was surpassing his father, and without anxiety; but on the other hand, he felt sad that his father was not alive to teach him to play tennis. He might outdo his father in skiing, but not in tennis. The situation was like that in which each of two men had his own woman and did not need to compete, since each excelled in a different sport.

Such resolutions of his oedipal problems were now more readily available to him, but they were not yet crystallized, and he was unable to remain in the "post-oedipal" state long enough to be considered no longer symptomatic. Situations symbolically representing oedipal stress could still make him regress to his oedipal struggles or even further back to his effort to find an idealized mother and bridge himself to her.

One night Dr. Albert tried to identify with his father's hortatory manner in telling him to stop sucking his thumb. He became unnecessarily testy with Pamela, who was not doing her homework. She did not respond as he had hoped, and he felt upset. "Fuck you, Volkan!" he thought and took a nightcap. When he came to his hour with me on Monday, March 10, he not only reported all this, but declared in a self-castrating, symbolic gesture that he had had no interest in sex for several days. There was to be a basketball game Monday night, and he said he was anxious at the idea that I might see him there with Jane. For the rest of the session, he played with a rather austere image of me he had evoked on the couch, and saw in a frame. I did not see him at the game that night. He reported that he had seen me sitting with two little boys, but no woman. He decided that I was divorced, and this made him anxious lest I, as oedipal father, steal Jane or kill him by pushing him into the path of a train. Throughout this session, he seemed extremely cautious in his choice of words and manner of utterance.

Presently Dr. Albert heard from the Internal Revenue Service that his tax return would be audited. He had no worry about its accuracy but regarded this scrutiny by authority as an expected punishment, and during the next two sessions he seemed to be awaiting the fall of my axe; I thought he awaited an attack from me, fearing that I would kill him to steal his woman. He was often silent and complained of one session as "the longest hour in my psychoanalysis." A week went by, and he saw me at another game. He was animated when he came to the session immediately after this and said, "Congratulations! You have a wife and kids." I did not tell him whether those accompanying me at the game were my family, but he was so firm in his assumption that they were that he continued to speak of a sense of being separated from me and a feeling of relief. On the previous day he had recovered his sled from his mother's house and taken it home. He planned to take it to the new house he, Jane, and Pamela would soon occupy.

It seems that he had seen me emerging from a restroom at the game, and this led him to recall how as a small boy he would look about him in restrooms to see the penises of adult men. This was a sort of self-castration, since he felt inferior; at the same time, he might have experienced a kind of narcissistic identification with men he considered superior. When he was in high school, Dr. Albert had found a book describing penises in terms of national differences; it maintained that whereas Americans and the English had short penises, those of Arabs were long. Nothing had been noted about Turkish penises, but it occurred to him that they might resemble the Arabian ones.

At his next session, he thought of me as Charles Manson sitting behind him as he lay on the couch, and the idea upset him. The university's basketball team was now one of the finalists in competition for a national championship, and Dr. Albert began comparing the teams involved. In the midst of this, he recalled having had a professor named Napier who had had hair like mine. He recalled that once a slip of the tongue had led Dr. Albert to call him "Rapier." This man had been seen as godlike by his students, who had once joked on seeing the man leave a restroom, "He is not *really* a god; he needs to pee!" Dr. Albert said of me, "You are not a god either; *you* needed to pee!" Nonetheless, I knew that in his eyes I could still be a "rapier" (the rapist), a sword, and rape him.

That night he sat up far into the night to watch the university's team win the National Invitation Tournament championship. Then he dreamed of an acquaintance he thought of as "a little kid," seeing him make a chemical mixture out of which he made fibers, string, and then yarn. The diameter of the string was about one millimeter, but its length was five or six feet. Dr. Albert was ready to make his own interpretation of this: the man in the dream represented himself as a child developing a very thin, long penis, like the one he thought his Turkish analyst had. The yarn reminded him of Turkish rugs. He concluded that he was not only identifying with me, but was surpassing me by making his penis five or six feet long. The phrase "spinning a yarn" came into his mind, along with "spinning a tale." This homonym let him believe that developing a "tail" represented his development of a backbone, a penis, but "spinning a yarn (or tale)" also reflected his anxiety at competing with or surpassing me. It was as though he were saying that the idea of his having a longer penis than mine was a "tale" rather than reality. Thus he protected himself from my retaliation for his competitive feelings.

Dr. Albert thought the dream was connected to the basketball game and its result. Throughout the game he had thought of his father and me. He had read on the previous day of a snake race in California, in which a garter snake (the name recalled Gar and Garner) finished first, and two snake owners were bitten. The real-life basketball competition reminded him of this, and the string in his dream was like the snakes. "Volkan, I expect you'll say snakes are also penises," he added. "Freud missed the boat, though! Snakes are not dangerous; vaginas are!" When I made no reply, he cried, "Should I compare everything about you with everything about myself in order to finish my analysis? Should I compare our women, our kids, our fish, our dogs? Maybe you have an elephant in your back yard. How do I find out what else you have so I can compare my things with yours?" I reminded him that an elephant's tusk might be said to resemble a penis, and that he might still be referring to the relative size of our penises.

He went into a silence that seemed comfortable. Then he broke it by wondering aloud how I raise my children. I replied that he might be wondering if I felt that I was "raising" him, too, from childhood to manhood. He protested that he was already a man and recalled that during his time at college he had dated little, but had once thought of dating a girl with the intention of bedding her. After much hesitation, he had asked his father what kind of condom to buy and had been surprised that his father advised him without anger, so that he had felt himself one man talking to another.

Dr. Albert's laboratory assistant returned to work from maternity leave in the third week of March, and he no longer needed the services of the woman with whom Dr. Sanders allegedly was having an affair. This removed one occasion for competition. As the move to his new house with Jane and Pamela approached, this "success" evoked new material for examination in analysis. He continued to be curious about where I live and wondered, for example, if my house were grander than his.

He began his session on March 26 by saying that he was going to see a new dentist that day, his former dentist having left town. He was afraid of dentists and afraid of their drills. He said his teeth were "tender," but in a slip of the tongue, he used the word "cinder" instead. When I called this to his attention, he began talking about being burned and a burning bush. God had spoken to Moses from a burning bush. Dr. Albert realized that he had recently made a number of references to the Bible. He had gone through a religious phase as a fat little boy of 13 and had been baptized. He recalled this with embarrassment, since he had worn a shroud and been dipped three times into water. Later he concluded, referring to the behavior patterns of some religious people he knew, that Baptists are hypocrites. He thought the reason for his not having been baptized earlier was that his father did not attend church, although his mother's side of the family had been extremely and rigidly religious. Brownie, for example, was so rigid she thought Jews and Catholics would go to hell.

I told him that I (fire-volcano) had burned Brownie's house. He had expected this; it had been prophesied, and after it had happened, he had felt relief. After all, I was not the most ferocious volcano; I had not burned the house to the ground. Once he experienced my power, he was not overwhelmed. Now he was about to move into a new house and to be successful. Therefore he remained cautious; I might burn his new house unless he gave in in competition with the analyst (God). But this prospect in turn made him feel silent rage.

Dr. Albert was well aware of being anxious. He had been unable to sleep the night before. His luck had recently been bad. Besides having trouble with the new house that involved confrontations with the contractor, he had to face the dentist. A representative of a drug company was coming on the following day to check his use of a certain drug, and the IRS examination of his tax return was still pending. But he assured me that he was now responding in a new way to all these external problems, and no longer felt, as he had in the past, that he was being attacked personally.

He talked more about how, at age 13, he had been stuck between going back to the mother and feminizing himself by getting fat, or turning toward the father, expecting punishment for doing so. Then, having to give each his due, he had cut off his toe.

Dr. Albert spoke of the move to his new house as being, in his perception, a move from adolescence into adulthood. Although his new house was in a neighborhood that represented a social advance, he was nostalgic for the one he was leaving. The move from a "starter" neighborhood into an "established" one symbolically represented mov-

ing into adult success from childhood. He mentioned again the story of
Gar, where the inhabitants moved from childhood to adulthood after the
loss of the magic power that depended on blandness and immunity. He
claimed he had felt no older than 20 for the past fifteen years and knew
only by the calendar that he was in fact in his mid-thirties. He now felt
his true age, although he realized that arriving at adulthood means
facing death. Since his father had not lived beyond his mid-fifties, he
worried about dying himself, perhaps even before he could psychologically attain adulthood, which was symbolized by the termination of his
analysis. His professional experience indicated that psychological expectations have much to do with people giving up and dying, and he did
not want to die young. Later, he said that now that he could face the
reality of death, he had come to believe that the notion of his dying
young was an illusion. He felt nostalgia about leaving a state that
allowed the illusion that he was "always at the breast." Although for a
year or so he had felt compelled to have a drink or two before going to
bed, he had recently been indifferent about having a nightcap and was
indeed almost bored with drinking.

After being silent for a while at the end of the session, he noted that he
felt as though he were in a swimming pool. I suggested that his mental
image recalled his baptism. In spite of his having felt embarrassed about
his baptism as a boy, this event had been a turning point for him from a
religious or cultural viewpoint. I told him that he wanted to leave his
childhood (the past) behind him and move ahead to his adulthood (the
future). The session ended.

At his last session before he moved to his new house, on March 28, Dr.
Albert accused me of sitting "like a computer (Gar)" behind him and
spoke of the volcano then erupting on the West Coast. On the previous
day, while passing an elaborately appointed house, he had wondered if it
were mine. He was then struck with anxiety that I might live in the
neighborhood to which he would be moving. He was both excited and
anxious about the move as a symbol of success but wondered if there
were room for the two of us in one neighborhood, or, in fact, in the
whole world.

A New House and
a New Beginning

The End of March through Mid-May

Our March 1 session was the first after he moved. When he appeared in short sleeves, I thought it was to display the many bruises on his arms. He complained of sore muscles, and I thought he was in effect bragging about how much work he had done during the moving, at the same time wanting me to know that he had suffered in consequence. I said nothing.

He and Jane had initial differences over who would run the kitchen of the new house, but agreed that this should be her domain after realizing that the move had had the psychological effect of fostering individuation from his mother, and that in claiming a measure of dominion over the kitchen he had been clinging to a bridge to her. On the first night in his new home, he dreamed about going to a basketball game; he could not recall whether he had played in it. His ex-mother-in-law was there, and he avoided her. His associations to this indicated that he and Jane had decided that he would refrain from any close association with his ex-mother-in-law; he had already decided not to invite her to their wedding. He thought also that the dream had something to do with leaving his mother behind and trying to identify himself with a good father (represented by the basketball players). His voice cracked as he spoke, and he sniffled as though weeping. I suggested that his physical symptoms reflected grief at leaving the old house, with its psychological investment, and that they might be in the service of his liberating himself.

His first week in the new house left him feeling exhilarated with his success at separating himself from old ties and moving up in status, but at the same time anxious lest the oedipal father or the powerful smothering mother assail him. Dr. Albert spoke with considerable insight about how he had been in the habit of defensively keeping a great many people of his professional circle at a distance. His psychoanalysis had opened his eyes and cured his "blindness" to the fact that he had isolated himself from his peer group. He now thought it appropriate to invite people of his own educational level to his new home and to seek out new friends. While showing Joe and Caroline around his new house, he accidentally cut his hand; he felt frustrated to observe the repetition of self-castration before a man who had once been his competitor for a woman and who came from a family more socially prominent than his own. But he could see humor in this, in spite of the pain in his hand.

On April 9, Dr. Albert reported a dream he thought had something to do with the new house. In it he stood on ground like the area that had later been seeded for a lawn. Then he saw himself walking on a path up to a cave, in which there lived a huge spider that tried to bite him. The day residue of this dream came from his having discovered some spiders in the new house and learning that his telephone was out of order. These imperfections made him fear that a "Charles Manson type" might come to kill him. Then he thought of being attacked by "foreigners," smiling as he reported this. He joked and seemed without any great anxiety. "I hope you aren't like the Ayatollah Khomeini," he said. When I urged him to continue, he confided that his concern about spiders, Charles Manson types, and foreigners might reflect his fear that his mother might suffocate him or his father kill him because of the evidence his new house and social surroundings provided that he had separated from his mother and surpassed his father. He suddenly remarked that he felt as though psychoanalysis were a poker game.

After being silent for a while, he explained his reference to a poker game. He had found my address in the telepone book on the day before having the dream he was reporting. When he located my house on a map, he realized that some time ago he had gone to my neighborhood with a friend to play poker. He then wondered if my house were like the one in which he had played. I told him he was also gambling in learning something about me and in comparing my house with his. He noted then that he had figured out the source of his anxiety; he had not expected that I could be pleased with his success.

By the next session he was busily turning his passivity and expectations of danger into activity and attempted solutions. He took his
daughter on a walk to help resolve her grief at leaving their old home.
They discussed Mamie, still in Europe, and Pamela's feelings about Jane
and the approaching wedding. Explaining what analysis is, he told her
that he had been in analysis for a little more than three years. "It helps
me to know myself, to be a better father to you," he explained. When
she learned my name, she joked with him and told him I might be Mr.
Spock from the planet Vulcan.

After surveying his land, he told me that there were no dandelions or
roses there and recalled his father's having planted a tree that grew to a
height of fifty feet. It was clear that he wanted to strike new roots as a
man. When he spoke of going to the authorities to check on his mother's
background, I felt that he wanted to know her last secret and to break his
bridge to her.

In mid-April, Dr. Albert had a visit from his physician friend who had
become a leader of the Young Turks. Dr. Albert reported being much at
home with him, no longer tormented by envy. He told his visitor about
his analysis and about his envy of his brother and the way in which he had
displaced this onto his friend. "Something is happening in me," he said in
his session. "I feel as if I have resolved all my problems. I am happy,
secure, and comfortable. Do I need your permission to finish analysis?"
When he asked where we were now, I told him that the move to the new
house symbolized individuation for him, but that he still had occasional
fears about frightening images of his childhood, as the spider dream
suggested, and that he displaced these on me. I pointed out that in the
past such anxieties had lasted for weeks or even months and that now he
understood them and dealt with them in a very short time. Moreover, I
told him that it would certainly be appropriate for him to think about
terminating his analysis but that meanwhile we would continue to take
stock on where we were.

Dr. Albert responded with affection and sadness at the thought of
ending work with me. Then he declared that he wanted to know me as I
am. "I know you are a computer," he laughed, recalling Gar. "You are
an administrator, a writer; you smoke cigars and drink coffee. But
perhaps I am still afraid that you may be the North German type I think
of as cold and lacking in feeling. On the other hand, I think you have
warmth." When he noted that off and on during the last three years he
had thought about reading a book on psychoanalysis in the hope of

learning my secrets, I made the interpretation that this off-and-on preoccupation was like his wavering interest in going to the records for reliable information about his mother's background. He still clung secretly and regressively to a bridge to his mother in case his move forward proved unsuccessful. It could remain an open question whether his mother were a dandelion or a rose if he did not find out the facts. If she were a dandelion, he could be a savior prince and make her better. If, on the other hand, she were a rose, he could bask in her glory. I told him that if he did not discover the facts about her—and thus about myself as her representative—he could be close to us, or distant, according to how the wind blew. Dr. Albert said my remarks made him dizzy. The session soon ended.

On the following day, he "accidentally" opened the door of Dr. Sanders's office and found him again in a close embrace with his laboratory assistant. Dr. Albert said that this time he felt relief, "as though I knew but didn't know that my parents had sexual relations . . . as if now I have proof . . . as if now I can really surrender my mother to my father."

On April 17, he reported having had a desire for a nightcap on the previous night. He had thought to himself, "Don't stop drinking, or you will finish psychoanalysis." It was as though the nightly drink were not only a bridge to his mother but a symbolic grasp on symptoms that kept us from separating. As he continued to speak of whether to end the analysis, his mood alternated between elation and sadness. Further warm memories of his father poured out. During his hour on April 22, he made a remark in passing about something he would do "after I finish my analysis next summer." This was his first mention of a specific termination date, and as he heard himself make it, he fell silent and then spoke of being sad.

Dr. Albert called to cancel one of his Monday hours, toward the end of April. He explained later that he had spent the weekend working on Brownie's old house, damaged in the volcano-like fire, and wanted to finish on Monday what he had undertaken. His time at Brownie's house had been full of physical activity, he said. "We worked in the midst of dust and ashes," and almost everybody got something in his or her eyes. "But I didn't," he was quick to say, in conscious reference to his eye symbolism. He had worked on the roof, tied by a rope to a railing, and was proud that he had conquered his fear of heights. The damage caused by the fire was now repaired. After finishing work, he had gone to his mother's house, collecting there a number of items from his childhood to take to his new house. He had felt close to his father while in the basement, and the tears had streamed down his cheeks while his mother, on the floor above, prepared for him an overabundance of sandwiches. As he left the basement, he perceived that she was ready to smother him, choke him with food, and he felt "like a gosling." He was vexed at her but handled himself with tact in spite of refusing to be "a gosling." "My mother was interfering again with my relationship with my father," he said, and he began to sob on the couch.

After this, Dr. Albert reported a dream that I am not at liberty to write about fully since it concerns his mother's real maiden name. In brief, in it he saw a representation of the idealized mother as a white animal accompanied by a baby animal that had "blind trust" in its mother. He dreamed of seeing the idealized mother representative die, and with a pun on his mother's real name, he changed the idealized mother into a more realistic one. He ended the session with a description of how the house he had been working on (Brownie's old house) now looked splendid inside, but about the same on the outside. Emphasizing the "inner change," he spoke of the inner change in himself and of feeling that he had repaired himself by making his mother more realistic. His associations to his dream continued as May began. He reviewed his knowledge of his mother's early childhood and told me that she was about to visit him in his new house.

I live in a rather small town, Charlottesville, the site of Thomas Jefferson's university. Nevertheless, Dr. Albert and I had not met socially or known one another until Dr. Albert became my patient. It was surprising that we had never seen one another outside of his analytic sessions, either by accident or design, save for the basketball games. But one sunny afternoon on the first weekend in May I went with my wife to a cocktail party given in the beautiful garden of a friend. Among the more than 300 guests was Dr. Albert, who came up to me as I stood apart from my wife, smiling and extending his hand, ready to introduce me to Jane, whom I thought a lovely young woman. I shook hands with them both, and we spoke of the nice weather. Soon we separated and lost one another in the crowd. I did not feel awkward meeting him with Jane in this unexpected way, perhaps because by now he had worked through with me many of his conflictual problems, and we had achieved a positive relationship in our psychoanalytic work. The garden was full of beautiful people and beautiful flowers, and my wife and I were soon involved with others in a most pleasant way.

When Dr. Albert came to his session on May 5, he made no reference to our having met but began the hour by explaining why he was ten minutes late; while washing his face he had lost his contact lenses, and it had taken him time to find them. I thought that his old symptom of "blinding" himself might be at issue in connection with our meeting at the party. I decided to say nothing at this point but to let him develop the session himself.

He said that he had had an eventful weekend. First of all, his mother was visiting and he was keenly aware of her behavior patterns, her competition with Jane, and so on. When his dog bit a neighbor that weekend and his mother made excuses for the dog, Dr. Albert had become very angry at her but did not display it. The intensity of his anger had surprised him. With my help, he made the formulation that he had seen something of his mother's treatment of his childhood self in the way she had excused the dog. He now realized that when he had been little, his mother had excused his aggression rather than providing him with an external model to fix a boundary to it and to tame it. He felt that over the years much unneutralized aggression had accumulated within him. He also sensed that the outward release of his untamed aggression was potentially dangerous, since it would attract the retaliation of others. If his mother had been better able to set boundaries to his impulses, he might have dealt better with his inner drives by identifying with her functions and would thus, in the long run, have felt less guilt over them. Guilt over untamed aggression had played a role in his having turned it inward, and this way of handling his aggressive drives had resulted in his self-mutilating behavior.

At his insistence, Dr. Albert's mother had given him more information about her background on this visit. I suspect it was information that had been available to her all along. It occurred to me that it was because of his own readiness to hear it that he pressed her for details. She knew her birthplace and her original first and last names; she also knew the profession of her father, who might have been involved in state politics. Certainly there were no grounds in what she said for her having sprung from "Spanish nobles." The "nobility" myth was something she had shared with her son without any real foundation. As his mother spoke of her birth, Dr. Albert made written notes, which included his mother's given name. There was some question about the spelling of the last name, which, of course, was the surname of Dr. Albert's real grandfather. When he looked at his notes the next morning, Dr. Albert was surprised to see that he had made a mistake; instead of writing one or another version of the surname, he had put down a rhyming word that expressed directly how peculiar and distant his background had been to him. I then learned that his mother, persuaded to do so by her son's recent active interest in her background, had brought some documents with her, which she left for his inspection when she went home. He had not yet had a chance to review them.

At this point, Dr. Albert asked if I had seen the medical school play, in which a cigar-smoking Freudian analyst was pitted against a psychiatrist. Dr. Albert had seen the play as the guest of a colleague of mine on the medical school faculty. He had decided that I was the Freudian psychoanalyst. He said that the medical students had a good opinion of me and that the conflicts depicted in the play reflected actual turmoil currently being felt in the department of psychiatry, which he admitted having known about; it had been a topic of gossip and discussion at some gatherings of local physicians. He had heard no mention of me specifically, but he might have known that I had stopped playing a major role in the department since my move to a new aspect of the hospital as medical director. He realized *now* that I might have been affected by the turmoil and thanked me for being able to exclude all that perturbation from my work with him.

After a brief silence, Dr. Albert changed the subject and made direct reference to having seen me at the cocktail party. He said that although Jane had been afraid of meeting me because I knew so much about her, she had felt comfortable with me. He added that at the party I looked taller to him than he remembered me to be. As he fell silent, I thought that he had indeed had an eventful weekend. He had repeated his old routine of "losing an eye" in response to the triangle involving him with Jane and me but soon recovered. He had unearthed secrets from his mother's past and reviewed her representation. He had reviewed his father's as well and had allowed himself to feel close to me in spite of so recently having shown a self-castrating response. He broke silence by saying how he was blending in his mind the image of me as I appeared at the party with that of the Freudian analyst in the play, who was like a wise man, or a priest sprinkling holy water on his flock. He said he felt very good about me, and to him this meant that the termination of his analysis was at hand. As the session ended, he seemed sad.

The next day he had an urge to buy a BB gun to shoot at his dog if he ever tried again to bite anyone. He reported on May 7 that he had made this purchase. His mother had never allowed him to have a BB gun as a child, and the one he now had was more powerful than would have been available thirty years earlier. I told him that the dog's aggression probably represented his own. He perceived his mother's inability to tame his aggression, which then was turned toward himself. He was substituting an active situation for a passive one by buying a BB gun with which to control his dog—his own aggression. While on the one hand his mother could neutralize his aggression, she could, on the other, deny its existence when she refused to let him have a gun. Their father's shotgun had been given, when he died, to the brother who had been a prime target of young Chris's aggression. Dr. Albert might indeed want to "bite" this brother as his dog had bitten the neighbor. His purchase of the gun was an active attempt to deal with his jealousy of his brother, who had, at least briefly, supplanted young Chris in their mother's regard.

After this session, Dr. Albert sought out Mamie's alleged lover, with whom he was on friendly terms although they had not recently seen one another. When they met, Dr. Albert realized that this man reminded him of his brother. I thought that what he was in fact trying to do was to seek out a representative of his brother to tell him that he no longer envied him. Dr. Albert told the man about his analysis and about the change that had taken place in himself; when the other saw no change in him, he felt injured, and advised the man to go into analysis himself!

When Dr. Albert and Jane gave a party in their new house, the guests were people on their educational level and included the superior of Dr. Albert's who was having a clandestine affair with his laboratory assistant. That night Dr. Albert dreamed of a steep driveway leading to his new house, where a party was taking place, as it had done in reality. His father came to the party in a car that he had always driven and tried to go up the driveway. Dr. Albert wondered if he would make it, but after being stuck for a minute, the old car went all the way to the top. "In the end, my father was successful!" he said. Then the dream scene changed, and he found himself talking to his superior, Dr. Sanders, telling him that he planned to build a pond on his property and showing him the site he proposed for it. The two men found themselves on a *bridge,* gazing down into a body of water. Dr. Albert felt for a second like jumping into the water, but this was fleeting and he soon realized that the water was shallow and seemed very far away.

After reporting this dream, Dr. Albert talked about how things were "looking up" for him. He had been very successful at racquet ball and had promptly sold his old house in spite of anxiety about the sale. He needed the proceeds to discharge some debts connected with the move to his new house. What was more important, however, was that the old house was a symbol of his self-castration, a "starter house" in a neighborhood of common people in which he had behaved as though he were unable to "move up." I also recalled that the street name there suggested the idealized version of his mother's real name. The old house was a *bridge* to his idealized mother, and its sale validated separation from her as well as the abandonment of self-castration. I thought that his dream dealt with these issues, but before I said anything he began explaining it, saying that he had been impressed by the fact that his father had been successful at the conclusion, whereas in reality he had not been notably successful in life and had worried his son by the prospect that he would die "whimpering." With pride in his voice, Dr. Albert added, "At the end, he died with his chin up." He had created in his dream the image of a father successful enough for him to identify with satisfactorily. I noted that he had perceived his father "good" and strong enough to identify profitably with this mental representation just before his father died. It seemed to me that in Dr. Albert's associations to this dream there was gratification of aspects of his oedipal wishes; not only could he identify with a strong father, but the father's death left his son room for success, an opportunity to become the male head of his own, new household.

He went on to tell me, without any prompting, that the second part of the dream, in which he stood on a bridge with a father representative (Dr. Sanders), had reference to his individuation/separation from his mother, who was represented by the "body of water." He had been momentarily afraid of being engulfed by her, but had managed to distance himself. Commenting that Jane was not like his mother, he said, "We don't engulf each other."

He and Jane decided to have a traditional marriage, and she planned to use his name in her professional as well as personal life. This pleased him, and at the party he had been aware of how much he wanted to show off both Jane and Pamela to his guests, as well as the new house. "I was not shy at the party," he noted, "but I feel shy around you because I still perceive you as a parental person. I am growing up. I don't think my parents ever really expected me to grow up. My mother does not even yet realize that I am an adult." He allowed that he had never really thought of his father as an adult with feelings, thoughts, and conflicts of his own but had seen him in a stereotyped way simply as big. Only recently had he grasped that he had been someone in his own right. "It is correct to say that I find many things in me that come from my father, and I like that. My ability for actual accomplishment is a paternal gift; Father was a doer. I used to think of him as a dreamer, though. That he might have been, but he actually did many things. Mother talked a lot but didn't do much except cooking. But I should give her credit, too. My ambitions come from her."

By mid-May, Dr. Albert had examined the documents left by his mother. The handwriting on some was very poor, and he could see two possible names for his real grandfather, one of which had "good" connotations, the other of which sounded "peculiar." He offered no given name for his grandfather at this time. I suggested that he might wish to keep two images of the grandfather, one as a dandelion, the other as a rose, just as he had clung to two images of his mother. In the end, he decided that the name with the good implications was the *logical* choice. The documents confirmed some of Brownie's recollections about his mother's background but offered nothing substantial. He could find no reason for his mother's having been put up for adoption. She now implied that her real father had been a politician, so Dr. Albert thought it might be helpful to check records of those in political office during the relevant time, to see if he could find a name that would fit his grandfather's surname. His most important find among the documents was the exact date of his parents' marriage, since he had surmised that his mother had been pregnant with his sister, and that this was the reason for the marriage. He now had documentary proof that his sister had been born a year after his parents married. He seemed surprised at the way his mind had distorted things and recalled another distortion: his persistent notion that it was he rather than his brother who had been obliged to wear protective straw hat.

Full of praise for analysis, Dr. Albert referred to a celebrity who had declared in a magazine interview that analysis had changed his life for the better. "I feel I changed, too," he said. "I spend time with my family and my house, and I spend less time with medicine. You know, I still feel a little guilty about this, but I know why: it is as though I am not fulfilling my mother's dreams for me, her ambitions for me."

He went on to speak of Mary Lou, a young patient afflicted with the illness in which he specialized. She seemed to have limited intelligence and to be fixed in a sort of symbiotic relationship with her mother. He not only gave her medical care over a long period but took pains to help her acquire some skills and to separate psychologically from her mother. He had recently seen her, and she expressed great gratitude for all he had done for her, saying that she wanted to write a book about her experience with him. It was a moving story and one I had heard nothing of previously. It seemed to me that Dr. Albert was identifying with me in helping someone with "mental problems." He said there was a parallel between what had happened to Mary Lou and what happened to him. "I even think about writing a book about my experiences in analysis," he said. I saw in this remark even more identification with me, since he knew that I had written at least one book. When he said that he sometimes wished he could paint his experiences in analysis, I asked what that would entail. "Black clouds—hands—toilets—coffins—a yellow brick road," he said, listing what he would try to get on canvas. He seemed sad. "All those belong to my experience." He reported a feeling state identical to that he had had while getting ready to leave home for college. "I am thinking of terminating my analysis, you know. I feel very sad!"

Dr. Albert suddenly asked, after a few moments of sad silence, "What kind of relationship did you have with your analyst?" As a medical man he knew that all proper psychoanalysts must undergo personal analysis as part of their training. I answered spontaneously that I felt that he was thinking that if I could separate myself from my analyst, he would be able to separate from me. He said, "Hm, hm," and asked why I refused the box of candy he had offered on our first Christmas together. I suggested that he imagine for a while that I had accepted it. After a thoughtful silence he said, "If you had, I somehow feel that you would really have seemed to be like my mother, and we would have bargained forever and ever with one another about who got what from whom." I said nothing but felt that he was separating me further from contamination with the image of his mother. He went on: "You are not really a colleague of mine. You are a doctor, and I am a doctor, but we are different. You are not really a friend of mine. You are different from all my other friends."

Dr. Albert proceeded to tell me that now he accepted his sister and brother as grown-up people "without giving them grades." He felt changes in himself but knew I would not grade him for his work in analysis or for undergoing change. "Now maybe I am waiting for a sign to stop my analysis. Why don't you give me a sign?" I referred to the concept of mutuality and suggested that we talk about this and learn together where we were, what we still needed to do, and when it would be best for him to stop. He replied by saying that the book *I Never Promised You a Rose Garden* (and the film derived from it) came to mind. It is the story of a young psychotic woman and her (female) psychotherapist, and it describes the young woman's journey into health, her affection for her psychotherapist, and her separation from her when she became well. As our session ended, I felt confident that Dr. Albert and I would move harmoniously toward the termination phase of his analysis.

Toward Setting a Date for Termination

Mid-way to June 17

In mid-May, Dr. Albert was busy tying together the loose ends of his analysis. I suggested that he could use further help in dealing with his task of taking his place in a man's world and consolidating his new image of himself and his occasional pull backward into ambivalent relationships with women. He began the May 15 session by saying that he had once again gone over the documents his mother had left with him and rechecked the dates of his parents' marriage and his sister's birth. "I was so sure my mother was pregnant with my sister before she married my father, but I know better now. I was so sure I was the one who wore the straw hat as a child, but my mother said it was my brother. There is seeing and seeing; there is knowing and knowing!" he repeated. He paused before adding, "The truth about my mother's background and my childhood does not matter to me psychologically now as much as it did, but I believe my curiosity about the reality of things will persist."

Since he had seen cut flowers in a vase in my office on the previous day, he asked if yesterday had been my birthday. When I made no reply, he reflected and said, "I am trying to talk about birth and independence, about the impending separation between us. I have mixed feelings, sorrow and gladness. Now, again, I recall a song from the movie of *I Never Promised You a Rose Garden.*" Some sounds outside reminded him of the sounds of a dump truck, and I told him to let his mind work on this. He thought the dump truck was unloading sand somewhere. His early memory of hesitating about jumping onto a pile of sand deep in a ditch came to mind again, and he suddenly reported feeling himself in the air. He himself associated this with his getting ready to jump off from his analysis.

Dr. Albert recalled a recent conversation with an acquaintance whose wife had undergone analysis. The man had told him that although he had anticipated she would be a completely different person after this experience, she had not been. Dr. Albert referred to the poem by Robert Burns about seeing ourselves as others see us. "I think seeing oneself objectively is so hard," he said but indicated that he thought he was succeeding. He spoke of other successes, such as getting rid of his somatic symptoms, achieving a better sex life, and so on. He added that recently he had felt no need of a nightcap.

I was silent through all this, and he taxed me with this. I asked if there were something special he wanted to hear from me. He began to sob. I offered nothing, and when he caught his breath, he said that he was thinking of "when the final bell will toll and the analysis will be all over." This had reminded him of how his father had died without a farewell from him. Once again he mourned his father's death, recalling how he had forced himself to tell his father that he loved him, and had made his father say the same to him. "I am really sorry that my father died," he said. "I wish he could see Pamela and Jane. I feel positive about him. How can you have positive feelings about someone you can't see? I guess I am also talking about you. I realize that I want you to tell me that you love me." He continued to cry, quietly. Then he recalled how his father had hugged and kissed him and tossed him in the air affectionately. He fell silent before reporting a bodily sensation of being tossed in the air. At this, he was all smiles!

That morning Pamela kissed him on the cheek when she said good morning. She had until then kissed him on the lips. "She is giving up her incestuous objects," he said. "I felt suddenly that she is no longer a little girl. She is growing up. I feel sad about it, but I am also so pleased. My mother did not allow me to give her up until I came to analysis. I can't believe what my daughter is doing. Oh yes! I do, and I am so proud of her!" He ended this session with reference to a paragraph in a psychiatric textbook he had read in the past. "It all makes sense to me now," he said. "I understand now how I could not compete with my father and then identify with him. I was the apple of my idealized mother's eye until I came to analysis, and she kept me away from my father. Then there was the idealized image of Daddy Doc, with whom I could never compete!" I made approving sounds. There was nothing to add to his remarks, and the session ended.

On May 16, the next day, Dr. Albert began the session by visualizing a bird learning to fly. In his imagination he let the bird free, but he could not see what happened to it. "Will it fly, or will it fall down?" he asked. "I have a nagging feeling that it will know when it can fly!" He then told me when he and Jane would be married. The wedding date was toward the end of July. He asked me impulsively if we could finish his analysis on July 14. I asked why he chose that particular date. He was consciously aware that that was Bastille Day, a day that represented to him a day of freedom from me. Referring to his analogy of a bird learning to fly, I spoke of his hesitation about termination and suggested that the selection of a magical day would not be in our best interest. I also suggested that we could keep on speaking of termination without setting a final date. He agreed and began talking about King Arthur and Merlin the magician, who had the power of assuming various forms, including those of animals and, Dr. Albert thought, birds. Dr. Albert began laughing affectionately at this and called me "Merlin the magician." He spoke of how Arthur had fought Lancelot, and said there was no end to such relationships and that one might yearn forever for Camelot. I made the interpretation that "Camelot" might represent blissful reunion with his good mother, and that although one might have memories of such a state, one cheated oneself to preoccupy oneself with this at the expense of a full and robust life. He began crying again, explaining, when he could collect himself, that he was grieving for the old relationships he was leaving behind. Moreover, he now thought of these relationships from a new perspective. "I did not kill my father," he said. "I did not give him cancer. I have only regrets and anger at his death."

Dr. Albert went on to explore feelings of guilt over matters other than his oedipal wish to kill his father. "I now understand how guilty I was in my behavior when my daughter was born. Her birth activated my feelings about my newborn brother." He let me know that he had worked through his jealousy of his brother and that he was enjoying his daughter very much now. He considered having children with Jane and asked if his old feelings about his brother would be directed toward them. He answered his own question by saying, "I am different now. I know I will have different feelings if I have other children."

Two days later, on May 19, Dr. Albert spoke of another dream, a new version of one he had had previously. There were oblong boxes in this dream, like coffins or graves side by side. Their lids were transparent, and he could see within them portraits, one of his ex-wife and two others, her parents. He had gone to bed that night thinking of a gift for Jane, which he had been unable to select during the day because of the press of business. He now thought of this dream as his gift to Jane since it depicted the burying of his old marital connections.

On the following day, he gave details of the coming wedding. He and Jane had decided to be married in a romantic little white chapel in the country, at no great distance from their new house. On a recent visit to the chapel, they had met the minister, a tall older man who was "fatherly" toward the young couple. Dr. Albert had liked him very much. After telling me this, he asked, "How does a bird know when he is ready to fly?" He then spoke of my mention of his wish to keep an open door—a bridge—to the representation of his mother in case he needed to return to her. He was thinking now of his preoccupation with keeping or not keeping a bridge to me.

The next day Dr. Albert reported a dream in which he was driving a truck over a gas conduit and worried about having broken it. He thought it represented an umbilical cord, except that it felt rigid. He spoke of noticing how much better able to separate from her mother Pamela was; she no longer displayed anxieties over Mamie's letters from Europe. Dr. Albert noticed behavior patterns of his own that suggested anxiety about separating from me. He had been overeating since we had started to talk about termination, and recalled becoming obese as a child when threatened by separation from his mother. "I think I am trying to fatten myself up in preparation to separate from you, as though I must keep all kinds of goodies in me for a rainy day," he observed, noting that this behavior pattern was the repetition of an old one, and must stop. He said he was able to avoid gaining weight by playing extra games of racquet ball.

The truck in his dream had the color of an army truck, and this reminded him of Danny's departure for boot camp one summer, at about the time young Chris left home for college. He recalled how they had become interested in different things in the months before they separated and that they had been growing apart. It was then that "Danny planned that he would die," Dr. Albert noted, feeling anxiety lest I die if our separation were really to come about now. He fell silent before reporting the visualization of a bridge once again. He saw the sun rising over it, and presently the bridge resembled a cemetery and the sun was shining on tombstones.

Dr. Albert and Jane drove to his sister's that weekend. He felt close to his sister but knew that the visit was in the service of "turning over a new leaf," and was designed to permit the sharing of his marriage plans. He encountered a couple he had known in the past and felt that he had grown away from. Although Jane was bothered by sneezing during the visit, where they were surrounded by flowering trees, Dr. Albert's nose stayed "crystal clear." As he and Jane traveled home, he had different mental images of me with which he kept toying, superimposing them on images of his father. Once he imagined me as a Turk of old, complete with robe and turban. He likened this image to that of the Wise Men, and called me "Allah," saying that this was his way of paying tribute to me. But I sensed a certain mockery in this. He agreed and admitted that he still related with ambivalence to me. While thinking of me as Allah, he had noted black clouds in the sky and had thought of the volcano then erupting in the West. His perception of me as an idealized Allah was condensed with his perception of me as a "black cloud." He was engaged in bringing together my good and bad images and playfully mending them.

Dr. Albert took a wrong turn "by mistake" as he approached the city; this took him past my office. He realized that after being away from me, he still needed "a visit with me" in a symbolic way. He was aware of struggling between separating or not separating from me. On May 27, after reporting that "the big push for the wedding" was on, he turned his attention again to the question of separation. He spoke of the lawn now thriving at his new house, how his allergy had completely disappeared, how well he had handled his mother when she stayed with Pamela over the weekend during their recent absence, and how there was nothing dramatic about his daily life. Was his analysis going to end "Not with a bang but a whimper"? he asked, borrowing Eliot's phrase.

Dr. Albert had found in his garden a bird's nest with two nestlings in it. They fascinated him in view of his recent references to birds getting ready to fly. When he later checked the nest, he found the nestlings gone. Birds know when they are ready to fly! But he had a nagging fear that they might have been the victims of some predator.

He began thinking of how he would feel when his mother died. During their recent encounter, he had been able to feel love for her even when she tried, as usual, to barge into his life. He now found himself able to handle her intrusion without anxiety or any allergic response. During her visit, she had insisted that her son leave his contact lenses in the downstairs bathroom she used during her visit, although he proposed taking them upstairs. Downstairs would be more convenient for him, she declared, but he asserted himself and spurned his mother's suggestion, which he regarded as an invasion of privacy. He had noted that Jane was appropriately assertive toward his mother. But he was particularly delighted that Pamela said she would find a private and secret place in the new house to be a place of her own, a place to go to when she needed to be by herself. When he heard this, Dr. Albert recalled how he had behaved toward Pamela in the past, intruding on her as his mother had intruded on him. It now suited him to honor the privacy of others. As the hour ended, I told him I was taking a two-week vacation in early June. I apologized for not giving him longer notice and said that my original plan had been to go in August. Only recently had this plan been changed. I did not give reasons for this, and he did not ask about them. But two days later he responded to my abrupt announcement of a separation between us, reporting a dream in which a door he thought of as that to a dining room was shattered by an act of violence. He had gone to bed with daydreams of violence, noting that this was the first time in many months he had had daydreams like that. He fantasied a shoot-out with a sinister man, which he survived. He was not then aware that his daydreams of violence had something to do with my abrupt announcement about my vacation, but he made the connection when he thought back on his dream. He recalled my having said once, in relation to his bridge fantasies, that he might want to keep a door open to his neurosis (his idealized feeding mother was represented in the dream as a dining room). Instead of working through in piecemeal fashion the remaining conflicts about separation between us to achieve a "normal" termination, he saw me slamming a door on him. He retaliated in the dream by tearing down the door. This exaggeratedly aggressive act led him to expect retaliation from me (now seen as the dangerous mother able to eat him up or cut him up).

Dr. Albert then referred to a song the Beatles sang about a walrus. The local radio station was running a competition for the best suggestion of a mascot, and Dr. Albert thought of suggesting a walrus. The image of a walrus coming to his mental view was the reactivation of that of his mother's vagina with teeth, just as "Pandora's box" had been in the image that led him to ask me, "What is left in Pandora's box?"

Once he realized how he had responded to the matter of my vacation, he relaxed and assured me that he really knew I was not deliberately and malignantly doing something hurtful to him, but that he felt in fact well able to tolerate our separation. He said that the Beatles' walrus song symbolized death and separation also. After being silent, he reported imagining no longer coming to his sessions with me. He tried to imagine who would be taking his place on my couch. When I asked for his associations, his brother came to mind, and he connected my "desertion" for a holiday with his mother's turning her attention from him to his newborn brother. But this was a familiar response that no longer jolted him. He told me *freely* of a fantasy of my having a car wreck and dying during my holiday. He was again associating me with Danny, and this also was a familiar association. Then he began talking about mutuality and his wish to join a social club with Jane after their marriage. The club he had in mind was one he thought I belonged to (as indeed I do), and he commented that he would be comfortable there since there was room for us both.

Our last session before I went away took place on June 2. On the previous day, Dr. Albert had tried to learn more about his mother's real father by calling a library in Maryland, but no information had been forthcoming. He then fantasied that his real grandfather was a wealthy man without heirs and that he himself might suddenly receive a fortune when it was discovered that he was the rightful heir. He realized he had entertained this notion before, but had suppressed it. He had been inhibited in his search for information about his mother's background by his unconscious desire to cling to this wishful fantasy, which also had something to do with the prospective separation between us. If I were not available to him, he could find a rich substitute.

When Dr. Albert found a small garter snake on his property, he was delighted to feel that he had gotten over his fear of snakes, in which he had imitated his mother's fear. "The snake is the symbol of the medical profession," he thought and felt protective toward the one he found. When he learned that afternoon that Pamela and a babysitter had killed it, he was angry, as though Pamela had done something destructive to him. Then he was able to consider in his disappointment that she might be responding, through her destruction, to his approaching marriage. So he sat down with her, talked about the marriage, and helped her to verbalize her feelings about it. In a sense he was identifying with the helpful analyst. I was separating from him, and in response he was keeping me in a useful identification.

We met again on June 16. In a friendly but assertive way, Dr. Albert offered me his hand, which I shook in welcome. This was now a man-to-man meeting. He told me of doing much work in my absence, and said he felt like a glider, that he needed to be let loose to fly on his own. Our short separation had enabled him to test how he could handle himself, and he felt that he had managed very well. He spoke briefly of a problem with Dr. Sanders, and commented that his handling of this had been appropriate. He did not elaborate on their differences, and I asked no questions. Their differences were not what was important; what was important was his telling me about his enriched repertoire of handling things. He had checked the records on his real grandfather again, without results. He had reviewed the medical records from his childhood for the occasions of his onset of allergy and for details of the operation on his toe. He was especially interested in the question of radiation therapy, being still uncertain as to which child had worn the straw hat, and he was disappointed in finding the radiation records unavailable.

Dr. Albert also had gone to Maryland to visit Daddy Doc's house, during my absence, taking a second look at the past, assessing its reality, and reviewing his childhood perceptions in light of the reality. He expressed readiness for deciding when his analysis would end. His mood was good, and his voice sounded assertive. On the following day (June 17), he suggested that we decide upon a date for termination. I noted that when his father and Danny had died, he felt left behind, with unfinished psychological business, and suggested that it might be well to establish a date a few months away. We had been talking about termination long enough without setting a date. We agreed that it might be useful to meet for a while after his marriage so he could review his unconscious perceptions of this event. Since I planned to take the rest of my vacation after the first week in September, we decided that the end of that week might be a good time.

Reactions to Setting
a Date for Termination

June 17 to the Third Week of July

As soon as the termination date was decided upon, Dr. Albert yawned, in what I saw as an effort to conceal his anxiety. I have learned that most analysands reactivate their symptoms in anticipation of termination, as though to have a last review of them. Thus the analysand's condition may seem to worsen at this time. However, in this phase he will possess very active observing functions, and it is time-tested technique to let him reactivate his symptoms with little interference, make his own observations of them and interpret and surrender them on his own. The analyst does not, of course, remain altogether silent while this takes place; he offers some interpretations and to some degree guides the flow of whatever material then surfaces.

The first thing Dr. Albert did after setting a termination date was to exhibit exaggerated ambivalence toward me. He spoke of a friend's nephew who had been hospitalized for mental illness in a well-known hospital. It was proposed that he undergo psychoanalysis while an inpatient, and Dr. Albert decried this as "a money-making gimmick" perpetrated by the psychoanalysts in question. I suspected that he included my image negatively among the analysts. After venting more feelings, he began talking about how great I was since I had undergone analysis myself, and it had been highly successful so that I was "about the perfect person."

The next day, Dr. Albert reported a dream in which he had seen a giant ice cream cone full of something brown. He said the cone contained my milk (breast) that had turned into feces. He kept laughing in a way I sensed was both anxious and friendly. "I think that when we set the date for termination, I felt bad breath from your mouth," he said. "The ice cream cone full of shit is your bad breath." He had gone to bed the previous night thinking that when his analysis was over, another physician, one he knew, would take his place on my couch. "I know that he stood for my brother, in a sense. I got the bad breath when my brother was born!"

Dr. Albert wanted to associate further to the material in the cone. It was shiny, as though "beaming." "You know," he said, "after we set the date, I felt as though I were toilet-trained. I felt very proud. The shit I produced in the dream is the first delivered autonomously by me." He told me how proud he was when he told Jane and some of his friends about the approaching end of his analysis.

He began to sulk, but then he laughed and told me that he knew he was sulking because of the termination, and with this understanding, he stopped. "I am so hostile and angry right now," he explained. "Do you have little boxes like little stages of termination?" He noted that a person with a malignancy goes through stages during the termination of his life. "Maybe we are now on stage number thirteen," he blurted. Although I had been silent until then, I asked an explanation for the number thirteen. He was uncertain about whether this was a lucky or an unlucky number. His reference to malignancy reminded him of his father's death. His father had gone through stages before dying. "It is so difficult to talk about termination," Dr. Albert said.

He began the next session by saying that his telephone was out of order, and accordingly he was unable to reach anyone. I sensed that he referred to our separation. After a silence, he said something in German that I did not understand. I sensed in this an element of differentiation from me since I suspected he knew I have no German. Then he translated: "Tomorrow is another day." He then offered that his using German was in deference to his father's side of the family, originally German.

Then, openly discussing the finishing of his analysis, Dr. Albert related it to death and noted than even Pamela was talking at home about death. He attributed her preoccupation not to our terminating our therapeutic relationship, but to his approaching wedding. His marriage to Jane would, he acknowledged, be a death blow to his relationship with Mamie, and he knew that Pamela was unconsciously perceiving this as a kind of death. Again, he had sat down with her for a helpful talk, encouraging her to verbalize some of her perceptions.

He then pulled a card from his pocket. On it was written the address and telephone number of an office that promised to have information about his real grandfather; he said he had just remembered having it, and that he planned to call there. He then changed the subject by saying that on the previous day in passing a bookstore he had wanted to go in and get a book by Freud. I connected this wish aloud with his desire to find another statement about his grandfather since he might fancy Freud to be my father. He then gave me some information he had obtained, mostly from his mother, about the real grandfather; he was not certain that it was accurate in its particulars, but it confirmed that his grandfather had held high public office, apparently in a neighboring state. The telephone number he had written down was that of a library in which rosters of superior public officials in nearby states could be found. Recently acquired information suggested that this grandfather had had an affair with his secretary, the issue of which was Dr. Albert's mother, who had been put up for adoption. There seemed some evidence that in spite of the adoption, the grandfather had married his secretary. Dr. Albert was again aware of his mother's need to idealize her real father and to displace her adoration onto Daddy Doc. Although she had known some of the stories all along, she had conveyed to her son the myth of the Spanish nobleman, his grandfather. He now knew that if the politician and his spouse, his erstwhile secretary, were his real grandparents, his mother would consider that her father had made a misalliance. Dr. Albert recalled that his mother had never spoken of her mother.

On the couch, Dr. Albert developed a mental image of his grandparents. He imagined a man in a grey suit, with a cigar and a cane; and a woman wearing a dress trimmed in lace, with odd shoes. She was carrying a fan. He put them on a riverboat in his mind. "If you are on a boat on a river, the past, the present, and the future exist all at once, all at the same time," he explained. "This is what happens in analysis. I have a peculiar fantasy of having my grandparents here with me, here in this room."

Just then I heard a noise outside my window and saw that window washers were at work. A man in a "cherry-picker" suddenly appeared in the uncurtained glass doors of my balcony and could see us. Since Dr. Albert was on the couch, facing away, he could not see him, but I explained what was going on and suggested that under the circumstances it would be awkward for us to continue. He agreed with my suggestion that we cut this session short. We would lose ten minutes by doing this, but I could add an extra ten minutes to the next session, if he wanted. He found this satisfactory.

Before his session on June 23 he had seen the film, *The Empire Strikes Back.* He began the hour by saying that a machine that could be heard outside my building reminded him of the sound of a machine in the film. The hero of the film, Luke, lost a hand when Darth Vader, the villain (whom he believed to be his father), cut it off. Dr. Albert reported having been greatly impressed by this incident and even more impressed when a new hand was sewn back in place. He associated Luke's hand with his toe. The loss by castration at the hands of a father was compensated for by a new member. He recalled that the previous hour, cut short as it was, had been a castration, but the extra time allowed for this session was compensating. He said he appreciated my having curtailed the previous session because of distractions too great for me to tolerate; this humanized me in his eyes.

Dr. Albert went on to say that in *Star Wars,* the precursor of *The Empire Strikes Back,* the good and bad characters were clearly differentiated. In the more recent of the two films, it had been harder to tell the good from the bad, since it had been revealed that Darth Vader was Luke's father. This reminded him of some of the situations in his analysis, in which bad and good were distinctly different but had been integrated as time went on.

He continued to refer to Luke of *The Empire Strikes Back* in his next session. The film left many questions unanswered. Who was going to kill whom? Would the father or the son murder? Was there any solution for Luke's triumph save killing his father? Darth Vader reported to a great and mysterious master; was the latter a representation of Dr. Albert's real grandfather? More information about the adoption of Dr. Albert's mother emerged; it was based on long-ago conversations between his mother and Brownie, now relayed to him by his mother. His mother's mother had spent six months of her pregnancy in a well-appointed maternity home. If this were so, she might not have been a poor girl after all.

Dr. Albert felt that there were many obstacles to his learning the truth about his background. "I have a sense," he said, "that I am looking for a needle in a bunch of clothes on the floor. If I want to find it, I must grasp the clothes, but the needle may stick me. Maybe I'm not doing all I can to find out the facts of my background because I don't want to be stuck by a needle. On the other hand," he added, "there are tremendous *real* obstacles in the way of my discovering them."

He reported nonetheless on June 2 that he had learned the initials of his grandfather from adoption papers, and his grandmother's first name. Each had the same last name, and this raised the question as to whether the couple had given up their daughter for adoption even after marrying. Was something shameful involved? He got help from one librarian who located mention of a man with the same last name and initials as this grandfather, who was not a politician, but listed as *an author*. Dr. Albert fell silent and then said, "You write, I write, we write." I asked if he fantasied that I might be his real grandfather, and he said he had not thought of the possibility before, but it had just entered his mind with my designation as an author.

He went into a silence he then broke by reporting that he was imagining driving stakes into the ground. "I think you are trying to secure your roots," I suggested. He laughed in a friendly way. Referring to his earlier interest in repairing Daddy Doc's house and thus salvaging his mother's fantasies, he spoke of the development of his own roots. "Now I am obsessed with completing the still unfinished parts of my new house before my marriage," he said. "I think houses have been important symbols throughout my analysis." He counted those referred to in his work with me. "My adopted grandparents' house was in the service of my mother's fantasy," he said. "The one I left to move to my present house represented my connection to my mother. Then the volcano burned my grandparents' house and left me with the option of building a stronger one if I wanted to. The white house of my dream implied identification with you and the good aspects of my mother. Now, my present house represents the building of my own roots."

On June 27, more information came from the library; there had been no political officeholder in the surrounding states with his grandfather's surname or initials. In spite of his disappointment, he felt well and integrated. "If I can summarize the results of my analysis in one word, that would be *integration*," he said. He told me that he had again been asked to head a division in a medical center in another state and commented, "In the past I would have gone into a frenzy about what to do about such a thing, but this time I feel all right, and I will consider this job possibility seriously. I am finishing my analysis, and I can leave town."

Dr. Albert opened his June 30 session with the account of a dream he called "amorphous," in which there had been great brightness. When he awakened from it, he was reminded of "a sense of space." He went into a long silence and then told me that this was not because he was anxious, but because while silent he caught the feeling of the dream and felt as though he could expand into the space of my room. His associations were to his childhood memory of going to the basement of the family home and watching in silence as his father worked. It was a good memory. His mother would fill her space with sounds, and would invade his, talking as she moved from room to room. Even if they were not in the same room, young Chris would feel that she was speaking to him from whatever room she was in. Now, growing into his space, he was pushing his mother away. He could remain silent in my presence without anxiety, but with the same comfortable feeling he had enjoyed toward his father in their unbroken silent companionship.

On July 1, he opened his hour by saying that my office smelled musty. I asked for associations, and he recalled the basement in which he had watched his father work. But then he was reminded of the basement's musty smell when he made love to Mamie with his father lying on his deathbed just above them. Once again he reviewed his father's death, with effect, and his lovemaking with Mamie. "I knew that she might conceive, and she did," he said. "I was giving life as another life was passing away. I wanted the baby to be a boy. When it wasn't, I think I paid too little attention to Pamela." He went on, "I have a 16-year-old boy helping put the finishing touches on the house. I thought of him as my son. The musty smell has something to do with termination of our psychoanalytic work. As if I am repeating the lovemaking scene I had with Mamie, with you." He confided that one day he had seen Jane as Mamie and had realized that, like Pamela, he was recalling Mamie's image as if to bring her back to be reviewed and grieved over. He began to cry and said he was not really disturbed about the return of Mamie's image; he knew much about the mourning process. In order to give up something, you must review it and then let it go. "I have not been with Jane sexually lately," he added, and began to laugh with relief. "I'll be sexy again when my grief is over."

When he resumed sobbing and used a handful of tissues he commented, "Thank God, you don't use scented Kleenex. I hate them." His tone was friendly. He then spoke of leaving me soon and of his understanding that he could carry away with him the experience we had had together. "I am like Luke of *Star Wars* and *The Empire Strikes Back*. I am going through a process of growing up." After a brief silence, he reported that this session felt as though it were the best we had ever had and that he was so very tired. The hour ended.

That night I dreamed for the first and last time about Dr. Albert. I believe my dream had reference to our forthcoming separation. I had kept notes about him throughout his analysis, noting every dream and key issues. After he left the office, I would write the details of the session. In the dream, I was holding my notes about Dr. Albert in my hand. The pages were not the originals, however, but copies produced by some machine, not of the contemporary kind, but of the sort used long ago when I was a psychiatric resident. The notes ended at one point and were followed by a letter from Dr. Albert to me. The letter was written and copied to resemble my notes. My name appeared on it and a German word that I decided, on awakening, might have been "damn."

Dr. Albert's letter said that he had heart trouble and had only a short time to live. He told how his analysis had opened up his conflicts. He was catching up with them, but before he could resolve them all he would die with the psychosomatic heart condition he had developed. When I awakened and recalled the dream, I remembered how much affection he had shown me at our recent session and how much I had been moved by his feelings.

I have for fifteen years or so had a bad hiatal hernia, and when I go to bed with a full stomach, there is always the possibility of food regurgitation during sleep. There have been occasions when food partially blocked my breathing until I would awaken gasping for breath, afraid of death by suffocation and cardiac arrest. I have to accommodate to this to some extent, and to take certain medical precautions before retiring. On the night I dreamt about Dr. Albert I had overeaten, and was concerned about this.

I thought that talking with him about the termination of his analysis, and his associating this with his father's death might have awakened in me anxiety about death, and anxiety with some foundation in reality given my physical condition. I represented (to myself) Dr. Albert's father upstairs who would die. I also wondered if my full stomach made me feel like the pregnant mother who had rejected him, or like Mamie, whom he had impregnated. However, in the dream it was Dr. Albert himself who had the cardiac problem. In my dream I made him assume my disability. I recalled that as a child he had assumed his brother's symptoms for himself. I wondered if I felt rivalrous toward him and wanted him to take on my physically bad, "castrated" side. Had I unconsciously to a degree made him a reservoir of some unwanted thing about myself? Once he was well and his analysis terminated, he would shake off these "castrated" aspects and I would lose him and might have to resume my unwanted aspects. I thought of the possibility that this might be a conflict we needed to work out, and I began to explore my negative feelings about him and the reasons for them. I recalled having felt "jealousy" of him on a few occasions, indeed at all times when he talked about resolving his guilt over Pamela and his having become a good father to her.

It happens that my first marriage ended in divorce, and I was not as fortunate as he in developing a loving relationship with my daughter from that marriage and resolving my guilt about having been separated from her and her brother for some years. Dr. Albert had integrated in himself an element of fatherliness and motherliness toward Pamela that I envied. I remembered at the start of his analysis having a tendency to protect Pamela myself when he was able to give her rather good care. I was in competition with him, as though I were Pamela's mother or father. Although on occasion I had been aware of this "jealousy," I had the impression that this so-called countertransference response (unconsciously determined feelings and attitudes on the part of the analyst, due to his own conflicts but directed toward his patient) had not interfered with the flow of his analysis. Now, however, the issue was reappearing in my associations to my dream; perhaps I needed to explore the possibility that it needed resolution in me. His knowledge of German language and literature also suggested that he had something that I did not.

My associations to my residency days took me to the conflicts in my first marriage and their resolution in the personal analysis I underwent after my residency. Unconscious competition with Dr. Albert apparently had induced some guilt in me, as evidenced by the appearance of the word "damn" in my dream. But during my residency, I might have been excused for not being above any countertransference feelings. It was as though I should have been able to reach to the "idealized" stage of not having countertransference feelings. In this I was identifying with my analysand in his reach for idealized images. I had to remember how countertransference feelings themselves could be used as therapeutic tools!

Although I am not at liberty to give further details about my associations to my dream, I want to state here that they led me to examine who and what it was that Dr. Albert represented to me, just as he had been reviewing his relations with important others, especially as they were displaced onto me. It seemed as though we were both trying to tie up loose ends in order to achieve successful separation. After pondering my dream, I was filled with affection for Dr. Albert that morning, as he was filled with affection for me. But I did not share my dream with him then.

At the hour after my having the dream, he told me that when he left the previous day's session, he had thought of a game show on the television, in which as players answer questions correctly, blocks with bits of a picture on them are turned toward the audience until the meaning of the entire picture becomes plain. He felt that in his analysis all the blocks had been turned face out. He said he felt as though he were lying in a meadow beneath a tree, gazing up at the sky and feeling nostalgic about different people in his life.

Toward the end of the first week in July, his mother, brother, and the latter's wife and children came two weeks before his wedding to help with preparations. He spoke to his brother about his efforts to learn about their grandparents and was at first surprised at his brother's opposition to this search. Then, realizing that he himself had wanted to deny their real beginnings because of a desire to perpetuate the family myth, he refrained from challenging his brother on the issue.

One day when a snake appeared at a window in his house, Dr. Albert watched it with some pleasure and without fear before recalling his old phobia about snakes and spiders. I told him, when he reported this, that snakes and spiders had represented to him the dark side of his parents' images.

He got in touch with the child psychiatrist who had previously been helpful to Pamela and told him about his approaching marriage and how Pamela was reactivating her mother's image in connection with this. He had the impression that she needed to grieve again, and the psychiatrist told him that the child's reactions were not surprising and that he would like to see her. They made an appointment for Pamela, and Dr. Albert thanked me, crediting his analysis for enabling him to keep his daughter relatively unscarred by the ramifications of his marriage. He had a dream of his father as a wraith.

By mid-July he "had butterflies in his stomach" about the marriage, now a week away. When he sought to buy a diamond for Jane, and to charge it, his credit was disallowed because of some bills Mamie had incurred and failed to pay. "Mamie's ghost appears just before my marriage!" he complained to me. The issue was soon settled, however, when he found a copy of a letter he had written three years earlier to the jeweler stating that he would no longer be legally responsible for Mamie's bills. When he spoke with excitement about his wedding, he called it "a celebration" not only, he explained, of his nuptials but also of "what I have accomplished in my analysis."

The wedding rehearsal came in the third week of July. The bride and groom had asked that the minister's words speak of their "individuality" and their joining together out of different life experiences. It was to say "each will bring his or her background experiences to the marriage," and during the rehearsal at this point Jane whispered to Dr. Albert, "and three-and-a-half years of analysis." In reporting this he said it had made him chuckle, but he added seriously that both he and Jane were aware how much his work in analysis was finding its way into their union.

Trilogies

Shortly before the wedding, Dr. Albert reported a long dream he referred to as his "trilogy dream" since it included three episodes. In the first episode, he had seen a rather dark brown, warm room in which were three people—both of us and someone in a white loincloth who was presumably an Indian guru and who had some of my facial characteristics. Some mysterious, special, and exciting event was taking place. It was as though we were all engaged in a psychoanalytic session.

In the second episode, I had offered to meet Dr. Albert and Jane at an aunt's brown house in his home town, and they waited for me there, but I did not arrive. There was a feeling of emptiness and chill. Then, after leaving Jane and Pamela at his mother's house, he decided to come to my house to find me. It was morning.

It was still morning in the third episode, in which he came to my house, which was next door to the real location of his own new house. My house resembled a medieval English inn or castle, and it contained three people. "The trilogy continues," he noted in reporting this. The three were my wife, my son, and myself. My son, in the dream a boy of 5 or 6 with blonde hair, was playing outside when Dr. Albert arrived and questioned him about my whereabouts. He told Dr. Albert that I was inside. When my wife went to the door, he noted that she greatly resembled a neighbor of his called "Sugar." She was blonde, and he felt relieved to see that she was good-looking. She was, however, very disagreeable when he asked to see me, and when he insisted, they argued. Then I appeared in the doorway. Dr. Albert could see a circular stairway behind me in the house. I told him that his notion of having had an appointment was a figment of his imagination. Later, however, I recalled that I had indeed made an appointment to meet with him, Jane, and Pamela. I told him I had something to give him and went into the house, getting a bottle of brown liquid that may have been whiskey. Using scissors, I made a sort of suitcase from a cardboard box, put the bottle in it, gave it to him, and told him he could leave. He began to walk up a steep hill. He was sorry to feel that his psychoanalysis was ending on a sour note.

In reporting the dream, Dr. Albert commented on the appearance of something brown in all of the episodes. My own association to the color, which I did not share with Dr. Albert, was feces, which, in his unconscious, I believe, represented his own autonomous creative production. His dream was a "production" that summarized the state of his analysis at the time. In his dream his activities, especially in the third episode, took place in the morning (mourning). He identified the guru in the first episode as Buddha or Freud. This had been a warm episode reflecting the security he had initially found in his analysis. The second episode, cold and empty, reflected his fantasied expectations of me—a gift, a million dollars, a Mercedes, love, status—and frustration because I did not deliver any such gift. He felt that the third episode, however, represented the practical, realistic issues between us, and this episode was what he emphasized at this point. He had felt uncomfortable in this part of the dream and said, "It represented how any involvement of my personal life with yours is impossible within the confines of our joint analytic work. As though you are telling me that the analysis is over and that I can expect nothing more from you. You ask me to take something away from analysis, and all you give me is a bottle of booze in a flimsy suitcase. Both are transient, ephemeral things. They have limited life. I felt sad. The saddest thing was that the analysis was ending on a sour note. I felt like a bird pushed out of the nest to fly, but at the same time I had the realization that this was necessary."

Dr. Albert went on to say that my leaving him "with booze" was somehow appropriate since we had so often talked about his keeping a link to his mother by means of nightcaps. He associated the name "Sugar" with a dog of the same name he had once had and to which he had been greatly attached. When a new puppy was introduced to the household, Sugar had undergone a personality change. Dr. Albert associated this recollection to his brother's birth and his perception of his mother's consequent rejection of himself. Again, he was recalling a separation "on a sour note."

As he reviewed his negative feelings toward me by talking about the third episode, he spoke of how the important separations in his life had caught him unprepared. He mentioned Danny's death and his father's, the sudden desertion of Mamie. "Maybe I never had an experience of mutuality at a time of separation. We have talked about mutuality here, but perhaps I still model the separation about to part us on past separations in my life. The fact is that I have warm, affectionate, and appreciative feelings for you, and it disturbed me to have this dream." After falling silent he suddenly spoke, as though he had discovered evidence of a positive relationship with me, saying in an animated fashion, "It is not true that I never had a separation with mutuality. There was one pleasant separation, and it also included a bottle of booze." He went on to tell about having made friends at college with a big man named Larry, with whom he often talked and drank Scotch in a very friendly way. "One day, just before we left college, Larry came to me and said, 'This is it. It has been fun to have known you and to like you. Probably I won't ever see you again. Goodbye!'" Dr. Albert went on: "His frankness surprised me. There was no lingering, but I felt that the separation came with mutuality and pleasantness." The session ended.

Dr. Albert had asked to change his hour with me on the following day to some time in the afternoon because medical duties would occupy his morning. He had put his request in a man-to-man way, openly, and since the time change was allowed by my schedule, I agreed. When the day came, however, he found himself released from the medical duty he had anticipated and came to my office at the usual time, only to find that I was not there. He did not recall the arrangements we had made for the afternoon until it was too late. On coming to the next session, on July 24, he expressed curiosity about having missed me and suggested that this had something to do with his trilogy dream, with his associating to the dream during his previous session. I might be angry, and he was interjecting a "sour note" by missing his hour and bringing about a separation. He then began to talk about the *stairs* he had seen in his dream. The word "stare" came to his mind. He was staring at my family, he said, when my wife interfered with his seeing the man of the house, as his mother had interfered with his attempts to see his father realistically. He spoke of having spent the previous afternoon and evening making some sawhorses, recalling how he had watched his father doing this and had felt warmth. "Also," he said, "I suddenly realized yesterday that I no longer dislike my mother. It is a very funny feeling. I don't accept all the crazy things she does, but I don't take any of them personally any more."

Dr. Albert began to laugh and told me that when he and Jane had been taking whiskey bottles for the wedding to the basement of their new house, he had unintentionally made Jane drop one. It broke, and he thought it had been a link to me (mother), like the bottle I gave him in the trilogy dream. He recalled now, however, that the contents of the bottle he had dreamed about were amber with an orange tinge that reminded him of a painting by Dali; this painting in turn reminded him of one called *Inner Space*. He knew that the dream reflected some activity in his inner space. There are many people in the *Inner Space* painting, but the boundaries between them are blurred. He noted that he was still trying to sort out his inner images. Although it occurred to him that the dream might concern his approaching marriage, he could not establish any connection. This was his last session before his wedding and honeymoon.

The next time I saw him was on August 4, although he had had one earlier appointment, which he canceled on the grounds of illness. When he came on August 4, he explained that he had not really been ill but had had a hangover. Although the wedding had been splendid, he said, his sister, then a houseguest, gave him two occasions of irritation. The wedding reception, with many guests, was held in his new house, and the presence of houseguests had led him to make arrangements to take Jane to a motel around 2 o'clock in the morning to start their brief honeymoon. His sister "pushed him out" at midnight, however, and he learned on returning from the honeymoon trip they had taken after the night in the motel that her teenage sons had used marijuana in his absence. He reported this to his sister, thinking that she was liberal and would just lecture the boys. She became furious instead, and Dr. Albert felt that he had betrayed his nephews' confidence, and he in turn became very angry at his sister, recognizing inwardly that his anger really derived from her having sent him off with Jane at an earlier hour than he had intended. On the following morning, when he was supposed to have an hour with me, he apologized to her, but he was so upset he could not have his session with me. As he told me this he said he sensed that all this had something to do with approaching termination, his being "pushed out" of his analysis.

Referring again to his brother's birth, Dr. Albert said, "He pushed me out from my special relationship with my mother. It seems that was the crucial trauma influencing my life." He then spoke of a book he had taken on his honeymoon. It was *The Last Enchantment,* and as he gave the title he said, "Oh, no! Here is the trilogy again. This is one of the three books by the same author on Merlin and King Arthur. It seems my associations to my trilogy dream continue."

In the third book, which he had read, Merlin ages and knows he will die. Dr. Albert said, "It is you or my analysis that is dying." Merlin taught his tricks to a new assistant, and Dr. Albert associated the latter with himself. While reading this book during his honeymoon, he dreamed about a certain person lying in a casket. He identified him as a 37-year-old man he knew who had failed to take action and had become the eternal student, still attending classes instead of going to work. He was the opposite of all that Dr. Albert aspired to be, and when he awakened, he knew that this man represented that part of himself that wanted to be "an eternal analysand." "I was killing that image of myself," he explained, "and my reading of *The Last Enchantment* influenced me to dream about it." He went on to say that Merlin did not in fact die, but lived on sealed in a cave, his magic lost. "This is like what is happening between you and me," he said. "Somehow the magic in analysis, in the way I see you, is disappearing." I thought he was referring symbolically to the resolution of the transference neurosis.

The transference neurosis, in which the analyst becomes the focal figure upon whom the analysand "transfers" his perception of important figures of his past, is an indispensable therapeutic tool. The feelings experienced by the analysand in this transference are vivid, and thus intepretations of the unconscious aspects of what the patient is going through are felt to be authentic. As analysis approaches termination, in the patient's mind the analyst begins to appear more and more as a "real" person and less and less as a transference figure.

Dr. Albert continued: "We have only one more month until termination. Termination will really come. It will be the demise of Merlin. Nothing spectacular. Things will dwindle away. Merlin's assistant will become more and more independent of Merlin and separate from him. I will carry Merlin's skills." He became very friendly and suggested that I read the trilogy, saying that the books had "great stuff" in them and that I would be interested.

He spoke of having ridden a horse while on his honeymoon. It was the first time he had been on one since he was 3, and a horse did not look so big now. He had enjoyed himself immensely. He gave details of his wedding and said he wished I had been there. He spoke of feeling very good at returning to analysis and said that that part of him he called "his childhood feeling" wanted to stay in analysis longer.

On August 6, he spontaneously returned to do further work on his dream, which he recalled as his "trilogy dream." It will be remembered that his associations to his dream and our attempt to understand its deeper meaning had come to an abrupt halt when he left his analytic work for a brief honeymoon. As he took the *stairway* to my office that day, he thought again of his trilogy dream. He now said that the three parts of the dream had something to do with the temperature; the first part was warm; the second, cold; and the third, "room temperature." "I think the third part is accurate concerning the present," he said. "It represents a combination, a mending, of the previous opposite temperatures: different and opposing feelings I had about the analysis and you now give way to a more realistic attitude regarding you."

I reminded him that just before leaving for his honeymoon he had entertained the idea that this dream had something to do with his upcoming marriage. I suggested that he let his mind wander, that he be receptive to this idea. In response, he told me that he might know why my wife in his dream had been represented by his neighbor Sugar. He said that before her marriage to him Jane had known Sugar's husband, Scott, slightly, but Dr. Albert had not. Jane had told Dr. Albert that while she was eating in a restaurant one day Scott had approached her and invited her to his house to see his new Jacuzzi. Perceiving this as a proposition, she had politely declined. While she and Dr. Albert were house-hunting, they learned that Scott and Sugar lived almost next door to the house they proposed buying, so they visited them "to ask about the neighborhood." During this visit, Scott showed Dr. Albert the Jacuzzi, having no idea that he knew of his earlier invitation to Jane. Dr. Albert, who was seeing the couple for the first time, found Sugar beautiful, and he thought it was a joke that Jane had taken Scott's invitation as a proposition since he already lived with a beauty, and this would keep him from stealing Jane away.

In describing Scott, Dr. Albert called him a "schmuck" and immediately realized that he had used the Yiddish expression for penis. Thus in the dream Scott was a father-penis-analyst, and he (I) was married to Sugar, whose beauty was a relief. As long as I were married to her, I would not compete with him for Jane. Thus he could go ahead and marry her. The dream protected him from oedipal rivalry and made his marriage to Jane comfortable. I said in a friendly way, "I have my woman and you have yours, so we can go on our merry (married) way." Then he laughed and said he had discovered what the stairs in the house stood for; he visualized a "circular, artsy, steel stairway" of the kind that it had always made him anxious to climb. The water in the Jacuzzi bath had made circular motions in its whirlpool activity, and matched the dream image of a circular stair. He now believed that circular stairways and the whirlpool represented a powerful vagina that would suck him in. In *The Empire Strikes Back,* Luke had fought with his father on a circular stair, and that is where he was castrated by having his hand amputated. Since Dr. Albert knew that Luke would gain a new hand (toe, penis), he had rehashed before his marriage his old fear of engulfment by a powerful mother and his oedipal fear of being castrated, finding solutions for them.

In the dream I had been wealthy, with a most ample house, and the lines from the Bible had come to him, "In my Father's house are many mansions." He recalled a story of a rich man giving crumbs to a poor one, as I had given him only a bottle of liquid in the dream. In the dream, I was also the fantasied adoptive grandfather of noble blood (or a powerful official) living in a medieval English mansion or castle, who could have given him something but never did, although perhaps he still expected to receive something of value from such a powerful figure.

Why had I given him a bottle in the dream? I asked at this point if he thought I might be jealous of him because he was forging ahead in his profession and was marrying the woman he valued so highly—and finishing his analysis. It was my own dream about him that led me to ask this question; I thought we should bring any possible negative feelings I might have into his analysis in an appropriate way. I especially wanted to examine with him his possible perception of negative feelings on my part toward him. If he had perceived such feelings and then hidden this knowledge, I wanted the issue verbalized so it could be resolved.

At first he seemed greatly surprised at my asking such a question. How could I have any jealousy of him? After all, I "had all my shit together," he said. "I feel flattered that you could even consider being jealous of me." Then he recalled a college friend who had also surprised him by saying that he should cheer up (when he seemed depressed) because he had a "steady girlfriend" (the Cuban girl), was making A's, and was preparing for medical school. Then he suddenly asked, "Are you jealous of me?" I did not want to burden him with the details of my dream about him, or even let him know I had dreamed about him, so I said it would not surprise me if, from time to time, I had been. He had gotten over the fear of powerful women, had fought with black panthers in black clouds, and faced men he considered unbeatable—and throughout all this turmoil he had managed to protect his daughter from all kinds of possible complications that might have arisen from his difficulties. So, after all, he might be an enviable man. I emphasized that I had no conscious feelings of jealous malice toward him, but I might harmlessly think of him as enviable from time to time. He listened intently and said that once again he had a feeling of relief, and once again I had proved myself to be a human being. I believe we felt very close to each other at this moment.

His association to the trilogy dream continued on August 7. He thought now of the contents of the bottle I had given him as some kind of potion. Merlin had used potions in *The Last Enchantment,* which represented to Dr. Albert the termination phase of his analysis. Now the trilogy pointed to three circumstances: psychological separation from his mother, psychological separation from his father, and psychological separation from his analyst. He had been satisfied that in his analytic work he had resolved his conflicts about his parents, but he still had mixed feelings about me. He had tried a type of separation from me modeled after separation from his mother; this would require that he become fat and cling to an internal bridge to her or have nightcaps and thus maintain an external tie. He now thought that his separation from me would be modeled after his separation from his father when the latter died. They had never spoken of their feelings until he was almost dead. "Now," he said, "I definitely see a parallel between my father's dying and my analysis ending." He had read somewhere about the several phases of mourning: denial, anger, grief, acceptance, and resolution. "The third episode of the trilogy dream dealt with anger," he said. "Today I am having a lot of grief." His voice trembled with sadness. "Emotions are interesting things; they are truly universal," he remarked. I added that this was indeed so since "an American and a Turk can communicate through them!"

He fell silent and then reported having recently felt very well. "I am satisfied with myself. I now know that integrated people also can have ambition. There are still things to do, like losing more weight, but everything is all right." Then he whispered, "I am appreciative of you!"

In the silence that followed, he reported that he had imagined an egg cracking and letting a bird fly out. His imagination was like a cartoon; he could see Pluto, the cartoon dog, sitting on the egg, and watching the bird turn to Pluto with the cry "Dad!" as it emerged from the shell. Dr. Albert began to laugh. He was the bird, but why was I Pluto? I told him that he thought of me as being clumsy like Pluto. I recalled the time when my car had mechanical trouble and I had been unable to fix it, and his surprise about my incompetence in such things. "All right," he said, "but Pluto is such a lovable dog!"

He opened the next session with talk about the phases of grief, and reported another dream that had something to do with me. It took place in a bright room with white furniture. Again the number three was featured: there were three people there, Dr. Albert, myself, and a child. The furniture suggested the place might be India; in a sense, I saw it as the fourth episode of his trilogy dream, in the first part of which there had been an Indian (or a Freudian) in the background.

This dream of his dealt with a discussion about separation with me. After rising to leave the session in his dream, he saw that the room was full of sunshine. I hugged him, and he hugged me back and was overwhelmed with emotion. He hugged the child also; he knew the child represented himself, the childhood he had brought into analysis. Then he felt tears in his eyes. He felt joyous and, walking downstairs, he joined a number of people dressed in light colors. He felt tremendous relief and suddenly realized that he had resolved his grief.

He then told me that Jane had told him on the previous day how certain people who worked with him had told her how much he had changed. "He is a different man, more relaxed," they told her. "He has a better sense of humor."

A Different Rose

August 11 until the End of the First Week in September

We were fast approaching the termination date of Dr. Albert's analysis. Discussion of his "trilogy dream" at the end centered around his review of his analysis and his preparation for leaving it. He began seeing himself as a kind of survivor. He had done so well in comparison with his brother; his career was progressing well; and he felt happy in his new marriage. He wondered about Mamie, still in Europe. He knew that while he was feeling secure, she continued to struggle with her conflicts. He seemed no longer driven to save her, but he was appropriately concerned about Pamela and was helpful to her as she adjusted to having a stepmother. Jane was feeling awkward about Pamela's calling her "Mom," and Dr. Albert suggested that she should continue calling her stepmother "Jane" in spite of the change in their relationship. When on August 13 he made reference to "a new trilogy," I felt that his seeing things in clusters of three had something to do with the triangular relationship of himself as an oedipal child relating to parents. He was trying to put such a triangle in perspective. He told me that on the way to my office he had had *three* different thoughts, which he reported in the following order.

The first came to him when he had to stop his car because a big truck stopped just ahead of him and prepared to dump gravel at the roadside. As it backed up, a bell in it signaled the traffic to be on guard. As he watched, Dr. Albert thought of Danny, who had once worked for the highway department. Then he thought that when Danny was alive there had been no such warning bell on highway department trucks, and once when a truck backed up suddenly, it had missed him by a hair.

His second thought concerned the woman who had been renting the family house in Maryland that had been damaged by fire. She had moved away, and a local physician showed some interest in renting the quarters. Dr. Albert, in pondering this, realized that the house symbolically linked him to his childhood, especially to the glories of Daddy Doc and Brownie as his mother had idealized them. He realized that he had worked on the house during the first phase of his analysis by way of resisting it but had come to work on it later as he worked on changes within himself. When the house was burned "by a volcano" (Volkan), the fire was something he had in a way expected, just as he had expected castration at his father's hands. The fire had led him to reassess his castration anxiety and to realize that when the dreaded event actually took place he could endure it and, in fact, rebuild for greater strength. He suddenly felt that the symbolic claim the house had on him was gone, that he would never return to live in it even in retirement; there were, after all, no good theaters or restaurants in that locale, and it might be well for him to sell it.

His third thought concerned his affection for me. He thought that a declaration of this would be "the final step" since his father had died the day after he declared his love for him.

He then wondered aloud how these thoughts could be connected. I suggested that his emphasis on triads during recent weeks might be concerned with the three key family figures, father, mother, and son. His first thought dealt with the danger of mutilation, castration, or death for the son who now had an "inner bell"—a warning signal to permit him to take appropriate steps to avoid a fate like Danny's. He referred in his second thought to his link to his mother's "glories" and to the symbolic stages in his analysis. He now thought that he would be able to leave behind all such links and separate from mother/analyst. His third thought was evidence of his facing up to his affection for his father/analyst as he prepared to separate from him also.

When I said that all three thoughts had much to do with the major themes of his analysis, he replied, "Pretty true! Pretty amazing!" and fell into a thoughtful silence in which he appeared to be assimilating what I had just said. Then I brought up the matter of his paying for his analysis at its termination. Since I am a salaried member of the university medical center staff, he would be billed by the center's computer office, and this could involve a month or so of delay. I had, however, adopted the method of having each of my patients bring payment to me each month. This allowed me to keep the matter of payment directly within the analyst-analysand interaction, as well as to keep an eye on the patient's account. I had on occasion told Dr. Albert that I disliked having a computer intervene between us but that we would have to do our best to adjust to its unavoidable intervention. (Here I was realizing another element in his identification of me as the computer Gar in the *Star Trek* episode.) My arrangements left me with the responsibility of forwarding the checks patients brought me to the office of computer billing. I explained that after our termination, Dr. Albert should expect a few bills not yet put through the computer, and that their receipt would represent some direct links to me that we would not have the opportunity to analyze. I asked if we could come up with a way to close out his account that would preclude any such loose ends when we terminated. It occurred to him that if he sold Daddy Doc's old house, he could have enough cash on hand to pay a lump sum that would cover all his debt at the time of termination.

On the following day we discussed the subject again. Dr. Albert agreed with me that receiving bills after termination might symbolically reflect unfinished business of the sort he associated with the unfinished business of seeking the truth about his mother's background. As the hour closed, he confided that whereas he had formerly had an image of me from the neck up only, he now saw me as a whole person.

On August 18, Pamela returned to her father's household, having stayed for a while with her grandmother to allow the newlyweds some time alone. When Dr. Albert saw his daughter looking over some pictures of her mother, he knew that she was checking on her own "links" to her own important "others" as her life underwent the changes brought about by his remarriage. When he told me this, Dr. Albert commented that he had always wondered about a picture I had kept in my first office, fantasying that the man in it was my analyst, to whom I maintained a "link" in this way. I said there were different kinds of links; those that were "magical" could absorb the energy of their creator to keep this investment in its magic active. I decided to tell him that the man in the picture, although someone important to me, was not my analyst. He commented that he did not need a physical and magical link to me, and he added with some insight that his analysis had altered his inner structure, although there were no physical changes in him to be seen. He added that he thought he would not consider the process of post-termination payment a magical link to me.

He was seriously considering the last offer of another position by August 20 and had decided to visit the institution that offered it in order to take a close look at what was involved. He planned this trip for a few months after his analysis would be over. After talking about his career plans for a while, he fell silent and then reported an image of a sled and a sensation of warm, brisk air. Since the sled symbolized the affection between himself and his father, he repeated the story of his father's purchasing it. He then noted that we had but two more weeks together and said he felt nostalgic. After another silent interval, he reported having a mental image of his birth. He had been told that his father had been so excited over the event that he slipped on the ice going about to tell the good news. Again Dr. Albert reviewed his mother's interference with his love for his father, whom she overshadowed in peculiar ways. She laughed so extravagantly at his jokes, for example, that her son felt they must be pointless. "You see," he said, "I'm telling you my mother was at fault. But I do realize she had enormous problems of her own. I'm not angry at her any more. I just feel sad."

He began his hour on August 21 by reporting a news item that had caught his attention. It told how a Muslim passenger on an airplane in Saudi Arabia caused a number of deaths when he tried to brew a cup of tea aboard the craft and set it afire. He then tried to change the subject, but I suggested we stay with the anecdote; I felt he was trying to tell me something about myself, or about us, in his reference to a Muslim, since Turks are Muslims. This brought up the subject of his possible prejudice against me; he claimed that he had no prejudice against Jews, but that he used to be prejudiced against people who spoke English with foreign accents. "You don't really have a bad accent," he allowed. "Besides, I feel so positive about you today!" I told him that in that case it might be a good time for him to get the negative feelings he had about me off his chest as the end of his analysis approached.

He began talking about two Turkish students he had known in college. Recalling that they drank very little, he wondered aloud if it were because of what he called "my religious bent" that I seemed to disapprove of his nightcaps. I suggested that whatever my "religious bent" might be, he might be making a last minute effort in speaking this way to challenge my interpretation about the nightcaps, in order to keep a link to the mother of his childhood, just in case. He began to laugh in a friendly way and, confirming my interpretation, reported having gone without his nightly drink for more than a month. "I even sleep well without a drink," he added.

After being silent for a moment, Dr. Albert said that throughout his analysis he could hear me behind him taking notes, and the thought had occurred to him that I might plan to use these notes for a book or a paper. (At this point I had no conscious idea that I would later use the notes to write this book, but I may have entertained some such idea unconsciously, and he apparently sensed this.) He commented that he himself had written papers on some of his interesting patients and that these were in effect "links" to them. I agreed that my notes were links to him that I hoped were in the service of being better able to analyze his conflicts. He wanted me to remember him without notes and complimented me on what he called my amazing memory of whatever he had discussed. He completed the hour by saying again that he had not been the same since beginning analysis and added that he did not consider his case unique.

He was ten minutes late for his hour on August 22. He apologized for this unusual circumstance and blamed his tardiness on Jane, who at the last minute had asked him to do something for her. He wondered if she might be jealous of me; she well knew that his relationship with me had been so intimate! I wondered myself if his tardiness had not also been a trial run of our forthcoming separation, but I did not share this with him.

Dr. Albert spent this hour reviewing how he had once sought to idealize other people, whether or not they deserved it. A letter received from his friend the "Young Turk" on the previous day provoked this train of thought. Dr. Albert had worked through his idealization of this man and his jealousy of him, and during his recent visit had developed considerable mutual understanding. The "Young Turk's" letter made reference to another physician about whom Dr. Albert had had jealous feelings also. This doctor drove a Jaguar and went about with rich and beautiful (idealized) women, but it was now disclosed that he had been arrested on forty-three counts of drug abuse.

Dr. Albert talked about having become more and more "average." Joking, he suggested that he was a good candidate for a club "for dull men" (apparently, there is such a club in California). After a silence, he commented that by calling himself dull he might be punishing himself for surrendering "idealization of the other" and added that he certainly was increasingly integrated, not dull. The session ended with his expressions of appreciation for his analysis.

He began the next session by referring to newspaper coverage of the supposed sibling rivalry between President Carter and his brother Billy. His association to this led to discussion of the "sibling rivalry" between us. He fantasied that I had done better in my analysis than he had in his, but further associations pointed to serious consideration of the possibility of his taking the new position offered out-of-state. He was afraid of my jealousy of him. Reference was again made to his perceptions of what his brother's birth had meant to him and how he had handled this by creating an idealized mother whom he could control, at least in his fantasy, and a correspondingly idealized self.

He spoke of a film I had not seen. It was called *A Thousand Clowns,* and in it Jason Robards portrayed an idealistic, dreamy person who was forced to become more realistic. Something like this had happened to him, he said, but he had not wound up in "Dullsville." "In fact," he said, "I am close to being as happy as I ever could be."

Again he spoke of dandelions and roses, saying, "The other day I was thinking about them. When I gave them up I thought I was a carnation, but suddenly I realized that I didn't want to be a carnation; when I pondered what came of crossing a dandelion with a rose, a carnation was no longer the answer. I want to be a rose! And I said to myself, 'Why not? This rose is a different rose!' " He laughed with pleasure, and we talked about the first rose, which was a creation of his to defend against the fantasied and real hurts of his childhood. The "different" rose was one of integration. "I want to be a rose," he said, "because now I can *choose* to be one." I felt very proud of him and filled with pleasure.

At the next session, on August 27, Dr. Albert reported that he felt his psychoanalysis had been completed in the session at which we talked about his being a different rose. "I feel as though you and I are simply having after-dinner coffee now," he said, "and I am enjoying it." Without waiting for a reply, he went into what I considered a spontaneous review of all the years with me. "When I first met you it was at a time that was bleak for me," he said. "I wanted to be happy but I didn't know how. I had emotions, but I could not name them. Now I know the emotions I had in those days were anger and envy." He then spoke of having "a surge of energy," after which he began weeping, as if to recapitulate his mourning for the separation from me.

During this recital, I was greatly taken by his beautiful description of his perception of what analysis had done for him. They appear here:

> It's as though I took off a few years and can now get back into the saddle again, but without any regret for taking time off.
>
> I am not perfect, thank God. I got mad at my daughter last night, and I knew what it was and corrected it. That's okay, too.

I think I belong to myself now. That's really good. I can actually give more of myself.

I actually feel good about my mother without feeling oppressed and smothered. She is the same old Mom. She has not changed. I changed.

Maybe I didn't get from psychoanalysis all I wanted, but I don't know what else I would get.

I still look at good-looking women, and I want to screw them, but it is an idle feeling. Idealized people are humans. There are no goddesses.

You [the analyst] must be the closest to being an idealized person, but you are not perfect, either. You occasionally forget things and you are not mechanically oriented.

At the end of the session, just before he left the room and while he still wept, he managed another quotable description of the effects of his analysis on his allergy: "It feels good to breathe through my nose again!"

The next session took place just a week before the day set for termination. Dr. Albert talked about the four remaining sessions and referred to a conference at which the moderator had stopped the speaker at the fixed time by saying, "We need to stop now!" "What has anything I'm telling you got to do with the price of rice?" he asked. I told him that we could say, "We need to stop now" at our meeting on the following week. He began to laugh and wondered about possible reluctance to leave me. He spoke of writing a scientific paper and his upcoming visit to a medical center where he had been offered a position. When he remarked that he had really nothing much to talk about, I said, "Follow the basic rule" to encourage free association. This brought into his mind the yellow brick road in *The Wizard of Oz*. He said that he had made miles and miles of "mental lines" on my ceiling and that they made up his yellow brick road. He kept gazing intently at the ceiling, and I felt that he was saying farewell to his "lines."

That night he tried to explain to Jane what it was like to face the termination of his analysis. On the following day he reported having had a melancholy feeling in the pit of his stomach such as he had had at the time of his father's death. But he explained to Jane, weeping, that the separation between us would be different from that with his father since I would continue to live.

When we met the day after Labor Day, Dr. Albert reported the last dream brought to his analysis. Unfortunately, I cannot give the details

since its manifest (surface) content concerned his professional preoccupations and would give clues to his identity that I feel inappropriate.
The dream referred to his having a certain physical ailment (which he
did not have in actuality), and to its being treated. His associations to the
treatment related to his analysis. Now that treatment was over, and he
was seeking a permanent cure, the dream was constructed in such a way
that if he were able to obtain this cure, his sister would die. Further
associations indicated the dream's deeper meaning, which had to do
with his psychological separation/individuation from his mother. Coming as it had on Labor Day, he saw this dream as a "birth," that is, a
separation from his mother/analyst as his analysis finished. He talked
about his old compulsion to save women and how this was connected
with his anxiety over individuating from his mother. Talking about all
this led him to discuss how he would pay his bills for my services; he
decided to borrow money to discharge his debt in full, after termination
and after being billed by the medical center's computer office. (In
reality, he did pay his bills soon after his analysis terminated.)

The day before we finished, he talked about his father's death. He felt
very tired and indicated that he felt his analysis was finished with this
session and that he might not appear the next day for his final appointment. I told him that I (father) was dead during that session, so
tomorrow would be my funeral. He disliked going to funerals. I
reminded him that when Clyde died he did not attend his funeral and felt
guilty for not going, thus perpetuating his unfinished business with the
deceased.

When Dr. Albert came for his last session, I noticed that he hesitated
about lying on the couch. I asked if he wanted to lie down, and he stood
before me for a moment as if deciding what to do. Then he sat down in a
chair opposite me, looking at the couch he had now left behind, and then
turning his attention to the different things in my office. He had seated
himself in a chair when we first met, in my first office, but in this
environment he had always been on the couch. I thought being seated
and looking about was giving him a new perspective of my office—a
new and "post-couch" experience. He noted how my lampshades
match, the kinds of plants I have, and so on. Joking, he said, "For a long
time I was blind in your office, but now I can see new things!"

After the scrutiny of my room was accomplished, Dr. Albert turned
to me and said, "You know, you were right yesterday. I felt that
yesterday's hour was an exact replica of my father's death. After I left

you, I kept telling Jane that I was separating from you, and I ended up having a big long cry." That night he had also noted anger in himself. Then he had recalled what he had been told about the phases of grief and thought that he should not be having anger at the last minute. But then he had thought that even the physiological phases involved in the healing of lesions do not go by the book. I suggested that the physical ending of his analysis did not mean that his psychological grieving over its loss would come to an abrupt end, and that his grieving might continue for some months. Awareness of this possibility might be useful for him, I thought. He indicated in reply that he already felt that what I said was true.

"I am happy to have eye contact with you as I sit in front of you," he said. I thought he was telling me that he was no longer "blind" "I used to have images of you from the waist up, in a frame, or else a bust view. Now as I look I can have an image of you from head to *toe,*" he said. His initial shyness at being seated before me seemed to disappear as the hour went on. He seemed comfortable and friendly. He said I was no longer a computer or some subhuman creature, and I said that I was glad we had made arrangements for paying his bills that did not make the medical center's computer (or computer Gar) an extension of me.

He then asked suddenly how I felt about the fact that this session was our last. Spontaneously, I replied that I felt as gratified as a parent who sees his child grow. He spoke of his appreciation of me and of the work we had done together and remarked that he should also thank Mamie, since it was because of her defection that he had come to analysis.

We had been sitting face to face for about half an hour. He seemed to have nothing further to say, and I felt that our work had indeed come to an end, and that he could take his leave. It was up to him to take his departure, and I told him this. He said he was still surprised at the way we could at times read one another's thoughts, that he felt the same. He rose and shook my hand and thanked me once again. I walked with him to the door and opened it. He left.

During the time left of his hour I sat in my chair, smoking a cigar, and I felt a great contentment.

Epilogue

A Few Years Later

A year after completing his analytic work with me, Dr. Albert moved with Jane and Pamela to a city in a neighboring state where he became the director of a division of his medical specialty in a well-known hospital. I knew this from reading a brief news item in a medical publication. Although he came to mind now and then during that first year after his analytic work with me ended, and occasionally thereafter, I had not considered reviewing my notes on his case and writing them up in book form until I was asked to be a member of a panel at a symposium on the psychoanalytic process. In preparation for this assignment, I was expected to read a book by Dr. Paul Dewald, a widely known psychoanalyst; this included a verbatim report of a young woman's psychoanalysis. Dr. Dewald, with his analysand's permission, had had her taped sessions transcribed, adding to the transcription his understanding of what had actually taken place in each session. The result was a valuable contribution to clinical psychoanalysis, a book for the professional study of the application to one case of one analyst's techniques. But although it was highly useful in our symposium, it seemed difficult reading to offer to a nonprofessional interested in learning more about the psychoanalytic process.

I was struck while attending the symposium by the paucity in the psychoanalytic literature of any studies reporting on the full course of a given analysis. Since the exchange between analyst and analysand is private and not to be shared with others, this paucity is not surprising.

However, I thought it might be useful, in view of the recent publication of popular books and articles on psychoanalysis, for a psychoanalyst to write about what happens in his office, using as an example the story of a single psychoanalytic case. It was this thought that led to the preparation of this book.

I chose Dr. Albert's story *on a conscious level,* selecting it from among the stories of many other analysands about which I have copious notes; it seemed the most suitable for my purpose. Being a psychoanalyst, however, I felt obliged to search for unconscious motivations that might underlie my selection of this case, and among these it seemed possible that I was unconsciously assuming the identity of Dr. Albert's real grandfather, about whom he had rather limited information, although at one time he thought of his grandfather as "an author." I was named for my mother's favorite brother, who was mysteriously lost in Istanbul while attending the school of architecture there and whose body was subsequently found in the Sea of Marmara. Upon my birth some years later, I replaced to a considerable extent this lost brother in the mind of my mother—and, indeed, in the mind of my grandmother, who was ever present to care for me. I was thus strongly linked to a man I never knew and had a sense that by "gratifying" Dr. Albert, by "becoming" his "lost" grandfather, by displacement, i.e., by standing for Dr. Albert, I was at the same time "gratifying" myself by "finding" my uncle, whose fantasied image was buried somewhere in my psyche. Such a find would further consolidate my identity.

I worked on the book without telling Dr. Albert about it, planning to put it aside if he did not give his permission for its publication when finished. I learned much about the psychoanalytic process as I worked on the manuscript. It was as though I had carried out a study with such satisfaction to myself that it would not be too great a disappointment if I could not share it with others. But when I called Dr. Albert after the writing was done, he was surprised and pleased to hear from me. He planned being in Washington at the National Institute of Health at times when, as it happened, I would be in Washington for my regular seminars at a psychoanalytic institute there, so we were able to meet in the District on four occasions, each time in the office of a psychoanalyst friend who kindly agreed to let me use his office in his absence.

At our first meeting, after telling him about the manuscript, I gave my conscious reasons for writing the book and shared with him my ideas about possible unconscious motives. At our next meetings, we agreed that none of the latter would invalidate the project, and after he read the manuscript and discussed it, on his own initiative, with Jane, Dr. Albert gave his consent to its publication.

Although during our meetings in Washington we did not discuss the details of our lives since the termination of his analysis, he delightedly spoke of a new baby born soon after he and Jane moved to their present home; he spoke proudly of how he had shared with Jane the excitement of her pregnancy and delivery and compared his responses with those he had experienced at Pamela's birth. He seemed happy and contented.

At our last meeting, I asked him if he would like to write his recollections of his analysis and his reactions to reading the manuscript, this material to be included in the book. A few weeks later I received a handwritten letter from him, which follows:

> I didn't really want to see a psychiatrist. However, I had encouraged my first wife to seek help and promised to do the same. So I was essentially making good on a promise, not that I really needed it. When you said I needed analysis, I thought it was bullshit, but I promised to see someone, and the concept of analysis was intellectually pleasing. I would never consider treating a fever without documentation of the etiology, and analysis at least approached the cause rather than just the cure. And I was depressed, with low self-esteem. No doubt of that. So I began, with little real anticipation that it would help, but also with the fear that if there really were anything to it, I might have my "personality" changed and cease to love those wonderful parts of my life consisting of attractive women, sex, good food and drink, aggressive competition, and achievement. I discussed the pros and cons with close friends and decided to pursue it.
>
> The time, as it happened over those years, is more carefully chronicled by you than in anything I might attempt. To me there were periods of frustration and despair in which nothing seemed actually to be accomplished. These were interspersed with the certain observation that the patterns of behavior I was learning to note in myself were truly present. This latter realization developed with time over many events, most marked in the early years by anger at the observation of their happening, and denial that any cause and effect existed. However, in time their presence became undeniably real and had to be accepted. With that, I am delighted to state, came also a near cessation of the bothersome traits.
>
> The course of analysis nonetheless always seemed marked by vagueness; when would I be part-way or half finished? when would I

be fully done? etc. And sometimes the parts of the puzzle would
seem to take interminably long to assemble. When you offered me
the opportunity to observe (read) my own analysis, I felt very
strange. Yet this rare and probably unique situation taught me little
that I hadn't already known. Instead, it made the whole process
much clearer, so that, in retrospect, I could see where I was and
where I was going—something laboriously slow in the actual process.
Reading the sequence of events has allowed me the chance to redo
the analysis in capsule form and confirm, to my own amazement,
that the multibranched pathways I strode mentally still led to the
same general conclusions, and I was more clearly able to observe
some of the patterns of behavior of those in the scenes with me, and
found the most major shock to be that I was considered to have (had)
a traumatic childhood. However, I understand that—it consisted, as
indeed I remember it, of years full of happiness and activity with my
family; love of my mother and father, brother and sister—only too
much of a good thing can be bad!! As paradoxical as it may seem, I
was loved "too much," and didn't adjust.

Now that I am finished with the formal side of analysis, I am
happier and wiser. I still get from point A to B as I did before, but I
feel differently. I can now accept the love of my mother, which I
once accepted and then rejected. There is peace and laissez-faire, and
love with my brother and sister. As I go forward day by day and
apply what I've learned, I feel anger and love and exhilaration and
all those other exciting human emotions except—oh, yes!—no
depression, and minimal anxiety. I don't think I could love my wife
more, nor my two children. I regret that I couldn't have had what I
have now in terms of myself for all those other times and years in
the past, but I have no regrets now, and I suspect few if any in the
future. I won't belabor the points dealt with in the text, but suffice
it to say that learning about myself has had a remarkable effect on
myself—essentially no allergies any more, hardly any accidents,
rarely any anxiety in public speaking and interaction with peers and
bosses, and the nice feeling of knowing a lot more about myself.

The formal analysis is long over, and I truly miss the opportunities
to talk. But my own observations of myself continue, and each day
provides me with greater enrichment. Yes, it was neat to read my
own story and so clearly see the patterns derived so laboriously at
the time, and fun to learn just a little more about you. But it
couldn't have been done by reading about it, only by doing it. That's
the way to learn how to cry and smell the flowers, to explode with
anger and feel the tender touch of love, to understand yourself and

yet succeed and accomplish more than jealous goals previously set, to waste no more energy trying to separate and combine the dandelions and roses. And yes, I still appreciate attractive women, love sex with my wife, adore good food and drink, and am doing very well, thank you. And Volkan, you were right. Thanks.

Chris